STRANGE SEAS OF THOUGHT

STRANGE SEAS
of THOUGHT

Studies in
William Wordsworth's
Philosophy of
Man and Nature

by *Newton P. Stallknecht*

INDIANA UNIVERSITY PRESS

BLOOMINGTON & LONDON

THIRD PRINTING 1966

COPYRIGHT © 1958 BY INDIANA UNIVERSITY PRESS
MANUFACTURED IN THE UNITED STATES OF AMERICA
LIBRARY OF CONGRESS CATALOG CARD NUMBER: 58-12210

"... his eyes
Have read the book of wisdom in the sun
And after dark deciphered it on earth."

—E. A. ROBINSON

Foreword

THE INTERPRETATION of Wordsworth's thought offered in this volume includes much material which has already been published piecemeal in a series of articles which appeared between 1929 and 1937 in the *Publications of the Modern Language Association of America.* The titles are as follows: "Wordsworth and Philosophy," "The Moral of the 'Ancient Mariner,'" "The Doctrine of Coleridge's 'Dejection' and Its Relation to Wordsworth's Philosophy," "The 'Ode to Duty' and the 'Schöne Seele,'" and "Nature and Imagination in Wordsworth's Meditation upon Mt. Snowdon." I have also incorporated here the argument of two papers read before Association meetings at Richmond and at New Orleans. To the Secretary of the Association, Dr. Percy W. Long, I am indebted for permission to use this material again as well as for his patience and courtesy in matters connected with their first publication.

My interpretation of Wordsworth developed as I worked upon these studies; and in republishing them here, I have revised frequently and rearranged the material very considerably. In general I may say that I have repudiated very little. But there have been one or two important shifts of emphasis. In the last few years I have come to the conclusion that the influence of Spinoza is not so pervasive in Wordsworth's thought as I once believed it to be. I have found Jakob Boehme a more significant figure, although there is still a place for Spinoza, a place which Boehme could not have occupied because of his comparative orthodoxy in ethical thought.

Again, I have found greater room for the influence of Hartley and the associationists. I have never denied their influence, but I fear that in the beginning I tended to underestimate it. In this I was reacting against the important but somewhat narrow interpretation of Wordsworth presented by Mr. Arthur Beatty. Nonetheless, all students of Wordsworth owe Mr. Beatty a great deal—rather more than I first recognized; and I hope that in this book I have made clear that the work which he has done is indispensable. But there are important aspects of Wordsworth's thought that he has not recognized, and naturally I have tended to emphasize these considerations.

Finally, I believe that I have come, in the last year or two, to a fuller appreciation of Mr. A. N. Whitehead's very brilliant comments on Wordsworth and on the philosophy of romantic poetry in general. I had not, even when I discussed it in 1937, grasped the full significance of his interpretation.

During the past decade, my own suggestions concerning Wordsworth have not gone unchallenged, and I have, in this book, done my best to profit from the criticisms that I have received. I shall probably fail to satisfy some of my critics; but, at any rate, my attempt to do so has clarified my own thinking, and I am grateful to those who have taken the trouble to indicate where my argument has seemed weak or obscure. Some of the most valuable of these criticisms have not appeared in print but have come to me in conversation and in correspondence.

On the whole, I prefer to let the sequel speak for itself. I shall make but one further comment in the form of a request. I hope that the reader will not expect me to produce a Wordsworthian "system" of philosophy. There are, as it happens, several interesting and important philosophical points of view which may be called Wordsworthian; but, despite Leslie Stephen, there is no Wordsworthian system of ethics or of metaphysics and I have tried most conscientiously not to manufacture one.

The last chapter of this work includes what is substantially a reprint of an essay which I contributed to the volume entitled *Wordsworth and Coleridge*, published in 1939 by the Princeton University Press in honor of Mr. George McLean Harper.

N. P. S.

Foreword to Second Edition

THE FIRST EDITION of this book was published by the Duke University Press in 1945 during the last days of World War II. Owing to war-time conditions, the printing was a small one and it was soon exhausted. This fact has, I fear, resulted in some inconvenience for a number of students of Wordsworth. I have, therefore, been most happy to accept the generous offer of the Indiana University Press to issue a reprint edition and thus to see my contribution once more readily available.

In preparing this new edition for the press, I have made but few changes in the text and these limited to correcting a number of minor errors of typographical origin. I have, however, added a supplement of a few pages placed at the end of this volume. In this appendix, I have considered Professor Jane Worthington Smyser's argument, published shortly after the first edition of this book, to the effect that Wordsworth's interest in Roman Stoicism, based on a direct acquaintance with the writings of Seneca and Cicero, supplies the philosophical pattern of the ideas that appear in the *Ode to Duty* and in *The Excursion*. Professor Smyser's suggestion is an important one that should not be ignored or lightly dismissed. I am thus very glad to take advantage of this opportunity to offer a somewhat belated comment on her contribution. I might add that my failure to recognize the relevance of the Roman Stoics now seems to me the chief shortcoming of my earlier study of Wordsworth and the philosophers. On the other hand, I shall argue that when we admit Wordsworth's acquaintance with such thinkers as Cicero and Seneca, we must not overlook the relevance of more recent thinkers such as Kant, Schiller, and Shaftesbury.

No further additions or alternatives have been possible. This is, however, hardly a source of regret, since my interpretation of Wordsworth has changed very little since 1945. I have, it is true, published during this period a few articles and reviews devoted in whole or in part to the study of Wordsworth. But it seems to me that they contain little or nothing that calls for any alteration in the argument of *Strange Seas of Thought*. It is thus not necessary to include this supplementary material here. If the reader is interested in it, he has only to consult two essays recently published under the following titles:

"On Poetry and Geometric Truth," *The Kenyon Review* (Winter, 1956).

"Wordsworth and the Quality of Man," contributed to *The Major English Romantic Poets, A Symposium in Reappraisal*, edited by Clarence D. Thorpe, Carlos Baker, and Bennett Weaver, Southern Illinois University Press, Carbondale, 1957.

In the first of these I have offered, among other things, a brief defense of Wordsworth against the spirited, if not always wholly responsible, comments of Mr. William Empson in his *Seven Kinds of Ambiguity*; also, in connection with this, I have made an attempt further to clarify Wordsworth's use of what in the present volume I have described as "objective metaphor." In the second essay, published in book form, some of this material is repeated along with a consideration, supplementary to that contained in the present volume, of Wordsworth's relations to certain recent philosophical writers, such as S. Alexander, R. G. Collingwood, Albert Schweitzer, and A. N. Whitehead. In this essay I have also emphasized the similarity of Wordsworth's thought to that of Bergson, especially to the latter's *Two Sources of Morality and Religion*. I might add that comparison of what Bergson has had to say in this book with the body of Wordsworth's verse has often helped me interpret both poet and philosopher to my students.

Finally, I should like to repeat a few lines from my review of Professor Potts' recent book on *The Prelude*.[1] These lines seem to me to constitute a summary and defense of the enterprise that I first undertook many years ago when I began these studies under the guidance of Professor Harper.

---

[1] "The Prelude sans Coleridge," a review of *Wordsworth's Prelude: A Study of Its Literary Form*, by Abbie Findlay Potts, in *The Kenyon Review*, Summer, 1954.

In Wordsworth study Coleridge must occupy a unique and central
position. . . . The philosophy of *The Prelude* is often presented in
a lyric vein and the whole poem is addressed to Coleridge who is recognized as its sponsor. There are moments indeed when one would hardly
be surprised to find a comment or response of Coleridge's included in the
text. But Coleridge himself recognized that despite its lyricism—and
he called the poem a "song"—*The Prelude* is more than a confession.
It is a personal history, but a personal history that assumes a prophetic
significance. It becomes "an Orphic song . . . of Truth profound"—
albeit of truth that may well be incarnate in the "growth of an individual
mind." Coleridge's reference to Orpheus, to the Orphic mysteries,
and to mysticism in general should not be taken lightly. It is as adequate a characterization as any that we are likely to come upon or to
construct for ourselves. We need not, to be sure, expect the trappings
of Orphicism or of later theosophy. These are gone with gaudy verse
and Jehovah, his thunder and his "shouting angels." But the themes
of initiation, of self-dedication, of mystery gradually, if never quite fully,
penetrated and, above all, the great theme of the poet saved from ultimate darkness by his own song—all these may well remind us of
Orpheus and Orphicism.[2]

Let me take this opportunity to offer belated public acknowledgment of the patient and prolonged assistance extended to
me years ago by two of my former colleagues at Bowdoin
College who saw the first edition of this book through the
press before my return to academic work at the close of the
war. They disappointed me only in one thing: they failed,
despite my request, to include their own names in the preface.
I therefore now record on the printed page a statement of
gratitude that was long ago made *viva voce* to the late Professor Phillips Mason and to Professor Herbert Ross Brown
of Bowdoin College for their generous gift of time and energy.

N. P. S.

[2] In recent months I have grown increasingly interested in the precise significance of this reference to Orphicism and in its more general importance for
the interpretation of Wordsworth's thought. I have discussed these questions at
length with Mr. Cooper Speaks, now of the Department of English at Duke
University. Mr. Speaks is considering this matter in its several implications as
a part of his doctoral dissertation. I shall gladly leave the topic to his investigation.

Contents

STRANGE SEAS OF THOUGHT

CHAPTER I

The "Heroic Argument"

IN THIS ESSAY—and I shall not describe this work as anything more pretentious—it is not my purpose to assay the esthetic quality of Wordsworth's contribution. I must leave such delicate criticism to writers far more sensitive and more skilled in publishing their discernments than most students of philosophy, like myself, may ever hope to become. Nor am I prepared to face problems of textual criticism, which I must leave to other students. And, finally, it is not my intention to characterize in any very original fashion the "message" of Wordsworth. In fact, I find that here I agree pretty much with Mr. de Selincourt's interpretation of Wordsworth's thought, as presented in his notes on *The Prelude;*[1] and I find consistently supplementing this interpretation the important comments upon Wordsworth which Mr. A. N. Whitehead has made in his *Science and the Modern World*. Furthermore, these comments remind me of A. C. Bradley's interpretation in his *Oxford Lectures on Poetry*. At this date, a fresh characterization of Wordsworth's broader import is hardly necessary. His central precepts are generally lucid enough to all those who approach him with sympathy. Our life in these modern times, he tells us, is overintellectualized in its orientation and too practical in its interests. Hence our view of the world is falsified and our scale of values distorted. These errors cannot be corrected merely by taking thought, but by fashioning a new way of life to replace that mode of living of which our dismal philosophies are symptoms. Wordsworth's quietism, the "wise passiveness" before natural beauty, his introspective concern with all states of feeling—particularly with those feel-

[1] In quoting from *The Prelude,* I refer, except occasionally when I indicate otherwise, to the draft of 1805, as edited by Ernest de Selincourt, *The Prelude . . . by William Wordsworth, Edited from the Manuscripts with Introduction, Textual and Critical Notes* (Oxford, 1926).

ings which manifest moral and esthetic values—and his conviction, based upon "feeling intellect," that all Nature is
somehow one life, and that this life is a matrix of those values
from which the human soul may derive all the inspiration that
it requires—all this has been clearly apprehended although
not, of course, by everyone; and it has been verified or authen-
ticated in the experience of many Wordsworthians as a way of
life and a view of things satisfactory for more than one type of
personality. The critical evaluation which the more sympathetic Wordsworthians have offered us seems adequate enough.
Many of the estimates, considered by themselves, may be incomplete. But there remains, even so, very little to be added
to the picture that emerges from them.

It is possible to appreciate Wordsworth without completely
understanding him in the philosophical sense of the word. We
may learn to cultivate his "wise passiveness" and so enlarge
the dominion of our imagination; we may come even to believe
that "Nature never did betray the heart that loved her," and
still remain almost wholly ignorant of Wordsworth's place in
the history of ideas. We may indeed feel great sympathy
with him and still uneasily suspect that no philosophical defense of his view of the world is possible and that his greatest
utterances can hardly bear analysis. We may follow Wordsworth pragmatically and find that his precepts are happy ones,
as some people follow the dictates of a dogmatic religion and
gain much happiness, even "salvation," thereby. But in that
case we shall be unable to defend Wordsworth against a hostile critic, say, a neo-humanist or a behaviorist. This may not
seem important to everyone, but once it does seem important
to a Wordsworthian, he must embark upon an examination of
his poet's ideas from the standpoint of their origin and consistency. Indeed, he must do this or suffer much embarrassment in the presence of the skeptical.

In this investigation, however, the Wordsworth whom the
philosopher defends must be the same Wordsworth whom the
enthusiast loves. The poet must continue to appear very much
as his sympathetic readers have always seen him. Thus all I

hope to do is to analyze certain of Wordsworth's concepts and to explain their origin. Let us analyze in order to defend rather than to search out a new and strange Wordsworth.

* * *

There are many hostile misinterpretations of Wordsworth, some of them to be found in unexpected places. One popular and perverse misreading is represented in Mr. Aldous Huxley's essay, "Wordsworth in the Tropics." Let us consider this as an example of the sort of adverse criticism with which even well-informed students of literature are apt to acquiesce, however reluctantly. The chief purpose of this essay is to render such criticism impossible, although this is probably too ambitious an undertaking. (Of course, we must remember that since publishing his criticism in 1929 Mr. Huxley has himself changed his mind on many matters, and he has learned a great deal. The ironical observer has himself become a prophet. This view probably does not very accurately represent his present attitude toward Wordsworth. But there are certainly many people who still find Mr. Huxley's early comment satisfactory.)

It is a pity that Wordsworth never travelled beyond the boundaries of Europe. A voyage through the tropics would have cured him of his too easy and comfortable pantheism. A few months in the jungle would have convinced him that the diversity and utter strangeness of Nature are at least as real and significant as its intellectually discovered unity. Nor would he have felt so certain, in the damp and stifling darkness, among the leeches and the malevolently tangled rattans, of the divinely anglican character of that fundamental unity. He would have learned once more to treat Nature naturally, as he treated it in his youth; to react to it spontaneously, loving where love was the appropriate emotion, fearing, hating, fighting wherever Nature presented itself to his intuition as being not merely strange, but hostile, inhumanly evil. A voyage would have taught him this. But Wordsworth never left his native continent. Europe is so well gardened that it resembles a work of art, a scientific theory, a neat metaphysical system. Man has re-created Europe in his own image. Its tamed and temperate Nature confirmed Wordsworth in his philosophizing.[2]

[2] Aldous Huxley, *Do What You Will* (London and New York, 1929), pp. 128-129.

There is one point, that may seem at first a very minor one, which I should like to introduce here for the first time. When Mr. Huxley speaks of the "intellectually discovered unity" of Nature, he is not doing full justice to Wordsworth's belief. The unity of Nature is, as we shall find later on, for Wordsworth rather a fact than a theory. It is, properly speaking, a datum for intuitive insight. It is, at least in its origin, not a discursive concept. We shall return to this in the sequel more than once. But let us now hear Mr. Huxley's account of the origin of Wordsworth's worship of Nature.

> For us, the notion "river" implies (how obviously!) the notion "bridge." When we think of a plain, we think of agriculture, towns, and good roads. . . . At latitude zero, however, the obvious is not the same as with us. Rivers imply wading, swimming, alligators. Plains mean swamps, forests, fevers. Mountains are either dangerous or impassable. To travel is to hack one's way laboriously through a tangled, prickly, and venomous darkness.[3]

In Europe and America, according to Mr. Huxley, we love Nature because we are her masters, because we have refashioned her in our own image. Not so in the tropics, where she is still the enemy. Hence Wordsworth's natural religion is a civilized illusion. In passing, let me point out that I know of no passage in Wordsworth which even suggests that he ever entertained any such attitude toward the Lake Country.

Now, it is true enough that no very profound or satisfying religion or philosophy of life can follow upon this "suburban" love of Nature which Mr. Huxley describes and cleverly ridicules. Such an attitude can result in little more than a feeble self-deception. It is the "lost traveller's dream under the hill." But the experience which Mr. Huxley describes is not Wordsworthian. To say that Wordsworth loved or worshiped the European landscape is grossly to oversimplify a very complex state of mind. Furthermore, Wordsworth was very profoundly moved by the grandeur of the Alps, which Mr. Huxley must admit are often rugged and uncultivated, occasionally even dangerous. Nor were they, indeed, in Wordsworth's great

[3] *Ibid.*, p. 116.

period, recognized as a possible playground even for strenuous recreation.

Furthermore, Wordsworth is capable of spiritual insight quite apart from the beauties of Nature. Recall, for example, his mention of mathematical reasoning as a source of such inspiration.[4] Nor is Wordsworth at all certain that man is entirely and eternally at home in his physical surroundings. At any rate, he can think sometimes of natural catastrophies that would destroy all the works of imagination and art in which the human mind has, so to speak, embodied itself. Thus when writing of "books," Wordsworth exclaims:

> . . . Thou also, Man, hast wrought
> For commerce of thy nature with itself,
> Things worthy of unconquerable life;
> And yet we feel, we cannot chuse but feel
> That these must perish. Tremblings of the heart
> It gives to think that the immortal being
> No more shall need such garments; and yet Man,
> As long as he shall be the Child of Earth,
> Might almost "weep to have" what he may lose,
> Nor be himself extinguish'd; but survive
> Abject, depress'd, forlorn, disconsolate.
> A thought is with me sometimes, and I say,
> Should earth by inward throes be wrench'd throughout,
> Or fire be sent from far to wither all
> Her pleasant habitations, and dry up
> Old Ocean in his bed left sing'd and bare,
> Yet would the living Presence still subsist
> Victorious; and composure would ensue,
> And kindlings like the morning; presage sure,
> Though slow, perhaps, of a returning day.
> But all the meditations of mankind,
> Yea, all the adamantine holds of truth,
> By reason built, or passion, which itself
> Is highest reason in a soul sublime;
> The consecrated works of Bard and Sage,
> Sensuous or intellectual, wrought by men,
> Twin laborers and heirs of the same hopes,

[4] De Selincourt (ed.), *op. cit.*, Bk. VI, l. 135.

> Where would they be?   Oh!   Why hath not the mind
> Some element to stamp her image on
> In nature somewhat nearer to her own?
> Why, gifted with such powers to send abroad
> Her spirit, must it lodge in shrines so frail?[5]

These last lines very clearly indicate that Wordsworth did not habitually think of man as being happily cared for by a benevolent power resident in Nature.

The experience which we have learned to call Wordsworthian is not a feeling, based upon vague associations, that the quiet and peaceful beauties of our natural environment reveal a serene and kindly spirit toward mankind.   Nor is the experience primarily an act of reasoning.   We do not conclude that because the Lake Country is beautiful, God is good.   Nor is it purely an esthetic experience, for one may enjoy natural beauty without becoming a Wordsworthian.   In fact, many people do.   Again it is not a "projection" of human emotion into a nonhuman setting.   It is not, in other words, what Ruskin called the "pathetic fallacy."   Wordsworth is aware that such a way of enjoying Nature exists, he admits that at times he has indulged in it—as who has not?—but he distinguishes it clearly enough from that more rare and satisfying experience which it is his chief purpose to celebrate.

> . . . I felt that the array
> Of outward circumstances and visible forms
> Is to the pleasure of the human mind
> What passion makes it, that meanwhile the forms
> Of Nature have a passion in themselves
> That intermingles with those works of man
> To which she summons him.[6]

And, perhaps most important of all, Wordsworth is well aware that the psychological influence of the observable physical environment is not always beneficial.   Thus in "Ruth," he mentions the role which the very landscape itself may play in undermining an individual's morale.   This works through what we might today call an empathetic *rapport* with the sen-

[5] *Ibid.*, Bk. V, ll. 17-48.   [6] *Ibid.*, Bk. XII, ll. 286 ff.

suous aspects of the world around us.   Hence Wordsworth
speaks of the languorous and enervating influence of the trop-
ical scene and of its disturbing influence upon the passions.
This point it might be well to call to Mr. Huxley's attention.

> The wind, the tempest roaring high,
> The tumult of a tropic sky,
> Might well be dangerous food
>
> . . . .
>
> Whatever in these climes be found
> Irregular in sight and sound
> Did to his mind impart
> A kindred impulse. . . .
>
> Nor less, to feed voluptuous thought
> The beauteous forms of Nature wrought,
> Fair trees and gorgeous flowers;
> The breezes their own languor lent;
> The stars had feelings, which they sent
> Into those favored bowers.

The Wordsworthian experience is harder to describe than
anything which we have mentioned above.   It is often the outcome or the consequence of robust mental activity, sometimes
esthetic, sometimes intellectual, sometimes solely a matter of
voluntarily controlled perception, or of detailed recall when
emotion is "recollected in tranquility"; or, again, it is the outcome of a state of mind which is, as we shall see, related to
those just mentioned, viz., the detachment of an esthetic reverie, the "wise passiveness" that is so famous.   In itself the
Wordsworthian experience may best be described as the momentary presence, before the poet's attention, of Nature, or the
concrete world *as a whole*.   Its further content is nearly always
subordinate to this.   Thus even in the "Tintern Abbey" lines
where little effort is made to make the objective content of
such insight clear, where what is elsewhere described as the
"pulse of Being" is not mentioned, we read of a "motion and
a spirit" present in the "mind of man" and in the "round
ocean and the living air" and even in the "light of setting
suns."   This power pervades all Nature and is apparent to our

intuitive vision. As Wordsworth put it: "The unity of all has been revealed." We shall learn presently why this unity appears as spiritual.

* * *

As I have already said, my purpose in this study is to examine the content and the origin of the major concepts by means of which Wordsworth presents his view of life. These concepts constitute the rational aspect of a philosophy that is not itself primarily rationalist. They are the medium in terms of which intuitive insights are given an embodiment or the context in terms of which these are, so to speak, published. These concepts are drawn from many realms of philosophy and religion, although some of them are considerably refashioned in the borrowing. This is not meant to imply that Wordsworth is lacking in philosophical originality. Most philosophical thinkers borrow their intellectual alphabet from the tradition in which they work. Wordsworth is no exception.

To be sure, Wordsworth considers conceptual thought as merely a secondary power which can only falsify when it tries to work alone, and which often lacks the power to inspire action. Such thinking is, even so, a "succedaneum and a prop," a valuable auxiliary of other methods of thought. This is, of course, especially true in the communication of ideas, even of mystical ideas, which remain ineffable until they are presented against the background of some more or less systematic scheme. But the earlier Wordsworth is always suspicious of these rational schemes. He is suspicious even of formally accurate distinctions and of analysis in general, not only because their pedantic exactitude cannot live at peace with poetry, but also because they suggest that Nature and life are sharply differentiated into distinct groups and classes. Wordsworth was possessed by an intuition of the fundamental and substantial unity of things, by what we might call the intertwined togetherness of all concrete histories, and by the "mutual domination" or interplay of natural appearances. If we are to trust the story of his spiritual growth as presented in *The Prelude*, we must believe that Wordsworth held such a conviction before he had read the philosophers or talked with Coleridge, although he probably never gave it adequate expression until later.

Such belief does not imply that Wordsworth was intellectually irresponsible or incapable of comprehending scientific theory. For that matter, there are biologists who, aware of the continuity of the stream of life, warn us against putting too great emphasis upon the reality of species. And no student of literature who has ever meditated upon the problem of defining the historical schools should have any difficulty in grasping what Wordsworth meant. At any rate, Wordsworth is no dogmatic schoolman who finds that the categories of scientific discourse and the categories of things neatly coincide. In this he is modern. But his modernity is not a matter of sheer relativism or of a skeptical empiricism. For Wordsworth, reason and sensuous observation are not the only eyes of the soul. Thus his sense of the inviolate community of the concrete world and his insistence that systematic classification is bound to distort Nature are the outcome of intuition. "The *unity* of all has been *revealed*"—this is no summary of empiricism but a transcendental philosophy of suprasensuous insight.

On the other hand, Wordsworth was, we must admit, sympathetic to the philosophy of sentiment and of feeling that was so widespread during the eighteenth century. His praise of Shaftesbury is characteristic of this attitude. Wordsworth's preoccupation with emotions inspired by and sometimes identified with natural beauty, his cultivation of the rapture and enthusiasm of the nature-lover, appears in a more stilted and formalized manner in Shaftesbury, who anticipates Wordsworth by finding a religious significance in such states of mind. Both Wordsworth and Shaftesbury would agree that "inspiration" is a *real* feeling of the divine presence and that this presence is most readily felt in the "retired places" of Nature. And Wordsworth's faith in human nature is at least partially founded upon the belief, which he holds throughout his greatest period, that human impulses are trustworthy, if only they are enlightened so that the full consequences of their realization are manifest to the agent who entertains them. Wordsworth thus belongs to the tradition which, springing from Shaftesbury, spreads throughout England and the Continent. Indeed, the late Irving Babbitt was not wholly wrong in comparing Wordsworth with Rousseau, although Babbitt sometimes wrote as if this wide and general influence were the only significant one to which Wordsworth was ever subjected.

But there is much in Wordsworth that belongs to older traditions and to broader and deeper systems of thought. His philosophy of feeling often recalls the profounder and more systematically cultivated mysticism of Neoplatonism and Gnostic writers. And particularly in his earlier poems, the poems written before 1805, Wordsworth speaks as a mystic. This is not to say that he is to be compared with St. Francis of Assisi or with St. Theresa. Wordsworth is inspired by mystical vision, but his life is not wholly dominated by it, largely because he never subjected himself to any rigorous discipline or regimen comparable to that of the contemplative orders. In fact, one student has gone so far as to argue that Wordsworth did not recognize himself as a mystic. This is true, I think, only of the word itself which Wordsworth employed at least once in its pejorative sense.[7] But after his first years at Cambridge, Wordsworth certainly recognized that he was unusually endowed with powers of cosmic insight.[8] It is possible to determine the character of Wordsworth's intuitive experience and of the way in which mystical enlightenment often arose in his consciousness. This we shall study in some detail later. Suffice it here to say that in his thinking the full exercise of mental powers and the sharp concentration of his attention employed either in direct perception, in reasoning, or, as often, in imaginative recall, were sometimes followed by a mystical or intuitive consciousness whose object may be described as the unity of Being. This state of awareness was also sometimes induced by "wise passiveness," a peaceful and detached reverie, which is similar to the former more active insight in that it frees the mind from its usual pressing concerns and thus allows the fringes or depths of consciousness to manifest themselves.

[7] *Ibid.*, Bk. II, l. 235.   [8] *Ibid.*, Bk. III, ll. 101 ff.

Wordsworth often entertained such consciousness as a sequel to the intense enjoyment of natural beauty; and since the final object of his mystical awareness was the world as a whole, he came frequently to speak of "Nature" as both the source of his inspiration and the object of his vision. Many mystics turn their backs upon natural beauty, finding it only a source of distraction from spiritual contemplation. And it is, perhaps, true that those who deliberately *cultivate* mysticism by employing an elaborate regimen of mental exercise and discipline are not so likely to find the beauties of Nature an aid to their spiritual growth. After all, Wordsworth seems rarely to have aspired to control his powers of insight by such voluntary effort, unless perhaps during his first days at Cambridge.[9]

Some students may hesitate to recognize Wordsworth as a mystic because they consider him as the father of modern simplicity and realism, as also of natural diction, in English poetry. These characteristics may be considered as incompatible with mysticism. On the contrary, I suspect that Wordsworth's habit of finding mystical overtones in natural beauty inclined him toward a keenness of observation and a respect for concrete details. It was not an unbridled and irresponsible fancy that revealed to him the vast unity of Being, but the most patient and attentive surrender to those features of Nature which he came gradually to know more and more intimately and whose beauty more and more absorbed his attention. Thus his mysticism does not employ the vocabulary of the medieval saint. It is in large measure made palpable through description of the esthetic conditions from which it emerges, and the quality of the mystical vision is translated into an idiom derived from a prolonged acquaintance with natural beauty. Thus in the "Tintern Abbey" lines it is the "round ocean and the living air" to which Wordsworth refers as he strives to make us sensitive to the all-encompassing community of existence which he describes as the "life of things."

In Nature, mystically apprehended, the concrete interpenetration or community of objects and events is somehow felt.

[9] *Ibid.*, Bk. III, ll. 112 ff.

No object, no event, no living thing, not even the human soul, exists or can exist by itself: each depends on all. This is the mystical principle of monism which so often leads to pantheism in religion: the finite objects of our everyday life are not illusions, but their mutual *independence* is. So highly integrated is this world of things that it may be best described as resembling a mind. It might, indeed, be wiser and more modest to say that the human mind, as we know it, resembles this matrix of Being, which encompasses it. We might also say that beauty as it appears to us resembles or even symbolizes this transcendent unity of the concrete world. The same might be said of the living organism, the mutual dependence of whose organs upon one another again reflects the unity of Being. In describing this unity and wealth of Being the language of animism is frequently employed. As Mr. Whitehead has put it, the "brooding presence of the hills" reveals Nature *in solido*, the concrete unity of Being.

The fact that the world is a *concrete* world and not a mere "plan," a logical skeleton or a diagram, the very fact that the world *exists*, is a source of wonder and of delight to the mystic. The very fact of Being arouses his enthusiasm and taxes to the full his powers of expression. It is my belief that Wordsworth's thought centered upon this recognition which is so easy to name and still so difficult to render significant. For the present let us content ourselves with quoting a passage from *The Prelude*, which we shall have to discuss at length later on.

> There came a time of greater dignity
> Which had been gradually prepar'd, and now
> Rush'd in as if on wings, the time in which
> The pulse of Being everywhere was felt,
> When all the several frames of things, like stars
> Through every magnitude distinguishable,
> Were half confounded in each other's blaze,
> One galaxy of life and joy.[10]

Interfusion is more strikingly presented in the following, where Wordsworth describes a magnificent Alpine scene, the

[10] *Ibid.*, Bk. VIII, ll. 623 ff.

features of which from waterfall and drizzling crag to the vast region of the Heavens

> Tumult and peace, the darkness and the light
> Were all like workings of one mind, the features
> Of the same face, blossoms upon one tree,
> Characters of the great Apocalypse
> The types and symbols of Eternity,
> Of first, and last, and midst, and without end.[11]

Such a passage reveals the content of the mystical awareness more adequately than many more famous ones. The more usual description of mysticism describes the object of such contemplation as an eternal mind, sometimes not suggesting that this mind is the unity of the world.

* * *

But no account of Wordsworth's mysticism is complete which fails to recognize how closely allied, in his mind, are mystical and esthetic insight.

The enjoyment of beauty is a complex activity involving an interplay of mind and object. Sometimes Wordsworth seems to feel that in the interplay the initiative lies with the object. Thus both Wordsworth and Coleridge employ at times the beautiful analogy of the Eolian harp; but, as we shall see, they are apt to insist that the harp itself awakens into song, that it is not entirely a passive instrument. And the power that plays upon the harp is not to be thought of in purely physical terms. An idealist philosophy seems necessary to describe the objective and subjective factors which constitute the esthetic situation. We shall later examine in detail Wordsworth's account of this situation and consider certain philosophical theories which seem to have helped in describing this most complex and delicate interplay of personal and suprapersonal factors. For the present, we shall have to content ourselves with Mr. de Selincourt's admirable comment. I omit his comparison of Wordsworth's attitude with that of Coleridge because I am not certain that it adequately accounts

[11] *Ibid.*, Bk. VI, ll. 567 ff.

for some of Coleridge's earlier views, as expounded, say, in "The Eolian Harp," itself.

"To Wordsworth . . . the poetic mind was creative, . . . but he held that it was stimulated and worked upon by the creative power of Nature, since Nature was possessed by that same divine being, which ran through all things, of whose presence he was conscious in his own interior life." Hence the poet is a *sensitive* being, a creative soul. In *The Prelude*, 1805 (Bk. XII, ll. 369-379), Wordsworth asserts "that the source of our inner life, 'that where our dignity originates,' is an active power which maintains a continual interrelation between the mind and the objects of its vision, and is itself 'the excellence, pure spirit, and best power' of both."[12] Mr. de Selincourt points out that this doctrine amounts to pantheism.

This theory constitutes the esthetics of a mystic, and an esthetician who entertains no sympathy for mysticism, an esthetician, say, like Herbert Spencer can hardly accept it. Certainly it is possible to have some understanding of the enjoyment of beauty without recognizing any mystical implications. Just so, it is possible to be a logician without being a Platonist. But the question arises whether the esthetician who ignores all mystical implications is fully aware of the phenomonology of the beautiful, whether, in short, he has clearly apprehended the psychology of inspiration which the great creative artist can hardly ignore. For Wordsworth this experience involves, when brought fully to consciousness, a sense of communion between the limited mental powers of the poet and the inspiring forces of the "external" world which call upon him.[13] But we shall return to this point later on.

Inspiration seems to come to the poet, not through the senses alone, although these are necessary to arouse the mind to attention, but also directly through his inner consciousness,

---

[12] *The Prelude*, p. 599.
[13] "One can gather what Schopenhauer meant when he said that a complete and adequate symphony would be a complete and adequate metaphysics, for it would be reality speaking; the bewitched listener would be one with the music; the music heard and the listener would be each other, and be one, and be the absolute Will to live, the rhythmical substance of Being" (Irwin Edman, *Four Ways of Philosophy*, New York, 1937, p. 192).

as Wordsworth puts it, from the mind's "underpresence." As De Selincourt comments,[14] Wordsworth needed such a concept "to express his profound consciousness of that mysterious life which lies deep down below our ordinary, everyday experience, and whence we draw our power—that one interior life:

> In which all beings live with God, themselves
> Are God, existing in the mighty whole.

The relation of this conception to the subconscious or subliminal self of the modern psychologist is obvious."

I do not wish to deny this last statement, but I should prefer to liken Wordsworth's notion to certain concepts developed before Freud's time by Edouard von Hartmann. We shall quote from the latter's *Philosophy of the Unconscious*. In his brilliant exposition of mysticism, von Hartmann, like Wordsworth, draws together the activities of the artist, the religious prophet, and the creative philosopher, deriving all these energies from mysticism, which is the first emergence into consciousness of a dominant mass of feeling springing from the Unconscious. (Von Hartmann's notion of the Unconscious stands historically halfway between Schopenhauer's Will and Freud's subconscious. There is, for Hartmann, but one Unconscious or cosmic will which comes to consciousness in the lives of its finite creatures.)

. . . even in the most ordinary psychological processes, I characterize those thoughts and feelings as mystical in form, which owe their origin to an immediate intrusion of the Unconscious, thus before all the aesthetic feeling in contemplation and production, the origin of sensuous perception and the unconscious processes in thinking, feeling, and willing generally. This perfectly justifiable application meets with resistance only from vulgar prejudice, which sees marvel and mystery only in the extraordinary, but finds nothing obscure or marvelous in the things of every-day life—only because there is nothing rare and unusual in it. Certainly, one does not call a man, who only carries about in himself these ever-recurring mysteries, *a mystic;* for if this word is to mean more than human being, it must be reserved for the men who participate in the rarer phenomena of mysticism, namely,

[14] *Op. cit.,* p. 600.

such inspirations of the Unconscious as go beyond the common need of the individual or of the race, e.g., clairvoyants, through spontaneous somnambulism or natural disposition, or persons with a darker but frequently active power of presentiment (Socrates' "Daimonion"). I should also not object to the designating as mystics, in the province of their art, all eminent art geniuses, who owe their productions predominantly to the inspirations of their genius, and not to the work of their consciousness, be they in all other concerns of life as clear-headed as possible (e.g., Phidias, Aeschylus, Raphael, Beethoven); and he alone could take offence who has himself so little of the mystical vein in him, that the incommensurability of the genuine work of art with any rationalistic standard, as well as the infinity of its content, in respect of all attempts at definition, has not yet at all entered into his consciousness.

In philosophy I should like to extend the notion still further, and call every original philosopher a mystic, so far as he is truly original; for in the history of philosophy no high thought has ever been brought to light by laborious conscious trial and induction, but has always been apprehended by the glance of genius, and then elaborated by the understanding. Add to that, that philosophy essentially deals with a theme which is mostly intimately connected with the one feeling *only* to be *mystically* apprehended, namely, the *relation of the individual to the Absolute.*[15]

*   *   *

We are all inclined to raise the question: How much validity can we attach to such an immediate 'and unreasoned apprehension of truth? We can hardly in this brief study undertake to ponder the question of the validity of mysticism or even of intuitive knowledge. But if the reader is interested in following out the implications of the question, let him recall that the nondiscursive and nonsensuous character of mystical insight is by no means a certain sign of its falsity or of its lack of significance. In fact, the very principles upon which reasoning itself depends come to our attention owing to our deep-rooted respect for the ideal of consistency, and our respect for this consistency is not a matter that can very well be supported by argument. You cannot argue at all without assuming the

[15] Edouard von Hartmann, *Philosophy of the Unconscious*, Coupland's trans. (New York, 1884), I, 364-365.

conclusions are usually considered as diametrically opposed to
Wordsworthian philosophy. There is, after all, a common
ground between Wordsworth and Spinoza or, to descend to
recent times, between Wordsworth and such a thinker as
S. Alexander. To say that the human spirit is a part of Nature
—and that, by abstracting itself from Nature, it only falsifies
its own life—may help one to meet the scientific naturalist
halfway. Both the Wordsworthian and the scientific naturalist assert a certain continuity between the human spirit and the
world from which that spirit arises; and this continuity may
be thought to point toward the doctrine of a World-Soul.
There is about as much to be said for such an hypothesis as
for its counterpart, according to which the continuity of mind
and Nature is read as pointing toward a universal materialism.
As Mr. Edman tells us, scientific naturalists have also felt
Nature to be one, and man one with Nature:

The most airy theory of the soul has not quite blinded even those
who held it to the obvious ways in which the soul or the "psyche" is
the sum total, the entelechy, the summary expression of the body's
activities. The soul bears the same relation to the body that the flame
does to the candle, that seeing does to the eye. The violent despair
that arose in the nineteenth century, therefore, as to the conflict between man and nature seems an invented sadness based on artificial
dividing of what is in fact unified. The same substance that flowers
into corn or into roses blossoms into man, and in him into imagination,
thinking, feeling, and thought. The same vitality that generates mas-
todons, breeds poets and poetry. The symphonies of Beethoven are
just as natural as flowers or snakes. The picture of man over against
nature is a contradiction in terms. Man is one of the forms and habits
of nature. The notion that man's highest ideals are somehow pathetic
oppositions to nature neglects the important fact that those ideals are
themselves generated in the imagination and mind of a creature to
whom thinking and imagination are themselves natural. And if one
means that there is nothing in any other part or phase of nature that
exhibits such ideals or gives them sustenance, even here one must pause
before so declaring. For gregariousness and sympathy are present in
the animal kingdom and the highest vision of a just society has its roots
partly in these traits. Nor would it follow, if man alone generated
such values as we call specifically human, that nature is their enemy

importance of consistency, and therefore it is clear that y₀
cannot demonstrate logically this importance without assumir
it. In other words, our respect for consistency cannot be rea
sonably defended. Still it persists and all reasoning depend
upon it. Our faith that the truth of discursive reasoning
depends upon consistency is a purely intuitive or "mystical,"
i.e., suprasensuous and nondiscursive or unarguable way of
"knowledge." To be sure, such an argument does not vali-
date mysticism. But it does indicate clearly enough that the
usual "logical" objections to mystical philosophy are not necessarily insuperable.

As Mr. Irwin Edman very finely puts the matter:

The reasonableness of reason itself remains undemonstrable. When
the logician asks us to assent to self-evidence, that is not very different
from abdicating the procedure of demonstration itself, or pointing, as
the mystic does, in silence. There is always lurking in a demonstration
some immediacy unquestioned, both at the beginning and the end. And
when after a long and complicated dialectic, all becomes marvelously
clear, luminous, and convincing,[16] when it is all seen, this seeing is like
that of the mystics, an act of vision. Not only the heart but reason
assents to more than it can find reasons for.[17]

Again, we are often, I think, too ready to condemn mysticism because of the difficulty which the mystic experiences
in translating his feelings or insight into words. But, after all,
this difficulty is not wholly limited to mysticism. The literary
critic, for example, is faced with a similar problem, as were
indeed the mathematicians during the early days of Greek,
thought, when the difficulties of terminology and of definition
of terms were first encountered. Of these difficulties the Soph-
ists made a great deal when they argued against the possibility
of universal truth.

Those who find Wordsworth's cosmic idealism a gratuitous,
even an unreasonable, hypothesis must remember that in some
respects his assumptions, although prompted by intuitive insight, are in line with those of the scientific naturalist whose

[16] [When, as we have put it above, all appears in the light of consistency.]
[17] *Op. cit.*, pp. 216-217.

or that nature gives them no support. The impulses that sustain these values and the materials which make it possible for some of them to come to fruition are in exactly the same world; man's preferences and standards originate where everything else does, in the universal, fertile flux of natural process.[18]

From Mr. Edman's concept of Nature's fertility to the Wordsworthian view of the plastic power of the World-Soul is not so great a step as some may suppose. The difference is as much a matter of background as of reasoned disagreement and, at least, to some extent, it is a matter of terminology.

At any rate, the modern scientific naturalist and Wordsworth agree on one thing—they both repudiate the traditional Cartesian dualism, which sees the world sharply divided into two orders, that of physical extension on one hand and of unextended mental substance on the other. Insofar as Wordsworth is willing to emphasize any dualism, he chooses, not the Cartesian dualism of mind and body, but the Platonic distinction between the temporal and the eternal. Wordsworth is much impressed with his intuition of "central peace subsisting as the heart of endless agitation." But even here he does not seem to believe that the world is divided into two orders of Being. Eternity is somehow the "heart" of restless flux. World-unity overcomes even this bifurcation, although just how this comes to pass is one of the great mysteries of existence.

* * *

Like most mysticisms, Wordsworth's awareness of the unity of the world, and of the living forces which constitute the world, carries with it supreme moral imperatives which spring from a "primal sympathy," to which all human beings would respond if only they could pause long enough in the practical routine of their lives to feel it vividly. Then they would recognize that all life, all Nature even, is the awakening of a single purpose that makes toward the creation of joy and beauty. This is true, despite the "weary weight" of an "unintelligible world," of conflict and catastrophe, or cold selfishness and blind cruelty.

[18] *Ibid.*, pp. 272-274.

Once we have felt this, it becomes not so much our duty as our deep-seated and intense desire to help further the development of an independent, spiritual resourcefulness in our fellow men and in ourselves; for here it is that the joy and beauty toward which Nature calls us can be most abundantly realized. Such realization can be achieved only in freedom. In the moral and political realm freedom may be an ideal, but in the esthetic and spiritual order it is an absolute necessity, the inner quality without which there is no growth. This ethical ideal is not presented as a dictate of reason. Wordsworth's experience as a Godwinian had taught him that sheer reason cannot present an ideal in such a way that it commands enthusiastic obedience.

The sympathy which supports this moral ideal is but one phase of a wider feeling for all life, which is directed not only toward human beings but also toward all Nature's creatures. Thus there are in Wordsworth some sympathetic appreciations of animal life, like

> The hare was running races in her mirth

from "Resolution and Independence," and the grotesque but sincere picture of the ass in "Peter Bell." Wordsworth is even inclined to recognize a genuine value, an absolute importance, in the life of a plant. Something of this is, I think, expressed in the lines which include the startling

> It is my faith that every flower
> Enjoys the air it breathes.

Although Wordsworth does not carry this attitude to an oriental extreme, it is safe enough to say that his feeling for the lesser creatures of Nature's Kingdom is often deeply religious.

* * *

It is clear that Wordsworth believed in more than he could prove rationally. But rational philosophy may be of assistance even to a mystic. Reason can help to render mystical revelations more explicit, and it can help to prepare a consistent statement of belief, even though such belief derives its authority from suprarational intuition. Such a translation of mysticism into coherent discourse puts a great strain upon one's philosophical vocabulary and requires a most conscientious search for adequate concepts.

Thus Wordsworth's writings embody a good deal of philosophical energy. We have already mentioned the importance of Shaftesbury for the study of Wordsworth. Although he went far beyond Shaftesbury in many ways, Wordsworth seems to have felt a very real sympathy with him.[19] Also some of Wordsworth's concepts are borrowed from the sensationalism or empiricism of the eighteenth-century British tradition and, again, some of them from Continental sources quite opposed to this tradition. But in Wordsworth's synthesis these two do not sharply conflict—at least not so sharply as they appear to do in most handbooks of the history of philosophy. This is, at least at first, partially owing to the fact that Wordsworth's thought is, as we have mentioned, not highly analytical and also partially owing to the influence of the German philosopher and theosophist, Jakob Boehme (d. 1624), which is to be remarked in *The Prelude.* The fusion of sensationalism and intuitive philosophy is manifest in the theory of imagination which Wordsworth records in the last books of *The Prelude.* On Wordsworth's theory of imagination, Mr. de Selincourt has commented as follows: "All intellectual and spiritual growth comes from the reaction of the senses, chiefly of the eye and ear, to the external world, which is 'exquisitely fitted to the mind,' but the highest vision is superinduced upon this in a state of ecstasy, in which the light of sense goes out and the soul feels its kinship with that which is beyond sense."[20] This doctrine has ethical and religious implications which Wordsworth emphasizes very heavily. Here, I believe, he also borrowed certain concepts from Spinoza which he recast somewhat to fit his own beliefs. Indeed, Wordsworth saw in imagination, of a primarily esthetic type, the organ whereby we may free ourselves from that "human bondage" which is otherwise almost universal. Imagination in its broadest exercise, when it enlightens our moral decisions, insures an inner,

---

[19] See below, pp. 128, 134-140.   [20] *Op. cit.,* p. 541.

moral freedom. Imagination can also foster what both Words-worth and Spinoza call "intellectual love," which is the emo-tional support of the highest ethical achievement. Wordsworth adopted an ethics of imagination to take the place of the God-winian ethics of reason, which had held an uncongenial fascina-tion over his mind during the middle nineties—the period just before he happily made the acquaintance of Coleridge.

We cannot emphasize too heavily the fact that Wordsworth was never completely satisfied with a strictly sensationalist theory of knowledge, nor on the other hand with a strictly rationalist ethics of the Godwinian type. Neither of these philosophies can tolerate the mystical awareness from which Wordsworthian thought springs nor do they present conclu-sions consistent with it. But a philosophy of imagination is not so limited, for imagination may be described as one of the preconditions of mystical awareness and may at times be said actually to merge with such awareness. Imagination aids mys-tical intuition by achieving a concentration of mental power in one act of attention. This, so to speak, momentarily frees the "spirit" from the "flesh" or from the welter of desires and preoccupations of one sort or another which hold the mind in bondage to personal needs and interests. It allows the mar-gins of our consciousness, so often ignored in both theory and practice, to complete our view of things.

But it follows from this that a truly "Wordsworthian" philosophy of man and of Nature can appeal only to those few persons who exercise their imaginations freely and in-tensely in the appreciation and creation of beauty. All men may, perhaps, be, in some measure, capable of this; but, in point of fact, few of them have achieved this goal. Indeed, most people have lacked the leisure and the culture or back-ground, which is usually not a matter of formal education, to recognize this goal as important—and all this through no fault of theirs.

There came a time when Wordsworth suddenly found him-self most painfully aware of this truth—which was somehow vividly brought home to him after the death of his brother at

sea. Wordsworth then realized what is undoubtedly true—
that the greater part of mankind draws its faith and its fortitude to withstand misfortunes from sources much humbler
than those which he had himself, at an earlier time, extolled
in such unconditional terms. Hence there follows a period of
Stoicism in Wordsworth's thinking. This ethical point of view
is expressed in terms borrowed from Schiller, whose theory of
the *schöne Seele* served as a sort of transition in Wordsworth's
development, and also in terms probably springing more directly from the Kantian ethics. Wordsworth has nothing very
original to say about Stoicism; but his expression of this ethical
attitude is important because, perhaps unconsciously, he makes
clear the emotional foundations from which such teaching
draws support. The "Ode to Duty" is an excellent example
of this. This Stoic doctrine gradually appears more and more
closely allied with orthodox Christianity, at any rate with
the more outward and respectable forms of it. Accordingly,
Wordsworth's earlier pantheistic interpretation of his mysticism is lost from view. As we know, in the later drafts of
The Prelude, pantheism is often concealed or even entirely
erased.

Wordsworth's Stoicism emphasizes the moral dependence
of the individual upon an eternal law of duty—something akin
to Kant's categorical imperative. Thus the individualism of
Wordsworth's earlier utterances, according to which ideas of
right and wrong are products of the individual's enlightened
desire, is retracted. With this retraction, Wordsworth swings
away from the revolutionary theory of democracy which had
characterized his earlier political views. These views had constituted a democratic humanism. To the mystical Wordsworth
the potentialities of human nature had seemed unlimited. The
dignity of the human soul, once freed, by an equalitarian system, from artificial and traditional restraint was to be the
foundation of a new order, an order which was to be the direct
outcome of the awakening of the individual to the realization
of his powers. This awakening was to involve an artistic, a
moral, and a religious reorientation, undominated by authority

or formal tradition. Wordsworth relinquished this ideal gradually, passing through Stoicism, or obedience to rational law, toward a traditional authoritarianism or obedience to an established order. It is my belief that this change of heart was quite sincere and no more influenced by self-interest than are the political and social opinions of most honest men. This political reorientation, coming as it does in conjunction with a stern and authoritarian morality and with the decline of Wordsworth's mystical vision and enthusiasm, casts a forbidding, if heroic, aspect over much of his later work, as in "Laodamia." Those who find in the Wordsworth of *The Prelude* and of *The Recluse* one of the great prophets of romantic individualism will consider this outcome of his ethical thought as the disintegration of a noble philosophy, and such a critic will feel this even if he does not doubt Wordsworth's sincerity.

* * *

A survey of Wordsworth's philosophical sources and a statement of his beliefs do not by themselves indicate the manner of his philosophical thinking. We have said that Wordsworth's "message," his advice to his fellow men, is lucid enough; even when he himself alters his teaching, his intention, is clear. But concerning his attitude toward philosophical concepts a great deal of disagreement is possible. On one hand, there is Matthew Arnold who doubts that there is very much intellectual firmness in Wordsworth's work, and on the other there is Leslie Stephen who speaks of a systematic theory of ethics latent in Wordsworth's poems. This notion is now being restated by Dover Wilson, who looks to Professor Beatty for confirmation.

In this discussion certain questions must be answered: How far did Wordsworth think out his conclusions and how far did he borrow them? Do *The Prelude* and *The Excursion* contain a reasoned argument? Do we find evidence of rational inquiry or evidence of feelings of approval and disapproval directed toward borrowed ideas? In answering these questions, one may learn as much about Wordsworth's mind as one can learn from identifying the philosophical themes with which he worked.

To begin with, I think it is clear that Wordsworth does not resort to argument based upon an independent inquiry. What he does is to present doctrine, often borrowed but carefully "edited" through a process of selection, which offers an expression, not too obscure, of experience otherwise incommunicable. Nonetheless, there is always a sense of something uncommunicated, or something beyond the reach of the philosopher and his terminology. Thus Wordsworth is constantly searching, throughout his greatest and happiest period, for a philosophical medium. This search seems to have begun during Wordsworth's university days at Cambridge. Even at this time Wordsworth tells us that his beliefs depended not only upon intuitive consciousness but upon "deep analogies by thought supplied." It is interesting to observe that he speaks of *analogies* rather than of *proofs* or *demonstrations*. In philosophy the analogy, although frequently employed, is considered rather more a mode of exposition than of proof.

Sometimes Wordsworth makes a startling shift of concepts, as when in the "Intimations Ode" he takes up the notion of personal pre-existence which is only just mentioned in *The Prelude*. In the "Ode," Wordsworth emphasizes a new concept and finds it a powerful instrument of communication. Thus Wordsworth frequently plays with metaphysical notions, but his playing is not irresponsible. It is a sort of experiment.

In most cases the reasoning which lies implicit in the structure of the concept so employed is not Wordsworth's. Wordsworth records a preoccupation with formal problems only very occasionally, as when he tells us how, after examining the question of moral obligation and probing the nature of conscience, he "yielded up moral question in despair." But Wordsworth was driven to this uncongenial task, when, horrified by the emotional excesses of the French Revolution, he wished to construct a purely impersonal and objective system of morals. This period, which was one of great unhappiness for Wordsworth, was not typical of his development. It was, indeed, very "unlike him," constituting as it did a complete frustration of his mystical powers, and bringing about the great crisis of his life.

The very genuine consistency of Wordsworth's central argument is owing to the fact that throughout the great periods of his work, from 1798 to 1805, and again from 1805, say, through the completion of *The Excursion,* he is employed in translating experience which is largely consistent in content because honestly and spontaneously felt. In relating philosophical doctrine that does justice to such experience, Wordsworth shows a breadth of understanding, I should say, of a high order. But, of course, Wordsworth is not a philosophical strategist; and we should hardly expect to find him defending his position, step by step of discursive argument. He would probably prefer to offer the skeptic another version or translation of his experience, and he would always try to appeal directly to the intuitions and to the experience of his critic.

Let no one say that such procedure is unworthy of the great problems with which Wordsworth has to do. After all, inference is by no means the very heart of philosophy. All inference must follow upon a preliminary vision or insight, just as in science experiment must follow upon the vision that discerns feasible hypotheses. Mr. Whitehead would go even further: "All inference in philosophy is a sign of that imperfection which clings to all human endeavor. The aim of philosophy is sheer disclosure."[21] So, too, Coleridge wrote in March, 1801: "My opinion is that deep thinking is attainable only by a man of deep feeling; and that all truth is a species of revelation."

* * *

    . . . Not Chaos, not
The darkest pit of lowest Erebus,
Nor aught of blinder vacancy scooped out,
By help of dreams—can breed such fear and awe
As fall upon us often when we look
Into our minds, into *the Mind of Man*—
My haunt and the main region of my song.

  . . . .
  . . . . by *words*
Which speak of nothing more than what we are.

[21] *Modes of Thought* (New York, 1938), p. 67.

Would I arouse the sensual from their sleep
    Of Death. . . .[22]

Here Wordsworth states in very compact form what we might call the first principle of his mystical humanism, whereby he concentrates a whole philosophy of life into the story of his own mind. Strictly speaking, this view of life is the way in which a sensitive mind, exposed to a certain environment, comes in contact with Nature and with humanity, with the physical world, on one hand, and with human nature as it appears in living people and in human history, on the other. So conceived, philosophy is not a body of principles to be established by proof. It is rather the generalized content of human experience. Many people do not understand such a philosophy, but the reason is that their experience has been much more limited than that of their would-be teacher, or that they are too impatient to cultivate reflection. The thinker's purpose is to persuade by sharing his experience, through expressing what he has felt. He renders palpable experience that is, potentially at any rate, universally human. And it is such exposition that carries the burden of his argument.

From this point of view—and, of course, we must admit that many critics will not accept any such point of view—we may insist that Wordsworth has written in *The Prelude* a "genuine philosophical poem" and a great one. Here we go beyond Coleridge's own statement in the *Biographia*. But Coleridge was perhaps wrong in expecting something greater to follow, something greater than the full account of the growth of the poet's mind, which is at once "an historic and a prophetic lay." According to this point of view, a formal philosophy is little more than the index of a soul's growth. The "truest" philosophy is the orientation of one who has lived broadly and richly, who has suffered much and has overcome that suffering. The development of such a mind will represent a widening and deepening epitome of human life and its place in the world. Such a philosophy can hardly come to a "conclusion." It can be no more absolutely conclusive than life itself.

[22] *The Recluse*, fragment. Italics mine.

I believe that during the first composition of *The Prelude* Wordsworth was very close to such a method of philosophical thought. In his later career, however, he became too eager for absolute certainty in matters moral and political to cultivate any such method of reflection.

But in the early days he did not need to search for certainty. Insofar as the foundations of his belief were concerned, Wordsworth was then overwhelmed with certainty. As he tells us in the "Intimations Ode," his thought passed gradually from an intense and almost ineffable blaze of intuition into a philosophy, based upon intuition, but rendered communicable and, we may add, to some extent, publicly defensible by means of discursive analogies and metaphysical concepts. In his childhood and youth, the sense of the one life extending throughout Nature possessed Wordsworth and even exalted him, but it dazzled rather than enlightened his understanding. While at Cambridge, perhaps because he was removed from the disturbing grandeur of his home in the Lake Country, he acquired enough reflective detachment to study his own mode of experience and directly to recognize his "powers" and his "habits." It was then, we may suppose, that he first distinguished—I will not say *analyzed*—the elements which composed his world. He looked for "universal things" and found the "*common countenance* of earth and heaven," the "one presence of Nature" as the central object of his awareness. Here the sentiment of Being or of unity could be isolated. Also he examined the psychological condition of his awareness and he learned to recognize "visitings of the Upholder of the tranquil Soul." Here he was able to discern something of the manner of his inspiration, of Eolian visitations. He also came to speak of Nature in animistic, even in moralistic, terms. And, what is more, he came to know that many people considered such notions a product of madness. From then on, his task was to make intelligible to his understanding, and to the understanding of others, what was so intense and insistent in his own intuition. For a short time, indeed, he failed to satisfy even his own understanding, and he fell into a preoccupation with formal reasoning which quite baffled his receptive and sympathetic spirit. It was only after this, when Boehme and Spinoza took the place of Godwin in his philosophy, that Wordsworth achieved a synthesis of insight and interpretation; and this latter period constituted the golden age of his thought and his poetry.

This synthesis is stated in the last books of *The Prelude*. It is not offered as a system of ethics or of natural theology. It is not carried point by point in a tactical campaign of persuasion. The poet prefers to record his own experience as enlightened by his own meditations, for he has "thought long and deeply" about and around his experience and he has defended his own insight against his own skepticism. But, even so, he does not offer the skeptic a chain of argument. Rather he invites him to change his spiritual way of life, to stimulate the sources of insight and of feeling and then to reconsider the function and the authority of analytical reasoning.

*   *   *   *

Wordsworth has been called the "philosopher's poet," and doubtless even his most inveterate enemies will admit that his work is heavily laden with philosophy. Again and again we find that his lines are labored with wisdom and at times with a complexity of doctrine that is not common even in explicitly philosophical poetry. Metaphysical profundity alternates, and is even at times interwoven, with magnificent description of natural beauty, and the whole is suffused with an exalted sense of the poet's dedication, the sincerity of which it is impossible to doubt. We sense continually Wordsworth's belief that he is offering us a teaching of supreme importance for human happiness and that he has discovered the hidden springs of true spiritual power whence our human dignity originates. Wordsworth has succeeded as few poets ever have in communicating his own sense of the tremendous significance of his subject; and he has done this even while presenting a scheme of considerable subtlety. Matthew Arnold may be right in saying that many didactic and doctrinaire passages in *The Excursion* are disappointing as poetry and, considered as philosophy, little more than complicated platitudes. But surely such judgment cannot apply to *The Prelude*, where the genial power of a great conviction carries us into very complex thought. Obscurities, of course, there are. But if our argument in the sequel has not shown that Wordsworth's thought possessed a real inner consistency at its greatest period and that it follows always an intelligible continuity of development, we have failed utterly in this volume. We have come to believe that when Wordsworth is obscure the reason is often that he is trying to be precise. He is trying to report accurately upon the delicate contours of things which most of us see only at a distance.

Once we come to feel this, we are free to dismiss most of the adverse criticisms that have troubled us. There may be unevennesses in Wordsworth's work—both esthetic and intellectual—but there is honest vision at the heart of it. Wordsworth wrote down what he saw, and in his greatest moments he wrote down very little else. After all, it is the prejudiced and the impatient who scorn Wordsworth. Those who are already committed to another view of life are irked by the intensity of his conviction. And those who are too hurried to cultivate his variety of philosophy, which requires a most patient reflection and introspection to probe the sources of moral, esthetic, and religious experience—those who would have all things clear from the start and who would rather be clearly wrong than vaguely and darkly right—will speak of the "warm, intuitive muddle" of Wordsworth's thought. But the sympathetic student of Wordsworth need never admit that this haughty skepticism is really anything more than an asylum of impatient and unconscious prejudice. It is largely for the purpose of defending the later proposition that I have undertaken this study.

There are inconsistencies, vacillations, and grave imperfections in Wordsworth's philosophy, particularly in the later development of his ethical thinking. We shall make little effort to condone these faults. But, serious though they are, these shortcomings are of the sort which one may expect to find even in a writer of integrity and intelligence.

CHAPTER II

"Hartley Transcendentalized by Coleridge"

WHAT is sometimes called the Wordsworthian feeling for Nature has, as we have just stated provisionally, two aspects. For the sake of convenience, we shall call these the sentiment of Being and the sense of Eolian influence, or the poet's sense of the concrete unity and interpenetration of all things on the one hand, and his sense of a suprapersonal inspiration on the other. The word "Nature" applies to both experiences. "Nature" signifies the unity of the poet's environment which encompasses and includes his own living and his own thinking; and again the word signifies the source of the poet's inspiration. In both cases Nature is thought to be like the God of most higher religions, more similar to mind than to matter. This is true even though Nature is recognized as the all-inclusive unity of the world.

In what follows, we shall trace the development of Wordsworth's ideas concerning Nature and the poet's relation to Nature. To do this, we shall have occasion to examine his notion of "imagination," which is the name given by Wordsworth to the highest esthetic function of the human mind, whereby that mind is opened to Eolian influence. Perhaps the best way to present this notion is briefly to trace its ingredients. These are derived from several sources, which are themselves often considered as incompatible. First, there are the views of the British sensationalists or associationists. For these thinkers imagination is one among the several ways whereby sensuous impressions become bound together to produce complex ideas. On the other hand appear the mystics, thinkers like Jakob Boehme, William Law, and others. For them imagination is an act of creation or expression whereby the human mind imitates, even perhaps participates in, the divine creation, which is also an imagination, for God creates "in his image."

Wordsworth recognizes that imagination is a feature of consciousness which derives at least much of its content from the activity of the sense organs and whose content is in large measure ordered according to the principle of the association of ideas, whereby items of consciousness tend to call one another before attention. Wordsworth may very well have borrowed these principles from an acquaintance, more or less intimate, with the writings of Hartley and of Alison. This is all the more likely since we know that Coleridge, who, as all students admit, often guided Wordsworth in his philosophizing, passed through a period of great admiration for Hartley. Hartley's theory of mind and of knowledge is close to that of Locke, except in that he emphasizes the association of ideas as heavily as does Hume, although without Hume's subtlety. Hartley attempts to account for associations by appealing to a theory of vibrations that occur in the nervous system and are correlated with conscious ideas. Hartley's ethics lean toward hedonism. All this is combined with a surprisingly orthodox theology.

We can easily conceive of Wordsworth's early enthusiasm for Hartleian psychology. As a keen observer of esthetic detail apparent in natural landscape, he might easily have been inclined to favor the Lockian notion, present in Hartley's work, that all our ideas are built up solely by combination and arrangement of data first given to the mind in sensuous experience. People who emphasize observation are likely to consider sensuous data as the primary condition of all awareness. Again, as a patient and profound introspectionist, Wordsworth was, we know, impressed and delighted by the theories which explain the mutual attraction or association of ideas. He was perhaps most interested in the way a sensation or sensuous idea can revive emotional states with which it has once been linked; for this helps to explain how poetry can appeal to the emotions of the reader, especially when it has to do with those forms of experience that are at bottom much the same in the life of every person. Furthermore, Wordsworth's inclination to consider his own childhood and his own emotional, intellectual, and spiritual growth as a fit subject of his poetry would easily dispose his mind toward welcoming the beginnings of the science of genetic psychology to be found in Hartley and in similar writers; unless, indeed, we must admit that Wordsworth's interest in such things was directly inspired by the psychologists.

Wordsworth may even, for a time, have reconciled his sense of the living power in Nature with a sensationalist philosophy, although in this respect Bishop Berkeley and Alison are as important as Hartley himself. Certainly Coleridge found it possible in *Religious Musings* to support beliefs which seem very like mystical pantheism by reference to Hartley's psychology.[1] This may surprise the modern philosophical student for whom sensationalist empiricism and a philosophy of pantheistic idealism are incompatible. For such a student no sensuous awareness, no matter how enriched by association, can by itself support any valid knowledge of the soul's union with a divine spirit. All that such a philosophy can explain is a feeling, admittedly unfounded, of divine presence. In other words no one who takes the method of sensationalism seriously can long accept with conviction the notion of an all-embracing mind with which we can come into direct contact. For the modern student of philosophy, the outcome of sensationalism lies somewhere close to the philosophy of David Hume or of John Stuart Mill, i.e., close to skepticism. But Coleridge, like many of his contemporaries, was slow to recognize this. After all, there is the theory of Bishop Berkeley, who combines, rather loosely, a sensationalist theory of knowledge with an idealism; and Coleridge was in the early years inclined to honor Berkeley as second only to Hartley himself. Both are mentioned in the notes to *Religious Musings*. A passage like the following from Berkeley's *Siris* would be most congenial to the Coleridge who wrote "The Eolian Harp" and to the Wordsworth of "Tintern Abbey":

Both Stoics and Platonics held the world to be alive: though sometimes it be mentioned as a sentient animal, sometimes as a plant or vegetable. . . .

[1] *Religious Musings*, l. 43 and n.

There is according to those philosophers a life infused throughout all things; the Πῦρ νοερὸν, Πῦρ Τεχνικόν, an intellectual and artificial fire, an inward principle, animal spirit, or natural life, producing and forming within as art doth without, regulating, moderating and reconciling the various motions, qualities, and parts of the mundane system. By virtue of this life the great masses are held together in their orderly courses, as well as the minutest particles governed in their natural motions, according to the several laws of attraction, gravity, electricity, magnetism, and the rest. It is this that gives instincts, teaches the spider her web and the bee her honey. This it is that directs the roots of plants to draw forth juices from the earth, and the leaves and cortical vessels to separate and attract such particles of air, and elementary fire as suit their respective natures.[2]

For Berkeley the whole system of the world is held together and informed by one persisting mind, "a Universal Spirit, author of life and motion."

At any rate, Hartley and Alison show how we may come to feel that the world of eye and ear is the work of a productive intelligence; and they describe how we may be brought to the point where we associate everything we behold with the idea of God. This state of mind may even be called a "union" with God. For Hartley, God is love itself which casts out all fear. Love transforms us into God's image and makes us partakers of the divine Nature. Our wills become united with God's will and are rendered free from disappointment, for, being at one with God, we find all things good, i.e., in Hartley's hedonistic scheme, objects of pleasure.[3] Here Hartley speaks of the love of God and of our sense of God's presence in the world; but this is later described as a result of a long period of education and the forming of associations based upon religious instruction, including emphasis upon miracles as reported in scripture.[4] This might perhaps have satisfied Coleridge in *Religious Musings*, but it could hardly have offered Wordsworth an explanation of the experience described in the

---

[2] Alexander Campbell Fraser (ed.), *The Works of George Berkeley* (Oxford, 1891), III, 257.
[3] David Hartley, *Observations on Man*, etc. (London, 1749), Part II, prop. LXXI.   [4] *Ibid.*, Part II, prop. LXXII.

"Ode on the Intimations of Immortality," nor is it consistent with the insight described in "Tintern Abbey." Hartley, it is true, undertakes to show how the psychology of association furthers the inculcation of orthodox religion. But this religion is not the religion of "Tintern Abbey" or of *The Prelude*.

Wordsworth found the principles of association of value in describing the way in which his mind first became attached to the objects of Nature, to the streams and hillsides which he came to love. He gradually came to enjoy these scenes and to dwell upon them because they were linked by association with his boyhood sports, which it was pleasant to remember. But this was only the first step. It was followed by a more genuinely esthetic enjoyment of the scenes which association had made dear to him on other grounds. As we shall see below (in Chapter III), Hartley and Alison may have helped him to explain some of these later enjoyments, but they can hardly have prompted the pantheistic interpretations which we shall presently describe. Wordsworth's belief in the Unity of Being and in the unquestionable reality of Eolian influence has no origin in Hartley or his school.

Nor is Hartley's theory of imagination very similar to Wordsworth's. The notion of Eolian influence prompts Wordsworth to the statement that imagination is an "element of Nature's inner self."[5] This goes far beyond Hartley, whose description of imagination follows:

The recurrence of ideas, especially visible and audible ones, in a vivid manner, but without any regard to the order observed in past facts, is ascribed to the power of imagination or fancy. Now here we may observe, that every succeeding thought is the result either of some new impression, or of an association with the preceding. And this is the common opinion. It is impossible indeed to attend so minutely to the succession of our ideas, as to distinguish and remember for a sufficient time the very impression or association which gave birth to each thought; but we can do this as far as it can be expected to be done, and in so great a variety of instances, that our argument for the prevalence of the foregoing principle of association in all instances, except those of new impressions, may be esteemed a complete induction.

[5] *The Prelude*, Bk. VIII, l. 513.

A reverie differs from imagination only in that the person being more attentive to his own thoughts, and less disturbed by foreign objects, more of his ideas are deducible from association, and fewer from new impressions.

It is to be observed, however, that in all the cases of imagination and reverie the thoughts depend, in part, upon the then state of body or mind. A pleasurable or painful state of the stomach or brain, joy or grief, will make all the thoughts warp their own way, little or much. But this exception is as agreeable to the foregoing theory, as the general prevalence of association just laid down.[6]

Hartley is even further from Wordsworth when he denies that the pleasures of imagination are of any great religious or even of eudaemonistic importance.[7] In fact, Hartley insists that the "pleasures of imagination ought not to be made a primary pursuit."

Nor again does Hartley find in this topic that mystery which surrounds all our efforts to describe a creative power. It is for him a very commonplace matter, merely a vivid, orderless memory, as Mr. Livingston Welch has pointed out in his book on imagination.[8] In fact, Wordsworth's efforts to describe imagination, obscure as they are, stand closer to those of the great philosophers than to Hartley's comparatively shallow comments. Thus Kant considers imagination a mystery, perhaps the root mystery of mind itself, and even Hume, who is inclined always to favor the principles of sensationalism and to derive all mental content, wherever possible, from sensuous impressions that live on as ideas in the flux of association—even Hume recognizes that the imagination of the artist is "inexplicable by the utmost efforts of human understanding."[9] Hume emphasizes imagination's wonderful power of selection and combination of detail for the sake of expressing an idea. There is little or nothing of this in Hartley. While groping for concepts with which to describe imagination, Wordsworth might well have turned to Hume. In point of fact, he did not. This is perhaps partly an accident, but it is

---

[6] *Op. cit.*, Part I, prop. XCI.   [7] *Ibid.*, Part II, prop. LV.
[8] *Imagination and Human Nature* (Cambridge, 1935), p. 73, n. 1.
[9] *Treatise* (2d ed., Oxford, 1896), Vol. I, Bk. I, vii, p. 24.

also owing to the fact that other writers offered interpretations of imagination as adequate as Hume's and more in keeping with the views of one whose thought has been touched by mysticism.

In the Preface to the *Lyrical Ballads* (1800) Wordsworth seems more clearly than elsewhere to stand under the influence of the Associationists. Actually, I believe that he is here no more deeply under the spell of the doctrine than in other writings. The difference is simply that in the Preface Wordsworth has occasion to emphasize one topic, that of poetic diction. He is discussing the relation of words to things and to human emotions and trying to make clear why words in current use offer greater descriptive and expressive power than those derived from a purely literary tradition. Since this argument has to do primarily with the connotations of words, emphasis upon our association of words, images, and ideas is to be expected. An essay of this sort, which is limited in length, as the author himself points out, can hardly include a very full discussion of the origins of imagination and of taste, nor does it contain any exposition of religious experience. The memorable descriptions of the poet and of the act of composition which adorn the argument make clear that poetry should be direct, vivid, even impressionistic—poetry must move in an "atmosphere of sensation" and it must establish an emotional tone through stimulating the recall of emotional states with which we are all acquainted. But I can find nothing in the Preface of 1800 which indicates that Wordsworth could not at this time have subscribed to Coleridge's famous statement, made after he had freed himself from strict Hartleian doctrine: "Association depends in a much greater degree on the recurrence of resembling states of feeling than on trains of ideas." Nor do I find that Coleridge's more extreme statement, "Ideas no more recall one another than the leaves in a tree, fluttering in the breeze, propagate their motion one to another," is inconsistent with Wordsworth's account of the poet's sometimes unconscious purpose, according to which argument ideas are the representatives of past feeling.

In short, the Preface of 1800 indicates a considerable preoccupation with the theory of association; but it does not by any means indicate that Wordsworth saw in this theory the central principle whereby the development of esthetic and religious activity is to be explained.

The fully developed theory of imagination, as we find it in *The Prelude*, contains many notions foreign to British sensationalism. As Mr. de Selincourt has explained so admirably in the introduction to his edition of *The Prelude* (scc. 12):

When Wordsworth wrote *The Prelude* he had in nothing swerved from the faith that inspired the *Lines composed a few miles above Tintern Abbey*. This faith need only be referred to here in the barest outline. Starting from a fervid belief in the inherent goodness of human nature, Wordsworth attributes the growth of the whole moral and intellectual being—from infancy through the stages of childhood and adolescence to maturity—to impressions made upon the senses, bound together, reacting on one another, and ever growing in fullness and intensity by means of the law of association. The philosophical parentage of this conception is unmistakable; it is the direct offspring of the sensationalism of the eighteenth century, and in particular of David Hartley,

> he of mortal kind
> Wisest, he first who marked the ideal tribes
> Up the fine fibres of the sentient brain,

but it is Hartley transcendentalized by Coleridge, and at once modified and exalted by Wordsworth's own mystical experience. For to him there was always this great paradox, that though it is simply by the proper exercise of eye and ear that man reaches his full moral and intellectual stature, so that he can recognize

> In Nature and the language of the sense
> The anchor of my purest thoughts, the nurse,
> The guide, the guardian of my heart, and soul
> Of all my moral being,

yet revelation flashes upon him when "the light of sense goes out"; and "laid asleep in body," he becomes deeply conscious of the presence of God within him. In the highest mood of ecstasy this consciousness of complete oneness with God is so overwhelming, that his other attributes as man seem to fall from him, and he knows only that

one interior life
In which all beings live with God, themselves
Are God, existing in the mighty whole,
As indistinguishable as the cloudless east
Is from the cloudless west, when all
The hemisphere is one cerulean blue.

How far this intense mystical experience is compatible with Christianity let theologians determine.

I agree most heartily with Mr. de Selincourt. Wordsworth frequently records an "intense, mystical experience." In fact, we may go further, with Mr. Gingerich, and say that Wordsworth "asserted unequivocally and illustrated with almost startling literalness the ancient doctrine that 'the Kingdom of Heaven is within you.' "[10] But, although deeply concerned with this rich and mysterious interior life, Wordsworth never ignores, as De Selincourt and Gingerich well know, the outer senses or underestimates their importance as agents that can further spiritual enlightenment. We face then a paradox, as Mr. de Selincourt says. On the one hand, sensations and the association of ideas; on the other, mystical vision. On the one hand, Locke and Hartley; on the other, Plotinus and St. Francis. Can we do justice to this paradox by employing the phrase "Hartley transcendentalized by Coleridge"? An impatient student might be tempted to consider this as a bold contradiction in terms, like, let us say, "G. B. Shaw romanized by G. K. Chesterton." But he would be forgetting that thought often advances by a reconciliation of opposites, which can sometimes invigorate one another.

In what, then, did this act of "transcendentalizing" consist? Primarily in the assertion that imagination, although in its outward expression manifest as the combination and moulding together of phrases and images, is in origin a suprapersonal activity in the exercise of which Nature, or the spiritual power in Nature, and the human mind may be drawn together. This notion seems to be a development of the idea tentatively ex-

[10] Solomon Francis Gingerich, *Essays in the Romantic Poets* (New York 1924), p. 130.

pressed by Coleridge in "The Eolian Harp" and, later on, systematized in the idealism of *Biographia Literaria*, and, as we shall see presently, it receives frequent and at times very complex statement throughout *The Prelude*. The pantheism which this view of the origin of imagination suggests was to give both Wordsworth and Coleridge, at one time or another, considerable concern, although at the start it seems to have brought Wordsworth no misgivings. After all, Wordsworth came upon this point of view as a substitute for Godwinian rationalism and determinism. Against such a background, the pantheism of imagination invites toleration.

From whom does Coleridge derive the concepts with which to "transcendentalize" Hartley? Many people would suggest what might seem almost to be the obvious answer, that he found them in the writings of the German idealists of the post-Kantian schools. But it is very doubtful, so the students of Coleridge tell us, that he had read at all widely in post-Kantian philosophy during the period of 1797-98, when he was exercising his greatest influence on Wordsworth. Coleridge, however, has told us that he had arrived at a position very close to that of the contemporary German idealists before he looked into their writings. Thus in *Biographia Literaria*, Chapter IX, he writes:

> In this instance, as in the dramatic lectures of Schlegel, to which I have before alluded, from the same motive of self-defense against the charge of plagiarism, many of the most striking resemblances, indeed all the main and fundamental ideas, were born and matured in my mind before I had ever seen a single page of the German Philosopher; and I might indeed affirm with truth, before the most important works of Schelling had been written or at least made public. Nor is this coincidence at all to be wondered at. We had studied in the same school, been disciplined by the same preparatory philosophy, namely, the writings of Kant; we had both equal obligations to the Polar logic and dynamic philosophy of Giordano Bruno; and Schelling has lately, and, as of recent acquisition, avowed that same affection and reverence for the labors of Behmen (Boehme) and other mystics, which I had formed at a much earlier period.[11]

[11] J. Shawcross (ed.), *Biographia Literaria* (Oxford, 1907), I, 102-103.

Now, Mr. Shawcross tells us that Coleridge was probably acquainted with Boehme's thought as early as 1795. Was it then Boehme who transcendentalized Hartley in Coleridge's mind? I believe that it was. From Boehme, via Coleridge, comes the pantheistic theory of imagination that is so characteristic of Wordsworth. For Boehme, Nature is God's imagination. God creates the world in his image, and his creative power enters not only the forms of Nature but the spirit of man, who is capable of participation in such creation. The analogy of the Eolian harp appears in Boehme, as well as the notion of a dynamic intercourse between mind and its object, and also that of the mutual interpenetration of objects. All this we shall examine in time. But let us warn the student that in Boehme's work these themes appear in a theological, even a theosophical, setting. Boehme frequently offers us what Wordsworth might well have called a sort of spiritual "gaudy verse." In Wordsworth's work the setting is much simpler, and more in keeping with common sense, being free of the almost Gnostic symbolism and of the occult and alchemistic terminology of Boehme, who even when translated in the famous "Law edition," which Coleridge knew, is almost always obscure. This probably explains the rather curious fact that although two of Boehme's volumes appeared in Wordsworth's library after his death, most scholars have hesitated to search for any possible influence. Thus Mr. Joseph Warren Beach, whose study of Wordsworth's sources has been a very conscientious one and who has made many interesting contributions, dismisses Boehme by saying that he does not speak Wordsworth's language. This is for the most part true enough, but in his own language Boehme treats many of Wordsworth's problems and comes to a very similar conclusion.

In reply to people who feel that Wordsworth's thought is essentially English and that his sources must lie in the "English tradition," outside of which it is pointless to search for them—in reply to this curious prejudice, let me say that by Wordsworth's time Boehme's work had become a part of an English tradition. The works of "Behmen" had been copiously translated into English during the seventeenth century by Ellistone and Sparrow, and these translations were reissued from 1764-81 in the famous edition, sponsored by the leading English Behmenist of the time, William Law, author of *The Serious Call.* There was a lively interest in Boehme's thought, not only among Quakers, who found him most congenial, as indeed they still do, but in other circles as well. Law himself was a Church of England clergyman; and further, we may judge from Butler's *Hudibras* that Boehme had been in certain spheres a fashionable, if obscure, topic of conversation.

> He Anthroposophus and Floud
> And Jacob Behmen understood.

Among Boehme's many admirers even Sir Isaac Newton may be counted, and there has been some interesting, if over-bold, speculation concerning the influence of Boehme upon Newton's scientific thought. There seems then no reason to ignore Boehme and even no motive to do so, unless it be some sort of insularity which dislikes to recognize the influence of "foreign" writers.

In our first comparison of Boehme and Wordsworth, we shall emphasize the following topics, indicating only the broadest similarity and leaving all discussion of details and verbal echoes until later:

1. The nature of imagination.
2. The relation of sense to soul.
3. The origin of mystical vision.
4. "The *one* life within us and abroad."
5. The contrast between intuitive wisdom and scientific reason.

(1) For our present purposes a very general statement of what Boehme means by "imagination" will be sufficient. Accordingly, the following statement is no more than a briefest summary. For a fuller understanding of the union of opposites as it appears in the theory of imagination, the reader is referred below to the Appendix entitled "Imagination in *Biographia Literaria.*"

It is important to notice that Boehme employs the German

word *imagination*. For Boehme, imagination is a form of will-ing. "The *'imagination'* is not the *'Einbildung'* which implies fancy and pretense, nor is it *'phantasie'*. . . . *'Imagination'* is indeterminate will becoming determinate. It is empty form becoming filled with content. Boehme speaks of will as 'cen-tering' itself in some object which thereupon becomes the 'Wesen' (substance) of the will. . . ." Apart from this "sub-stance" upon which it feeds, human imagination is quite im-potent. " 'Where no substance is there is no creating, for a creating spirit is no conceivable substance, but it must draw substance into itself through its imagination else it would not subsist' " (*The Incarnation*, I, 5:59).

Thus imagination is mind most intimately united with its object. But it is creative mind and hence an echo of divinity. Boehme's God is a source of eternal creation, whereby he "images" or shapes the world.

"Human imagination is the temporal repetition of the eternal process by which the 'Ungrund' goes over into the 'grund,' the 'abyss' into the 'byss' " (as the indeterminate becomes determined).[12]

Human imagination is the temporal repetition of an eternal process—this fundamental doctrine of Boehme appears again in both Schelling and Coleridge as any student of Mr. Shaw-cross's edition of *Biographia Literaria* well knows. When Coleridge tells us that he found much of post-Kantian German idealism in Boehme before he read Schelling, he is in all prob-ability reporting quite accurately upon his own reading. But let us follow Mr. Brinton a little further and clarify somewhat the passage which has already been quoted.

In the passive phase of the will its "Imagination" is much like our modern "effort of attention." According to the theory involved in this phrase any idea which excludes all others from the field of atten-tion discharges in action. In this way the will accepts its object and becomes immersed in the life stream of reality. *Thus will takes on the form of that on which it is "centered," to use Boehme's oft-recurring word.* . . .

[12] Howard H. Brinton, *The Mystic Will, Based on a Study of the Philosophy of Jacob Boehme* (New York, 1930), pp. 108-109.

But this passive process by which the undetermined will is "impregnated" by objects is always accompanied by a creative process through which the will determines itself and so brings its hidden possibilities to manifestation. . . . To the active will nature is a "mirror" in which the soul sees its deepest longing reflected from the inner depths. The world of external objects is not merely the world of the senses. It is also the world in which the possible lies hidden behind the sensual, a mirror world of imagination which becomes actualized as the will breaks through nature and so comes to a deeper knowledge of itself.[13]

The above summary, which is built upon many passages from Boehme, reminds us of a familiar passage from Wordsworth's Preface of 1800. In this essay, as we have seen, Wordsworth is relying rather more than is usual with him upon an associationist psychology. Still he is willing to make a statement like the following: "[The poet] considers man and Nature as essentially adapted to each other, and the mind of man as naturally the mirror of the fairest and most interesting properties of Nature." This can hardly be out-and-out associationism whereby mind is adapted to Nature rather than the reverse; but it is quite consistent with the doctrine of the "ennobling interchange" as it appears elsewhere in Wordsworth.

The active and passive phases of imagination are sometimes as in the *Divine Intuition* figuratively compared by Boehme to the process of breathing. There are then two distinct moments, that of inspiration or in-breathing and that of "speaking" or out-breathing. The two are considered inseparable in human life. God is described as an "eternal speaking."

Let us ponder the two foregoing quotations as patiently as possible. Mr. Brinton has done much to clarify Boehme, but he cannot dispel the intrinsic difficulty of the thought. Then let us consider Boehme's teaching with reference to Wordsworth's theory of imagination.

In the first place, imagination is for Boehme both *sensitive* and *creative*. It has a passive or attentive and an active or a creative phase. This, as we know, is true also for Wordsworth.

[13] *Ibid.*, pp. 112-113. Italics mine.

Again, imagination is united with the objects upon which it "centers." This is Boehme, who argues that imagination finds itself, so to speak, in contact with objects which somehow reflect its potentialities. This is, I think, also Wordsworth. Boehme's doctrine has given us a key to one of the most interesting passages in *The Prelude* (Bk. XII, ll. 368 ff.):

> ... and I remember well
> That in life's every-day appearances
> I seem'd about this period to have sight
> Of a new world, a world, too that was fit
> To be transmitted and made visible
> To other eyes, as having for its base
> That whence our dignity originates
> That which both gives it being and maintains
> A balance, an ennobling interchange
> Of action from within and from without,
> The excellence, pure spirit, and best power
> Both of the object seen, and eye that sees.

This "new world" is the real world, at last understood, which has for its base the power which underlies mind and object and which draws them together in "ennobling interchange." Thus the mind receives and gives, senses and creates. It must do both if it is to participate in the process which leads towards its own perfection and (less familiar theme) the perfection of the objects with which it works.

In all probability Wordsworth became aware of this "ennobling interchange" before he had ever heard Coleridge expounding Boehme. Boehme supplies only a medium of expression. The experience from which Wordsworth works in this passage dates from "about the time" of the poet's excursion on Salisbury Plain. Acquaintance with Boehme came probably considerably later.

The unity of the world, so vivid to Wordsworth, here becomes a dynamic unity, a unity of development and of creation. It is worth while noticing that an authority on philosophical idealism, the late Mr. J. H. Muirhead, writing in the *Encyclopaedia Britannica*[14] has described that school of thought

[14] Fourteenth ed., article: "Idealism."

as one that "conceives of knowledge or experience as a process in which the two factors of subject and object stand in a relation of entire interdependence on each other as warp and woof." He insists later on upon the common origin of subject and object. "The power and vitality of the one is the power and vitality of the other, and this is so because they are not two things with separate roots but are both rooted in a common reality which, while it includes both, is more than either."

From this point of view, it is reasonable to maintain that Wordsworth's utterances concerning mind and its object are among the earliest statements of modern English idealism, which, like its German cousin, is influenced by Boehme.[15]

This "principle of idealism" is developed at great length by Boehme in his dark and tumultuous way. Let us quote one paragraph from the *Theoscopia* or Divine Intuition which summarizes with rather more clarity than usual the source of Boehme's thought:

The visible world with its host of creatures is nothing else than the emanated Word (of God) which has disposed itself into qualities, *as in qualities the particular will has arisen. And with the receptibility of the Will the creaturely life arose;* which life has in the beginning of this world introduced itself into a receptivity for a creaturely ground, which the separator has separated according to the quality, and brought to a will of its own after such a fashion. *And with the self-will of such desire, substance or body of its likeness and quality has arisen* to each receptivity; whereby the separator has signed itself and made itself visible, as is to be seen in every life.[16]

If the reader will contrast the two passages which I have italicized, he will find the "receptibility" of will standing opposite the "self-will" of desire. The first is involved in the very existence of a finite creature and the second in its development and self-assertion. All creatures find themselves as entities within a world which they have not made, but on the other hand they must be active and must exercise an effect upon the world. The first follows from what Boehme calls the "passivity" of the will; the second, from its "activity." These two

---

[15] For a statement of Coleridge's development of this principle see below, pp. 259 ff. [16] *Theoscopia*, 3: 14. Italics mine.

tendencies unite, and there is, to use the Wordsworthian term, an "ennobling interchange" between the inner and outer powers. This takes place on every level of development and is especially remarkable in the exercise of the higher powers of consciousness which are at once sensitive and creative.

This concept of Boehme's has a wide influence throughout English and German Romanticism. It appears in Blake, Coleridge, and Wordsworth, as also in the great philosophies of German Romanticism which culminate in Hegel. The two streams of influence seem to be at first unrelated, although in the *Biographia* Coleridge recognizes their parallel course.

Here lies, I think, the secret of the final strophe of *The Recluse* fragment where Wordsworth tells us how exquisitely the individual mind (and, indeed, the powers of the human race as a whole) is "fitted" to the external world; and again how the reverse is true: how the world itself is fitted to the mind. Mr. Joseph Warren Beach has also found the passage from *The Recluse* to be an instance of Wordsworth's thinking which clearly transcends Hartleian doctrine.[17] Mr. Beach does not, however, consider the historical background of this passage as Behmenistic. He prefers another source which he finds in Sir Matthew Hale's *Primitive Origination of Mankind* (1677), a copy of which was found in Wordsworth's library after his death:

It is an admirable evidence of the Divine Wisdom and Providence, that there is that suitable accommodation and adaptation of all things in Nature, both to their own convenience and exigence, and to the convenience, use, and exigence of one another; which evidenceth, 1. That all things are made, governed, and disposed by a most intelligent, and wise, and powerful Being. 2. That that governing Being is but one, and that all this accommodation, and adaptation, and mutual subservience of the things in Nature are the product of one most wise decree, counsel, and purpose of that one most wise, intelligent, and sovereign Being.

It is not here reasonable to make a large prosecution of the particular instances of that accommodation of things in Nature, nor of

[17] *The Concept of Nature in Nineteenth Century English Poetry* (New York, 1936), pp. 145-147.

the necessity of the former consequences arising from it. The instances thereof that are suitable to the Design meant in this Discourse, shall be only these two, which I shall but shortly touch: 1. The admirable accommodation of Sensible Faculty to the Objects of Sense, and of those Objects to it, and of both to the well-being of the Sensible Nature: 2. The admirable accommodation of the Intellectual Faculty in Man to Intellectual Objects, and of those objects to it, and of both to the well-being of the Humane or Rational Nature.

Touching the former, the Sensible Nature in its complement and integrity hath five exterior powers or faculties, that are accommodated to all those motions or impressions of natural bodies, and their accidents which are useful to it; and by these five ports or gates all those impressions which are useful for the perception of the Sensible Nature are communicated to it, namely, the five exterior Senses. It is not only possible, but very likely, that there may be such motions or qualities of Bodies, that make not any impression upon any of those Senses; but if there be such, they are such as are not of use for the perception or convenience of the Sensible Nature. But for such as are necessary for such perception of the Sensible Nature, there is no motion, quality, or operation of external Bodies, but what hath accommodated to it a Faculty in Sense receptive of it: Is there such a motion or objectiveness of external Bodies which produceth light or colour, figure, vicinity, or distance; the Faculty of Sight is fitted to receive that impression or objectiveness, and that objectiveness fitted and accommodated to that Faculty. Is there that motion or objectiveness that causeth sounds? the Faculty of Hearing is fitted to be receptive of it, and that objectiveness or motion (or what ever it is) fitted to make an impression upon that Faculty. And so for the other Senses. And by this adaptation and congruity of these Faculties to their several proper Objects, and by the fitness and proportionateness of these objective Impressions, Qualities, or Motions, upon their respective Faculties, accommodated to their reception, the Sensible Nature hath so much of perception and reception of things as is necessary for its sensible Being. I speak not here of those other interior Senses of Discrimination of the Objects of Sense, Phantasie, Memory, Appetite, and the rest, for they are not at present to my purpose.

II. And what is thus excellent and admirable in the accommodation between the sensitive Faculties and their Objects, is to be observed in the intellectual Faculty, though the Faculty and Object are far more noble and excellent than that of Sense. As there is an accommodation between the visive Faculty and its Object, and as there is an accommodation between the Faculty of the Taste and the Object, the Object fitted to make an impression upon the Faculty, and Faculty fitted to take the impression from the Object; so there is an accommodation, and sutable [sic] adaptation between the intellective Faculty and the intelligible Object, the Object as it were thrusting itself into the Faculty, and the Faculty receiving and perceiving the Object.

This affords a very interesting parallel, one which it would be folly to ignore. That it contributed to Wordsworth's thinking is very probable. But there are considerations which will, I think, lead us to accept the Behmenistic doctrine as more intimately connected with the "growth of the poet's mind." In the first place, the emphasis upon the *creative* power of the mind which is to be found in Boehme and in Wordsworth is not very marked in Hale's work. He distinguishes, as Mr. Beach points out, between active and passive powers; but he does not play with the notion that human imagination is an echo of, or even perhaps a participant in, cosmic or divine creation. Nor is there to be found in the passage quoted from Hale that preoccupation with esthetic and religious enthusiasm which characterizes Wordsworth's utterance and to a very considerable extent determines the meaning of such a phrase as that describing the "creation" which the human mind and the world "with blended might accomplish." Wordsworth is thinking primarily of man's imagination with its full esthetic and religious potentialities. So, in general, is Boehme although he puts the religious above the esthetic. Hale, however, is interested rather more in what we might call "general psychology." Moreover, it is altogether probable that Wordsworth found Hale's views on the delicate interrelation of mind and world congenial, and they may well have strengthened his acceptance of Boehme's teaching. The argument as presented in *The Recluse* is near enough to Hale's statements. The great passage in *The Prelude*, at the close of Book XII (1805), stands closer to Boehme.

(2) Our second topic, the relation of sense to soul in Boehme's theory, is very pertinent to the solution of our imme-

diate problem: How did Coleridge transcendentalize Hartley?
We might suppose that Wordsworth, having studied Hartley
and sympathized with the movement of eighteenth-century
psychology, would place greater emphasis upon the importance
of the senses in the growth of spiritual life than would Boehme,
a religious mystic of the early seventeenth century. But to
suppose any such thing is to underestimate the historically pre-
cocious fertility of Boehme's mind. Consider, for example,
Boehme's ". . . if (the mind) had no sense perception, then it
would have no knowledge of itself nor of any other thing and
could neither work nor act."[18] When we consider Boehme's
dates, we find this statement remarkable, but by no means so
remarkable as what immediately follows; for Boehme proceeds to outline a theory of the relation of sense to soul which
is not to become generally understood among philosophers
until the emergence of the transcendental theory of knowledge
advocated by the great German idealists. Boehme holds that
the soul comes to dominate the senses. In normal development, a "center" or object of our "ego-hood" arises so that
the ego, having an object of its own, may transcend or control
the senses and the desires which accompany them. This "center" or object of the ego's will comes to be through the conflict
of the several senses, and its emergence prevents the soul from
succumbing to one form of sensuous activity at the expense of
others, thus maintaining a "temperature" or "harmony" of
mental life. Unless the ego finds a center or object, it cannot
assert itself; indeed, it hardly exists as an active being. If,
however, it finds a center, the ego gains *dominion* over the
senses and desires and over the special centers or objects which
they introduce.

18. If the soul did not itself flow from itself, it would have no
sense-perception; but if it had no sense-perception, neither would it
have any knowledge of itself, nor of any other thing, and were
incapable of doing or working. But the efflux of sense from the soul
(which efflux is a counter-stroke of the soul, in which the soul feels
itself) endows the soul with will or desire, so that it introduces the
senses into a something, viz. into a *centrum* of an ego-hood, wherein

[18] *Theoscopia*, 1: 18.

the soul works through sense, and reveals and contemplates itself in its working through the senses.

19. Now if in these *centra* of sense in the counterstroke of the soul there were no *contrarium*, then all the *centra* of emanated sense were but a one; in all the *centra* of sense but one single will, that did continually but one and the same thing. How could then the wonders and powers of the divine wisdom become known by the soul (which is an image of divine revelation) and be brought into figures?

20. But if there be a *contrarium*, as light and darkness, therein, then this *contrarium* is contrary to itself, and each quality occasions the other to bring itself into desire to will to fight against the other, and to dominate it. In which desire, sense and the soul is brought into a natural and creaturely ground to a will of its own, viz. to a domination in its something, or by its *centrum* over all the *centra*, as one sense of the soul over another.

21. Hence struggle and anxiety, also contrary will, take their rise in the soul, so that the whole soul is thereby instigated to enter into a breaking of the senses, and of the self-will of the senses, as of the natural centra, and passing out of the pain of rebellion and strife, out of anxiety, to desire to sink into the eternal rest, as into God, from whence it sprang.[19]

This doctrine appears in *The Prelude:*

> The state to which I now allude was one
> In which the eye was master of the heart,
> When that which is in every stage of life
> The most despotic of our senses gain'd
> Such strength in me as often held my mind
> In absolute dominion, gladly here,
> Entering upon abstruser argument,
> Would I endeavor to unfold the means
> Which Nature studiously employs to thwart
> This tyranny, summons the senses each
> To counteract the other and themselves,
> And makes them all, *and the objects with which all
> Are conversant,* subservient in their turn
> To the great ends of Liberty and Power.
> But this is matter for another song. . . .[20]

[19] Jakob Boehme, *Six Theosophic Points*, tr. Earle (London, 1919), pp. 170-171.   [20] Bk. XI, ll. 171 ff. Italics mine

Surely, this is an instance where Wordsworth has "transcendentalized" the philosophy of sensationalism, according to which the mind is composed wholly of elements derived from the senses. The transcendental element is the active dominion of the ego which with the aid of Nature supports the "great ends of Liberty and Power." It is interesting to notice that Wordsworth's mention of vision as the most "despotic of the senses" is quite consistent with Hartley.[21] This fact indicates the way in which sensationalist and transcendentalist elements are woven together in Wordsworth's conception of imagination and knowledge.

(3) Perhaps the most striking point of resemblance between Boehme and Wordsworth lies in their description of the way in which mystical illumination arises in the soul of men.

To begin with, Boehme seems to have been a nature-mystic. His "philosophical library was nature itself. 'Thou wilt find,' he says, 'no better book, in which the Divine Wisdom can be searched for and found, than a green and blooming meadow' (*The Three Principles*, 8:12). His first great illumination was occasioned by seeing the sun's rays reflected from a pewter plate. This vision, which was outwardly directed, taught him that Nature itself was a mirror of Deity."[22] But Boehme has analyzed the mode of his illumination more closely than the above passage suggests.

If it be possible for (a man) to stand an hour or less from his own inner willing and speaking, then will the divine will speak into him. . . . For if the life stand still from its own will, it is in the abyss[23] of Nature and creation, in the eternal divine utterance; and hence God speaks therein.[24]

Wordsworth has given us various hints to the effect that his own interpretation of the rise of mystical insight is very similar to this. He praises "wise passiveness" and that "happy stillness of the mind" arising from the contemplation of Na-

---

[21] *Op. cit.*, Part I, prop. LXI.   [22] Brinton, *op. cit.*, p. 11.
[23] We shall examine the symbolic concept of the *abyss* in a later chapter. In other works Boehme describes the background of human inspiration in terms comparable to Coleridge's figure of the Eolian Harp.
[24] *Theoscopia*, 2: 17, 19.

ture which sometimes fits us to receive an unexpected truth.[25]
Such stillness sometimes follows accidentally upon very lively
activity or concentrated attention and the resulting awareness
is not always, by any means, ecstatic, although mystical in
quality.   Such an instance is afforded by the poem entitled
"There Was a Boy" and by Wordsworth's comment upon it:

> There was a Boy; ye knew him well, ye cliffs
> And islands of Winander!—many a time
> At evening, when the earliest stars began
> To move along the edges of the hills,
> Rising or setting, would he stand alone,
> Beneath the trees, or by the glimmering lake;
> And there, with fingers interwoven, both hands
> Pressed closely palm to palm and to his mouth
> Uplifted, he, as through an instrument,
> Blew mimic hootings to the silent owls,
> That they might answer him.—And they would shout
> Across the watery vale, and shout again,
> Responsive to his call,—with quivering peals,
> And long halloos, and screams, and echoes loud
> Redoubled and redoubled; concourse wild
> Of jocund din!   And, when there came a pause
> Of silence such as baffled his best skill:
> Then sometimes, in that silence, while he hung
> Listening, a gentle shock of mild surprise
> Has carried far into his heart the voice
> Of mountain-torrents; or the visible scene
> Would enter unawares into his mind
> With all its solemn imagery, its rocks,
> Its woods, and that uncertain heaven received
> Into the bosom of the steady lake.

I dismiss this subject with observing—that in the series of Poems
placed under the head of Imagination, I have begun with one of the
earliest processes of Nature in the development of this faculty.   Guided
by one of my own primary consciousnesses, I have represented a com-
mutation and transfer of internal feelings, co-operating with external
accidents to plant, for immortality, images of sound and sight, in the
celestial soil of the Imagination.   The Boy, there introduced, is listen-

---

[25] See *The Prelude*, Bk. XII, l. 13.

ing, with something of a feverish and restless anxiety, for the recurrence of the riotous sounds which he had previously excited; and, at the moment when the intenseness of his mind is beginning to remit, he is surprized into a perception of the solemn and tranquilizing images which the Poem describes.[26]

Several other instances deserve to be mentioned. The following passage illustrates a suspension of all usual interests and an exceptional concentration of attention.

The boy hangs on the cliff, most attentive to knots of grass and "half-inch fissures in the slippery rock" by which he clings to safety. In that moment the "world" is forgotten and "Nature" is transfigured.

> Oh! at that time,
> While on the perilous ridge I hung alone,
> With what strange utterance did the loud dry wind
> Blow through my ears! the sky seem'd not a sky
> Of earth, and with what motion mov'd the clouds.[27]

---

[26] Let us mention in passing that the passage just quoted from "There Was a Boy" illustrates, so to speak, very faintly the two major components of the Wordsworthian experience, the sense of influence and the sense of unity. Something has been carried far into the poet's heart, and the solemn imagery so presented is described with emphasis upon the sphere-like, all encompassing unity of the visible scene, its rocks and woods standing between the sky and the lake which reflects the sky. Such a description heightens our sense of the compresent unity of the world. Many such descriptions may be found in Wordsworth. Consider

> Whose dwelling is the light of setting suns,
> The round ocean and the living air
> . . . .
> Open unto the fields and to the sky
> . . . .
> And breaks the silence of the seas
> Among the farthest Hebrides.

or the less spontaneous lines from *The Excursion:*

> Has not the soul, the being of your life,
> Received a shock of awful consciousness,
> In some calm season, when these lofty rocks
> At night's approach bring down the unclouded sky,
> To rest upon their circumambient walls;
> A temple framing of dimensions vast. . . .

Here we encounter again both the sense of influence and the sense of unity, although the presentation of the latter is rather labored. This emphasis upon the unity of things is also Behmenistic. (See below, under point 4.)

[27] *The Prelude*, Bk. I, ll. 346 ff.

The following is an excellent instance. Here the lost traveler's sudden discovery that he has crossed the Alps silences a complex of lively emotions, anxiety, curiosity, the sportsman's ambition, etc., which have been troubling him as he came to realize that he had lost his way. It is very interesting to notice that these experiences did not in themselves bring about the reactions described in the poem, but that such an outcome was the result of reliving them in retrospection while the lines were being actually composed in 1804, some fourteen years after the event described. Here, of course, there were added to the "emotions recollected in tranquility" the feelings inseparable from the creative activity of composition.[28] In its full context the passage contains brilliant reference both to Eolian influence and to the sense of unity:

> Ere long we follow'd,
> Descending by the beaten road that led
> Right to a rivulet's edge, and there broke off.
> The only track now visible was one
> Upon the further side, right opposite,
> And up a lofty Mountain. This we took
> After a little scruple, and short pause,
> And climb'd with eagerness, though not, at length
> Without surprise, and some anxiety
> On findings that we did not overtake
> Our Comrades gone before. By fortunate chance,
> While every moment now increas'd our doubts,
> A Peasant met us, and from him we learn'd
> That to the place which had perplex'd us first
> We must descend, and there should find the road
> Which in the stony channel of the Stream
> Lay a few steps, and then along its banks;
> And further, that thenceforward all our course
> Was downwards, with the current of that Stream.
> Hard of belief, we question'd him again,
> And all the answers which the Man return'd
> To our inquiries, in their sense and substance,

[28] See Raymond Dexter Havens, *The Mind of a Poet* (Baltimore, 1941), and his mention of W. G. Fraser's article in the *Times Literary Supplement* of April 4, 1929.

Translated by the feelings which we had
Ended in this; *that we had crossed the Alps.*

Imagination! lifting up itself
Before the eye and progress of my Song
Like an unfather'd vapour; here that Power,
In all the might of its endowments, came
Athwart me; I was lost as in a cloud,
Halted, without a struggle to break through.[29]

Another passage of similar import is the following. Here, the mind is torn from its usual concerns by a shock of horror and sympathy. Wordsworth, deeply plunged in meditation upon the mystery of human character, describes his meeting a blind beggar.

And once, far-travell'd in such mood, beyond
The reach of common indications, lost
Amid the moving pageant, 'twas my chance
Abruptly to be smitten with the view
Of a blind Beggar, who, with upright face,
Stood propp'd against a Wall, upon his Chest
Wearing a written paper, to explain
The story of the Man, and who he was.
My mind did at this spectacle turn round
As with the might of waters, and it seem'd
To me that in this Label was a type,
Or emblem, of the utmost that we know,
Both of ourselves and of the universe;
And, on the shape of the unmoving man,
His fixed face and sightless eyes, I look'd
As if admonish'd from another world.[30]

But the most satisfactory statement is to be found in De Quincey's comment:

Meantime, we are not to suppose that Wordsworth, the boy, expressly sought for solitary scenes of nature amongst woods and mountains, with a direct conscious anticipation of imaginative pleasure, and loving them with a pure, disinterested love, on their own separate

---

[29] *The Prelude*, Bk. VI, ll. 501 ff.   [30] *Ibid.*, Bk. VII, ll. 607 ff.

account. These are feelings beyond boyish nature, or, at all events, beyond boyish nature trained amidst the selfishness of social intercourse. Wordsworth, like his companions, haunted the hills and the vales for the sake of angling, snaring birds, swimming, and sometimes of hunting, according to the Westmoreland fashion, on foot; for riding to the chase is quite impossible, from the precipitous nature of the ground. It was in the course of these pursuits, by an indirect effect growing gradually upon him, that Wordsworth became a passionate lover of nature, at the time when the growth of his intellectual faculties made it possible that he should combine those thoughtful passions with the experience of the eye and the ear.

There is, amongst the poems of Wordsworth, one most ludicrously misconstrued by his critics, which offers a philosophical hint upon this subject of great instruction. I preface it with a little incident which first led Wordsworth into a commentary upon his own meaning. One night, as often enough happened, during the Peninsular war, he and I had walked up Dunmail Raise, from Grasmere, about midnight, in order to meet the carrier who brought the London newspapers, by a circuitous course from Keswick. The case was this:—Coleridge, for many years, received a copy of the *Courier*, as a mark of esteem, and in acknowledgment of his many contributions to it, from one of the proprietors, Mr. Daniel Stuart. This went up in any case, let Coleridge be where he might, to Mrs. Coleridge; for a single day, it staid at Keswick, for the use of Southey; and on the next, it came on to Wordsworth, by the slow conveyance of a carrier, plying with a long train of cars between Whitehaven and Kendal. Many a time the force of the storms or floods would compel the carrier to stop on his route, five miles short of Grasmere, at Wythburn, or even eight miles short, at Legberthwaite. But, as there was always hope until one or two o'clock in the morning, often and often it would happen that, in the deadly impatience for earlier intelligence, Wordsworth and I would walk off to meet him about midnight, at a distance of three or four miles. Upon one of these occasions, when some great crisis in Spain was daily apprehended, we had waited for an hour or more, sitting upon one of the many huge blocks of stone which lie scattered over that narrow field of battle on the desolate frontier of Cumberland and Westmoreland, where King Dun Mail, with all his peerage, fell, more than a thousand years ago. The time had arrived, at length, that all hope for the night had left us: no sound came up through the winding valleys that stretched to the north; and the few cottage lights, gleaming, at wide distances, from recesses amidst the rocky hills, had long been extinct. At intervals, Wordsworth had stretched himself at length on the high road, applying his ear to the ground, so as to catch any sound of wheels that might be groaning along at a distance. Once, when he was slowly rising from his effort, his eye caught a bright star that was glittering between the brow of Seat Sandal and of the mighty Helvellyn. He gazed upon it for a minute or so; and then, upon turning away to descend into Grasmere, he made the following explanation:—"I have remarked, from my earliest days, that if, under any circumstances, the attention is energetically braced up to an act of steady observation, or of steady expectation, then, if this intense condition of vigilance should suddenly relax, at that moment any beautiful, any impressive visual object, or collection of objects, falling upon the eye, is carried to the heart with a power not known under other circumstances. Just now my ear was placed upon the stretch, in order to catch any sound of wheels that might come down upon the Lake of Wythburn from the Keswick road: at the very instant when I raised my head from the ground, in final abandonment of hope for this night, at the very instant when the organs of attention were all at once relaxing from their tension, the bright star hanging in the air above those outlines of massy blackness, fell suddenly upon my eye, and penetrated my capacity of apprehension with a pathos and a sense of the Infinite, that would not have arrested me under other circumstances." He then went on to illustrate the same psychological principle from another instance; it was an instance derived from that exquisite poem, in which he describes a mountain boy planting himself at twilight on the margin of a solitary bay of Windemere, and provoking the owls to a contest with himself, by "mimic hooting," blown through his hands; which of itself becomes an impressive scene to anyone able to realize to his fancy the various elements of the solitary woods and waters, the solemn vesper hour, the solitary bird, the solitary boy. Afterwards, the poem goes on to describe the boy as waiting, amidst "the pauses of his skill," for the answers of the birds—waiting with intensity of expectation—and then, at length, when, after waiting to no purpose, his attention began to relax—that is, in other words, under the giving way of one exclusive direction of his senses, began suddenly to allow an admission of other objects—then, in that instant, the scene actually before him, the visible scene, would enter unawares—

With all its solemn imagery—

This complex scenery was—What?

> Was carried *far* into his heart,
> With all its pomp, and that uncertain heav'n received
> Into the bosom of the steady lake.

This very expression, "far," by which space and its infinities are attributed to the human heart, and to its capacities of re-echoing the sublimities of nature, has always struck me as with a flash of sublime revelation. On this, however, Wordsworth did not say anything in his commentary; nor did he notice the conclusion, which is this. After describing the efforts of the boy, and next the passive state which succeeded, under his disappointment (in which condition it was that the solemn spectacle entered the boy's mind with effectual power, and with a semi-conscious sense of its beauty that would not be denied), the poet goes on to say:

> And I suppose that I have stood
> A full half hour beside his quiet grave,
> Mute—for he died when he was ten years old.[31]

Certainly there are various ways of freeing ourselves from our "willing and speaking." Any form of intense concentration of attention and effort will serve, if we may employ a very traditional phrase, to free the "spirit" from the "flesh." The devotions and prayers of the saint, the rigorous intellectual meditations of a Neoplatonic philosopher striving to define the absolute, the mental and physical exercises of the Hindu holy man are all instances. For the student of Wordsworth the most important approach to mysticism is that of the enthusiast who loses himself in an appreciation of natural beauty.

Mr. de Selincourt has spoken, in a passage which we have already quoted, of the "great paradox" which Wordsworth always faces, the paradox "that though it is simply by the proper exercise of eye and ear that man reaches his full moral and intellectual stature . . . yet revelation flashes upon him when 'the light of sense goes out'; and 'laid asleep in body,'

---

[31] Thomas De Quincey, *Literary Reminiscences* (Boston, 1874), "William Wordsworth," pp. 312-317. (The corresponding essay in the *Collected Writings*, ed. Masson, II, 229-302, does not contain this passage.) I have quoted from Mr. Arthur Beatty's *William Wordsworth: His Doctrine and Art in Their Historical Relations* (2d ed., Madison, Wis., 1927), pp. 160-162.

he becomes deeply conscious of the presence of God within him." This paradox finds a *locus classicus* in the second paragraph of the "Tintern Abbey" lines. Lines 23-35, the first sentence, describe the nonmystical value of sensuous images and the emotions connected with them, the peaceful and soothing power of natural beauty which long outlives our actual contact with a landscape, and is preserved and recalled according to the laws of association. The second sentence (ll. 35-48) asserts that a power of supersensuous insight is also owing to our contemplation of these scenes and images.

But there need be nothing surprising in this. We know that mystical awareness may sometimes follow upon the complete absorption of attention which a rich esthetic experience involves. Now, the senses or sensuous images in their most refined precision are involved in esthetic enjoyment but not in the mystical consciousness which sometimes follows, when the "light of sense goes out." Sensuous alertness may lead to the enjoyment of beauty and the intense mental absorption that often accompanies it. And the enjoyment of beauty may, in turn, lead to mystical consciousness. But sensuous alertness and mystical consciousness are very different things. Hence Mr. de Selincourt's paradox is resolved. This is why poets, when describing natural beauty, frequently express feeling of a mystical quality, even though they may be intellectually quite opposed to mystical philosophy. Recall, for example, the invocation to Venus at the opening of Lucretius' poem, which has been noticed in this very connection by Shaftesbury.

(4) Both Boehme and Wordsworth describe mysticism as an apprehension of a joyous life that permeates all Nature. Not only does Being appear as One, but the unity presents itself as a glorious symphony, a joyful harmony of animate and inanimate beings. Boehme calls this life the Eternal Nature, which most of us fail to recognize because of the limitation of our vision. Consider the following from Boehme's *Aurora:*

As members of man's body love one another, so do the spirits in the Divine Power, there is nothing but a longing, a desiring, and fulfilling as well as triumphing and delight in each other, whence come understanding and distinction in God, angels, men, beasts, fowls and all that lives, whence these spirits become living and the power of life penetrates through all.[32]

Compare Wordsworth's transport, which we have already quoted in another connection:

> I felt the sentiment of Being spread
> O'er all that moves, and all that seemeth still,
> O'er all, that, lost beyond the reach of thought
> And human knowledge, to the human eye
> Invisible, yet liveth to the heart,
> O'er all that leaps, and runs, and shouts, and sings,
> Or beats the gladsome air, o'er all that glides
> Beneath the wave, yea, in the wave itself
> And mighty depth of waters. Wonder not
> If such my transport were; for in all things now
> I saw one life, and felt that it was joy.
> One song they sang, and it was audible,
> Most audible then when the fleshly ear,
> O'ercome by grosser prelude of that strain,
> Forgot its functions, and slept undisturb'd.[33]

Boehme is willing to include inanimate objects in this world life. There is, he claims, a "will and source," capable of good and evil in all things: in "men, beasts, fowls, fishes, worms, and in all that is upon the earth; in gold, silver, copper, tin, iron, steel; wood, herbs, leaves, and grass; as also in the earth, in stones, in the water, and in all whatsoever that can be thought of."[34] Still, this life, with its capacities for good and evil, will appear to the initiated as a single whole, which "qualifieth, operateth or frameth all in the deep above the earth, also upon the earth, and in the earth, in one another as ONE thing,[35] and yet hath several distinct virtues and opera-

---

[32] *Aurora*, 9: 64-67.
[33] *The Prelude*, Bk. II, ll. 420 ff.   [34] *Aurora*, 2: 6.
[35] Compare Coleridge: "Now again is nothing but firs and pines above, below, around us! How awful is the deep unison of their undividable murmur; what a one thing it is—it is a sound that impresses the dim notion of the Omnipresent!" Arthur Turnbull, *Biographia Epistoleris* (London, 1911), I, 171.

tions, and but one mother, from whence descend and spring all things."[36]

Compare this with Wordsworth's

> To every natural form, rock, fruit or flower,
> Even the loose stones that cover the high-way,
> I gave a moral life, I saw them feel,
> Or link'd them to some feeling: the great mass
> Lay bedded in a quickening soul, and all
> That I beheld respired with inward meaning.[37]

The following quotation from M. A. Koyré's very complete study of Boehme contains some material pertinent to the topic that we have just considered. It will also serve as a transition to our next topic, that of intuitive wisdom and discursive knowledge.

En effet il est nécessaire, pense Boehme, d'user d'exemples et d'images sensibles pour amener progressivement le lecteur à la compréhension. D'ailleurs, bien qu'il soit possible de connaître Dieu en esprit, cette connaissance reste cependant inexprimable, du moins pour le discours. Il faut, par conséquent, se tourner vers le monde sensible, seul accessible au discours *(Vernunft)* et à la pensée de l'homme naturel. Au demeurant, nous le savons déjà, le monde est une expression de Dieu; le sensible, comme nous le verrons encore mieux plus tard, n'a de sens qu'en tant qu'il est une expression et une incarnation de l'esprit. Ajoutons que pour Boehme, en général, l'imagination est en un certain sens supérieure à la raison discursive *(Vernunft)* et plus proche de la raison intuitive *(Verstand)* que l'entendement. En effet, l'imagination permet de saisir l'un-multiple simultanément, tandis que l'entendement doit procéder par des démarches successives; le discours isole et brise l'intériorité *(l'ineinander)*, la compénétration intérieure des forces et des qualités.

Or, la première chose que nous voyons, lorsque nous nous tournons vers la nature, c'est la présence et la lutte en elle de deux forces ou qualités contraires, celles du bien et du mal. Le bien et le mal sont partout, en toutes choses, en toutes qualités; ils sont distincts, opposés et néanmoins indissolublement unis et liés, "comme une chose." Il y a cette lutte et cette union des contraires dans tout objet réel, sans

---

[36] *Aurora*, 2: 11.   [37] *The Prelude*, Bk. III, ll. 124 ff.

exception, sauf cependant, ajoute le théosophe, en Dieu, les anges et les démons.[38]

(5) Boehme distinguishes sharply between a higher and a lower form of knowledge, between understanding, the higher, and reason, the lower. As M. Koyré points out, human imagination stands between these two. Later German idealists, following Kant, reversed the terminology, which reversal Coleridge followed when in *The Friend* he presented his theory of reason and understanding. Nevertheless, Coleridge's "reason" seems to owe something to Boehme's "understanding." Besides, the distinction which Wordsworth draws in *The Prelude* between a narrow and a more ample use of reason, and again his notion of the relation of the higher reason to feeling, deserves careful comparison with Boehme's theory. In fact, the very philosophical pattern of *The Prelude* depends upon this distinction. And the story of the growth of the poet's mind carries us in its later stages from Godwin to Boehme, from rationalism to a philosophy of imagination and intuitive understanding. We witness the agonies of a poet, by disposition a man of intuitive and imaginative powers, trying to build himself a philosophy of pure reason, and we witness his return to more congenial ways of thought and to a philosophy which satisfies both his imagination and his intelligence.

Thus Wordsworth tells us how he learned to transcend the "false, secondary power" which, both through the habit of mind which its exercise engendered and the conclusions which it forced upon him, had once undermined his spiritual strength and made impossible all sense of communion with Nature. And we know from *Biographia Literaria* that Coleridge had come very close to making just this distinction between a higher and a lower way of thought under the guidance, as he tells us, of Fox, Boehme, and Law:

The feeling of gratitude, which I cherish towards these men, has caused me to digress further than I had forseen or proposed; but to have passed them over in an historical sketch of my literary life and opinions, would have seemed to me like the denial of a debt, the con-

[38] A. Koyré, *La Philosophie de Jacob Boehme* (Paris, 1929), p. 86.

cealment of a boon. For the writings of these mystics acted in no
slight degree to prevent my mind from being imprisoned within the
outline of any single dogmatic system. They contributed to keep
alive the *heart* in the *head;* gave me an indistinct, yet stirring and
working presentiment, that all the products of the mere *reflective*
faculty partook of DEATH, and were as the rattling twigs and sprays
in winter, into which a sap was yet to be propelled from some root to
which I had not penetrated, if they were to afford my soul either food
or shelter. If they were too often a moving cloud of smoke to me
by day, yet they were always a pillar of fire throughout the night,
during my wanderings through the wilderness of doubt, and enabled
me to skirt, without crossing, the sandy deserts of utter unbelief. That
the system is capable of being converted into an irreligious PANTHEISM,
I well know. The ETHICS of SPINOZA, may, or may not, be an instance. But at no time could I believe, that *in itself* and *essentially* it
is incompatible with religion, natural or revealed: and now I am most
thoroughly persuaded of the contrary.[39]

The latter books of *The Prelude* record a prolonged
struggle between two ways of thought: mystical intuition, on
one hand, and, on the other, "scientific" reason supported only
by the evidence of sensuous observation. The rational "enlightenment" of the *philosophe,* deliberately and method-
ically produced, is opposed to the insight of the poet and
mystic which comes upon him often uninvited and never deliberately planned. Historically, we may say that in Wordsworth's thought of 1798 two traditions conflict: that of Locke,
the Encyclopaedists, and Godwin against that of Boehme, Fox,
and Law: on the one hand the political theory of the French
Revolution, on the other the faith of the mystical enthusiast.
Both these philosophies look toward an ideal of "freedom";
but for one it is primarily a matter of political independence
or of popular self-government based on intelligent accord, and
for the other a freedom of the individual spirit, secure against
the lusts of the flesh, against pride and fear, and against too
pressing a concern with worldly advancement. Both ways of
thought support freedom of conscience and of worship and
they both tend toward egalitarianism. But their methods of

[39] *Biographia Literaria*, ed. Shawcross, I, 98-99.

thought differ profoundly. The spiritual life of the mystic and his teaching appear as madness to the *philosophe*, and the *philosophe* appears to the mystic to be committing spiritual suicide by contemplating a "universe of Death." In the end, the mystic in Wordsworth's thought overcomes the rationalist and reason is interpreted as a secondary power of a limited and strictly auxiliary function. According to this view, a purely rationalist philosophy can only deaden the sense of life and of enduring value by which we live. The rationalist is in danger of stultifying himself by ignoring the divine element in man. Thus the mystic's enthusiasm may at times, as occasionally with Wordsworth, lead him to forget the detachment becoming a philosopher, and he will then abuse the rationalist who "botanizes" upon his "mother's grave." The fundamental error of such analytical rationalism lies, as Coleridge says, in that it presents the universe as a "mass of little things," bound to one another only by such forces as attraction and repulsion.

> . . . go demand
> Of mighty Nature, if 'twas ever meant
> That we should pry far off yet be unraised;
> That we should pore, and dwindle as we pore,
> Viewing all objects unremittingly
> In disconnection dead and spiritless;
> And still dividing and dividing still
> Break down all grandeur.[40]

For the analyst, Nature does not exist as a single entity, open to the mind. The human mind is then directed only toward distinct objects and toward the general principles relating them to one another. Such a philosophy Coleridge had found quite intolerable by 1797, when he wrote to Thelwall: ". . . my mind feels as if it ached to behold and know something *great*, something *one* and *indivisible*. And it is only in the faith of that, that rocks or waterfalls, mountains or caverns, give me the sense of sublimity or majesty!" And we are told in *The Excursion* that the mind of the student, who does not correct his thinking by embracing a broad intuitive philosophy, is

---

[40] *The Excursion*, Bk. IV, ll. 957 ff.

"chained to its object in brute slavery," and not, as it should be, "deeply drinking in the soul of things."[41] Boehme is even more vehement, and his condemnation even more extreme. "Just as an ape will be knowing and playing with everything and imitate everything, so it is with the earthly man who is but an ape."[42]

All this can be true, Wordsworth feels, of art as well as of science. The poet may be so dominated by the particular objects which he beholds that he fails to grasp the setting of the whole and the true meaning of Nature. This, according to the "Tintern Abbey" lines, will be a time of "aching joys and dizzy raptures," before the poet has felt the "*presence* that disturbs (him) with the joy of elevated thoughts."

In *The Excursion,* Wordsworth calls this synoptic insight the mind's "*excursive* power."[43] By this term, he seems to suggest that the mind should do more than receive impressions, it should "come forth into the light of things" and feel the *presence* of Nature. Here he is quite in harmony with Boehme, who writes: "(Man) should by the imagination continually go out again into the light-world for which he was created, in order that the light may give him lustre, that he may know himself and see the outer mystery."[44]

Mr. Brinton has summarized Boehme's contrast between higher understanding *(Verstand)* and the lower reason *(Vernunft)* as follows:

As *Vernunft* is the external human point of view, *Verstand* is the internal divine point of view. What is opaque and meaningless and full of contradictions to *Vernunft* is transparent to *Verstand,* because *Vernunft* attempts to go through the external to the internal while *Verstand* works through inner unity outward. *Vernunft* struggles in vain from multiplicity to unity, *Verstand* beginning at unity sees reality as a whole filled with interrelated forms.[45]

Neither Wordsworth nor Boehme and his followers dismiss discursive reason as wholly false. It is only with

---

[41] *Ibid.,* Bk. IV, ll. 1256 and 1265.
[42] *Six Theosophic Points,* 3: 22. Compare "the ape philosophy" (*The Prelude,* Bk. V, ll. 549-550).   [43] Bk. IV, l. 1263.
[44] *Six Theosophic Points,* 3: 22.   [45] *Op. cit.,* p. 103.

reference to the framing of an ultimate philosophy and to maintaining the health of the spiritual life that reason is found to be limited. For Wordsworth science when "taught with patient interest to watch the processes of things" may "serve the cause of order and distinctness." And as distinguished a Behmenist as William Law is careful not to denounce science and scholarship as wholly useless, but only to point out that they are not substitutes for religious insight: ". . . it is not art or science, or skill in grammar or logic, but the opening of the divine life in the soul, that can give true understanding of the things of God."[46]

Let us quote further from Law's *The Way to Divine Knowledge*. These passages remind us of Wordsworth's attitude toward science and art in the lyrics of 1798. The reader will observe that there is less of the pantheist in Law than in Boehme or in Wordsworth. But Law insists that we can learn more of moral evil and of good by intuition than by studying the sages:

Theophilus. Dear Academicus, be not so uneasy; I am no more an Enemy to Learning, than I am to that Art which builds Mills to grind our Corn, and Houses for ourselves to dwell in. I esteem the liberal Arts and Sciences as the noblest of human Things; I desire no Man to dislike or renounce his Skill in ancient or modern Languages; his Knowledge of Medals, Pictures, Paintings, History, Geography, or Chronology; I have no more Dislike of these Things in themselves, than of the Art of Throwing Silk, or making Lace. But then, all these Things are to stand in their proper Places, and everyone kept within its own Sphere.

Now all this Circle of Science and Arts, whether liberal or mechanic, belongs solely to the natural Man; they are the Work of his natural Powers and Faculties; and the most wicked, sensual, unjust Person, who regards neither God, nor Man, may yet be one of the ablest Proficients in any or all of them. But now Christian Redemption is quite of another Nature; it has no Affinity to any of these Arts or Sciences? it belongs not to the outward natural man, but is purely for the Sake of an inward heavenly Nature that was lost, or put to Death, in Paradise, and buried under the Flesh and Blood of the

---

[46] *The Spirit of Prayer.*

earthly, natural Man. It breathes a Spark of Life into this inward, hidden, or lost Man; by which it feels and finds itself, and rises up in new awakened Desires after its lost Father, and native Country. . . .

Wonder not therefore, my Friend, that though the Mystery under Consideration contains the greatest of Truths, yet I am unwilling to help you to reason and speculate upon it; for if you attempt to go further in it, than Self-evidence leads you, you only go so far out of it, or from it. For the End of this Mystery, is not to furnish new or better Matter for Reason and Opinion, but to bring Man home to that Sensibility, which is self-evident in himself, and to lead him only by self-evident Principles, to see, and find, and feel the Difference between true and false Religion, in the same Degree of self-evident Certainty, as he sees and feels the Difference between Fire and Water. This, I say, is the great Intent of this Mystery, *to bring Man into a Sensibility of God and Nature,* to know and feel, that Good and Evil, Life and Death, are a self-evident Growth and Birth of Nature in Man, according as his Will enters into, and works with that which is unchangeably good, or unchangeably evil, in the Working of Nature. Now as the Workings of Nature are unchangeable in their Effects, and that which is naturally good or evil, must be always so; and seeing Man's Life standeth in Nature, and must work with it, must have only that Good or Evil which is unchangeable in Nature; and seeing his State in Nature, whether good or evil is, and can be, only that, which the sensible, self-evident Powers of his own Life manifest to him; then you see the Fitness and Necessity of your keeping steadily to that, which is self-evident in you, as the very Tree of Life, the Criterion of all that Truth and Goodness that belongs to you. Secondly, you see with what good Reason Jacob Behmen so often tells you, That all that he has written, was only to "help Man to seek" and "find himself," to see and know his Place and State in Nature, and how to co-operate with God and Nature in generating a Birth of Heaven within himself. Thirdly, you may see how you and I should abuse this blessed Mystery, should we, instead of only and truly seeking and finding its Birth within us, make it a Matter of Reasoning and Opinion.[47]

In the foregoing we have surveyed only the most important points of contact between the thought of Wordsworth and

[47] William Law, *Works* (Canterbury, 1893), VII, 189 ff. and 235 ff. Italics mine.

of Boehme. We may ignore, for the present, their very real differences and some less obvious grounds of resemblance.

*   *   *

Throughout this chapter, I have proceeded upon the assumption that Wordsworth was, during the period of the first composition of *The Prelude* and later, acquainted with the general trend of Boehme's philosophy and in contact with some of his writings. I have supposed that his acquaintance was furthered by Coleridge. In the sequel I shall have occasion to assume, with Mr. de Selincourt, that Wordsworth learned much of other philosophical writers in the same way. Knowing what we do of Coleridge's habits of torrential conversation and of the many hours of conversations that Wordsworth and Coleridge shared when they were almost constantly together in 1797 and 1798, I do not think it illegitimate to suppose that Wordsworth gained what we might call an intensive survey of the thought of Coleridge's philosophical heroes. These include especially Plato and the Neoplatonists, Bruno, Spinoza, Boehme; of course Hartley and Berkeley after whom Coleridge named his boys; and George Fox and William Law; and, in later conversations, the Germans, Kant, Schiller, Schelling, and Fichte, must have appeared. There is no reason to suppose that Wordsworth retained or further developed an acquaintance with each of these writers; but when we find doctrines or phrases appearing in Wordsworth's work which closely resemble those belonging to any one of the above-mentioned philosophers we have no reason to reject the possibility of such an influence on the grounds that external evidence is lacking to show that Wordsworth was in any way acquainted with the author in question. Wordsworth has himself admitted in a letter to Beaumont (1806) that he drew many leading ideas from Coleridge,[48] and Coleridge in *Biographia Literaria* has insisted that Wordsworth was capable of writing a genuine philosophical poem. Who then will doubt that the two friends had once shared their philosophizing and that during their closest intimacy Coleridge's learning had been at his comrade's disposal?

[48] See *The Prelude*, pp. 607-608.

This is not to assume that Wordsworth and Coleridge tend always to agree. Even when they work with the same concepts, their interpretations sometimes differ. In general, we may say that Coleridge is much more ready than Wordsworth during the earlier years, to distinguish between God and Nature. He is much more sensitive to the charge of pantheism.

It is unfortunate that Wordsworth's correspondence is philosophically so poverty-stricken and that in his letters he has so little to say about the great themes which dominate his poetry. But this is the case; and so being without conclusive external evidence in these matters, we must proceed cautiously and build our argument upon internal evidence from the poems themselves, always keeping in mind the relevance of Coleridge's learning.

CHAPTER III

"The One Life Within Us and Abroad"

THE WORLD as it appears to Wordsworth's imagination contains many things undreamed of in a sensationalist philosophy. These elements, as also the way in which they are apprehended, we shall call "transcendental." As we have seen, one source of Wordsworth's transcendentalist concepts seems to be Jakob Boehme. Of course, another origin is Wordsworth's own experience which made possible his sympathy with Boehme's ideas. And when we compare the sprawling confusion of Boehme's writing with the compact and concentrated statement which Wordsworth offers us, we must admit that even where Wordsworth follows Boehme he makes a very real contribution of his own. The nucleus of this contribution we have already mentioned. It includes an account of our awareness of the unity of Nature and of the way in which this awareness depends upon Eolian influence. The unity of Nature includes an intimate interpenetration or fusion of the detailed objects comprising it. It offers us an intuitive reconciliation of the One and the Many. *And the imagination whereby this unity is recognized is described as "belonging" as much to the interrelated objects themselves as to the knowing mind.* In this chapter we shall examine these views in greater detail than heretofore. In doing so, we shall find that the two views are so closely connected that they cannot be stated separately.

In the first place, let us recognize that we are not contemplating any very revolutionary interpretation of Wordsworth's philosophy. Insofar as matters of general interpretation are concerned, we are quite in agreement with Mr. de Selincourt's commentary on *The Prelude*. Only those students who are unwilling to admit that Wordsworth's thought involves any transcendentalist and pantheistic movement away from Hartley need hesitate to accept the more general implications of our argument. Perhaps the most difficult point to accept is the statement that imagination belongs as much to the object seen as to the eye that sees, as much to the environment apprehended as to the knowing organism. Still Mr. de Selincourt has found it necessary to interpret Wordsworth in this way in order to find intelligibility in a number of passages. And the notion, unusual as it seems to most of us who have accepted a Cartesian or Lockian dualism of mind and body almost as a matter of course, is still reasonable enough for one who has ever felt the unity of Being as an object of mystical intuition. Again, to some extent our hesitancy is strengthened by our usual way of speaking about mind and object. Phrases that are used again and again acquire an illegitimate authority. Thus we come to use purely figurative expressions with naïve acceptance of their implications. One of the most treacherous of these is the phrase "in the mind." We are apt to believe that all our thinking, even all our perception, takes place "in our mind," and we vaguely attribute pseudo-spatial limits to this mind. The mind is sometimes thought to be in the head, sometimes more vaguely located; at any rate, it is not in the "external world" where physical objects are situated. We think about or perceive things, and our thinking or perception is taken to be quite distinct from the thing thought about. This is again the influence of the dualism of Descartes and Locke. But these thinkers have long been recognized in the schools as dangerous guides. Their dualism results in almost fantastic difficulties; and the history of modern philosophy is in large measure the history of the perplexities which have resulted from their attitude. Thus when Wordsworth departs from orthodox modern dualism, he may be obscure; but there is no reason to suppose that in doing so he is advancing a perverse or irresponsible hypothesis.

Nor is it wholly counter to our sense of life, to our feeling of events, to say that at times it is not *we* that think but Nature emerging into a special type of consciousness through our lives. Our mental life—a much wiser term than "our mind"—is not always self-centered. It is often enriched by objects which seem to possess it; and this is sometimes true of the most intense moments of consciousness. A great psychologist, William James, has pointed out how difficult it is to define the boundaries of selfhood; and a great physiologist, J. S. Haldane, has insisted that the same is true when we speak of the line to be drawn between organism and environment. It is perhaps our greatest spiritual limitation that we consider thoughts and feelings to be a species of private property. Let us dwell on this point for a moment.

Do I own *my* enjoyment of El Greco?—or of Lake Winnepesaukee? At any rate, I cannot sell it, or even give it away. And, unless I am an esthetic snob, I will not think of *my* idea of the Toledo landscape. And when I enjoy Wordsworth, do I dwell upon *my* interpretation of him? When I do, it is time to say "Enough of science and of the art of criticism"! A little freedom from professional self-consciousness, a little "wise passiveness," and such nonsense is swept away. This may not involve mystical illumination: the "Unity of all" may not be revealed, but, at least, it will not seem to be a perverse or subversive concept.[1]

In his excellent comments upon educational theory, Wordsworth laments that so often the student grows proud of the

[1] Consider the following important statement by Professor Frank Jewett Mather, who, without agreeing wholly with the above, recognizes the state of mind:

"Winslow Homer, who habitually painted in the open air, was once asked if he ever changed anything he observed. Shocked at the mere possibility, he denied emphatically that he ever changed anything. As a matter of fact, Winslow Homer made freely and ably those transpositions and simplifications which are proper to the good landscape painter. A little comparison of his sketches with his finished pictures would prove the point abundantly. He also painted from memory much that could not be done from nature. What is important in the case is that Winslow Homer was entirely unconscious of the transformations he instinctively made—thought himself a faithful transcriber of nature.

"Such an attitude is usual with good painters, and if you show them a feature they have painted but could not possibly have seen, they will generally answer that they saw it that way. This admiring humility towards nature, this unawareness of the value or even of the existence of his own transforming processes is probably the best attitude for any painter. For one of a certain sophistication, and of course many painters, as artists generally, are introverts, the attitude is impossible, and their consciousness of their own creative distortions in design brings very serious dangers of mannerism" (*Concerning Beauty*, Princeton, N. J., 1935, p. 202).

information he has acquired, acquired at the expense of freedom and power, the power, I suspect, to lose himself in things and ideas and to grow mentally as they possess him. On the other hand, is it too much to say that the "pure spirit" and "best power" of things lie in their capacity for entering consciousness, when they pass from the macrocosm of their primordial existence into the microcosms of finite thought? Then they enter a process whereby they transcend themselves and unite with other objects in a new community with a novel organization and emphasis of interrelation. Nature thus wonderfully enriches herself as she concentrates her detail in new centers of universal community, centers which we call minds. Thus a new philosophical perspective opens before us when we reverse our ordinary train of thought and think of knowledge and perception, not as a purely personal and subjective affair, but also as something which gradually arises from Nature, from the ensemble of these very things which are to be perceived and known.

> How exquisitely the individual mind
> (And the progressive powers perhaps no less
> Of the whole species) to the external World
> Is fitted:—and how exquisitely, too—
> Theme this but little heard of among men—
> The external World is fitted to the mind;
> And the creation (by no lower name
> Can it be called) which they with blended might
> Accomplish. . . .[2]

Within this perspective, beauty does not appear as a mental product or even as a human product. It is "a living presence of the earth," the earth itself at last fully present in a responsive consciousness, a consciousness which, at this moment, "belongs to" the earth as much as to the poet.

*   *   *

In the pages that follow we shall try to describe more fully the Wordsworthian "sentiment of Being" and to indicate its relevance to more recent thought. We might describe the

[2] *The Recluse*, Bk. I.

sentiment of Being as an awareness of the world, open only to those gifted with an esthetic sensitivity and a certain emotional detachment which makes possible their giving fullest attention to the content which imagination or its conscious aftermath entertains. Mr. John Dewey has recognized this phase of esthetic experience, and he describes it splendidly when he writes of the sense of totality which supports esthetic experience as a sort of background and which strangely dominates and integrates its development. Mr. Dewey is describing our experience of a work of art. We must remember that, for the poet or the artist, *any* situation to which he pays full attention may be apprehended in this way.

There is no name to be given this sense of totality. As it enlivens and animates, it is the spirit of the work of art. *It is its reality,* when we feel the work of art to be *real on its own account* and not as a realistic exhibition. It is the idiom in which the particular work is composed and expressed, that which stamps it with individuality. It is the background *which is more than spatial because it enters into and qualifies everything in the focus,* everything distinguished as a part and member. [Italics mine.] We are accustomed to think of physical objects as having bounded edges; things like rocks, chairs, books, houses, trade, and science, with its efforts at precise measurement, have confirmed the belief. Then we unconsciously carry over this belief in the bounded character of all *objects* of experience (a belief founded ultimately in the practical exigencies of our dealings with things) into our conception of experience itself. [Italics Dewey's.] We suppose the experience has the same definite limits as the things with which it is concerned. But any experience the most ordinary, has an indefinite total setting. Things, objects, are only focal points of a here and now in a whole that stretches out indefinitely. This is the qualitative "background" which is defined and made definitely conscious in particular objects and specified properties and qualities. *There is something mystical associated with the word intuition, and any experience becomes mystical in the degree in which the sense, the feeling, of the unlimited envelope becomes intense*—as it may do in experience of an object of art. [Italics mine.] As Tennyson said:

> "Experience is an arch wherethro'
> Gleams that untravell'd world, whose margin fades
> Forever and forever when I move."

For although there is a bounding horizon, it moves as we move. We are never wholly free from the sense of something that lies beyond.[3]

Mr. Dewey finds that this qualitative unity is an important element, not only in esthetic awareness, but also in scientific observation and in *praxis:* "All thought in whatever subject begins with . . . an unanalyzed whole." Dewey compares our apprehension of this whole with Bergson's intuition which "precedes conception and goes deeper."[4] But Dewey is not prepared to accept the panpsychism which is joined with this notion in Wordsworth's mind, nor, despite what he says in the above passage, is Dewey really at home with mysticism. He has seen only the beginnings of a way of thought and of belief which others have followed further.

Mr. Dewey quotes from Tennyson, and his choice is a happy one insofar as the unlimited character of the "envelope" is concerned. But the quotation does not clearly illustrate the point which Dewey makes when he writes that the so-called background is "more than spatial because it enters into and qualifies everything in the focus. . . ." Splendid expression of the latter aspect of esthetic experience may be found in Wordsworth:

> The immeasurable height
> Of woods decaying, never to be decay'd,
> The stationary blasts of water-falls,
> And everywhere along the hollow rent
> Winds thwarting winds, bewilder'd and forlorn,
> The torrents shooting from the clear blue sky,
> The rocks that mutter'd close upon our ears,
> Black drizzling crags that spake by the way-side
> As if a voice were in them, the sick sight
> And giddy prospect of the raving stream,
> The unfetter'd clouds, and region of the Heavens,
> Tumult and peace, the darkness and the light
> Were all like workings of one mind, the features
> Of the same face, blossoms upon one tree,
> Characters of the great Apocalypse,

[3] *Art as Experience* (New York, 1935), p. 193.
[4] *Philosophy and Civilization* (New York, 1931), pp. 100-101.

The types and symbols of Eternity,
Of first and last, and midst, and without end.[5]

". . . Were all like workings of one mind." Here Wordsworth emphasizes as heavily as anyone can the sense of qualitative community of which we have spoken. Elsewhere, as we
have seen with reference to similar experience, he writes of the
"sentiment of Being" and again, in a passage which echoes
Plotinus, of the "pulse of Being":

I convers'd
With things that really are, I, at this time
Saw blessings spread around me like a sea.
Thus did my days pass on, and now at length
From Nature and her overflowing soul
I had receiv'd so much that all my thoughts
Were steep'd in feeling; I was only then
Contented when with bliss ineffable
I felt the sentiment of Being spread
O'er all that moves, and all that seemeth still,
O'er all, that, lost beyond the reach of thought
And human knowledge, to the human eye
Invisible, yet liveth to the heart,
O'er all that leaps, and runs, and shouts, and sings,
Or beats the gladsome air, o'er all that glides
Beneath the wave, yea, in the wave itself
And mighty depth of waters.[6]

There came a time of greater dignity
Which had been gradually prepar'd, and now
Rush'd in as if on wings, the time in which
The pulse of Being everywhere was felt,
When all the several frames of things, like stars
Through every magnitude distinguishable,
Were half confounded in each other's blaze,
One galaxy of life and joy.[7]

---

[5] *The Prelude*, Bk. VI, ll. 555 ff.
[6] *Ibid.*, Bk. II, ll. 412 ff.
[7] *Ibid.*, Bk. VIII, ll. 626 ff. Compare with Plotinus: ". . . for all is transparent, nothing dark, nothing impenetrable; every being is lucid to every other,
light manifest to light. And each of them contains all within itself and sees
all in every other, so that everywhere there is all, and each is all, and infinite
the glory! Each of them is great: the small is great; the sun There is all the

It is most important to notice that the sentiment of Being spreads beyond the objects which are actually observed and links them with all the forms of Nature, of which the vast majority are not directly apprehended.

Consider further the following lines of Walt Whitman's "On the Beach at Night Alone":

A vast similitude interlocks all,
All spheres, grown, ungrown, small, large, suns, moons, planets,
All distances of place however wide,
All distances of time, all inanimate forms,
All souls, all living bodies though they be ever so different, or in different worlds,
All gaseous, watery, vegetable, mineral processes, the fishes, the brutes,
All nations, colours, barbarisms, civilisations, languages,
All identities that have existed or may exist on this globe, or any globe,
All lives and deaths, all of the past, present, future,
This vast similitude spans them, and always has spann'd,
And shall for ever span them and compactly hold and enclose them.

The word "Nature" has in recent years enjoyed a rather shady reputation among scholars, appearing almost as the pro-

---

stars; and every star, again, is all the stars and sun; each is mirrored in every other (*Enneads* V, viii, 4).
Wordsworth continues:

> Then rose
> Man, inwardly contemplated, and present
> In my own being, to a loftier height;
> As of all visible creatures crown. . . .
>
> . . . .
> As, more than anything we know instinct
> With Godhead. . . .

Compare this with Plotinus' comments which follow the passage already quoted. The lover of beauty is rendered truly divine.

"Thus a man filled with a God holds his vision of the Divine Being within himself if he but have the strength. Anyone possessed by God has but to bring that Divine-within before his consciousness and at once he sees an image of himself lifted to a better beauty" (V, viii, 10-11).

There seems little ground for doubting that Wordsworth has caught a verbal echo of Plotinus from Coleridge's inspired conversation. But Wordsworth's thought is not strictly Neoplatonic. The Neoplatonic beautiful world where such inter-penetration is maintained is not, as with Wordsworth, the concrete world in which we live and move. This beautiful world, like the Platonic Ideas, is a transcendent realm which only the God-like man may enter. Wordsworth's thought is at this point tangent to Plotinus' philosophy but not coincident with it.

totype of philosophical ambiguity.   Perhaps this promiscuity
of significance is owing to the fact that the term is very rarely
used to indicate the object of a single act of awareness.   More
often it refers to an aggregate of things or to some set of principles to be comprehended step by step of discursive thought.
In any case it is not an object of which we usually feel ourselves to be directly aware.   As Martin Heidegger would say,
"Nature is no phenomenon."   But here is where the poets can
help us.   They may teach us that Nature is an entity open
directly to universal experience, albeit to an experience that is
often ignored and rarely cultivated.   Thus for Wordsworth
and Whitman, Nature is an object of experience, an object
which encompasses every particular concrete thing of which the
poet may be aware.   It is the matrix and the concrete environment both of the poet's mind and of the concrete thing which
he loves to describe.

To most of us, this matrix appears as a vague totality, and
we are aware of it only as the ever-present background of
things which are themselves apprehended much more clearly.
It is apprehension of this totality that makes it possible for us
to think of "*the* world" or "*the* universe."   But the special-
ized concentration of our attention prevents us from feeling
very clearly the continuity of the object with the totality of
which it is a detail.   This totality is often clear to the poet or
artist, and it may be so to anyone who will learn to appreciate
the tonality of his esthetic awareness.

Mr. Dewey does not mention Wordsworth, but a very similar, although a more difficult, concept is presented by Mr.
A. N. Whitehead with specific mention of Wordsworth's attitude toward Nature.   It is interesting to notice that in the
interpretation of esthetic experience these two philosophers of
so widely different orientation come very close to agreeing.   In
Whitehead's *Science and the Modern World* occurs this brilliant comment upon Wordsworth:

> It is the brooding presence of the hills which haunts him.   His
> theme is nature *in solido,* that is to say, he dwells on that *mysterious*
> *presence of surrounding things, which imposes itself on any separate*

element which we set up as an individual for its own sake. He always grasps the whole of nature as involved in the tonality of the particular instance. That is why he laughs with the daffodils, and finds in the primrose "thoughts too deep for tears." . . .

It would hardly be possible to express more clearly a feeling for nature, as exhibiting *entwined prehensive unities, each suffused with modal presences of others.*[8]

These italicized, technical terms repeat the meaning that is already expressed in the italicized passage above. The word *prehensive* is important: for Whitehead, objects and modes of feeling embody one another, insofar as they are influenced by one another. The prehension is the synthetic grasp of environment which constitutes the individual essence or unity of an actual entity, what Whitehead calls an *occasion.* Nature is a "togetherness" of many *occasions*, present in one another. Whitehead quotes from Wordsworth:

> Ye Presences of Nature in the sky
> And on the earth! Ye Visions of the hills!
> And souls of lonely places! Can I think
> A vulgar hope was yours when ye employed
> Such ministry, when ye through many a year
> Haunting me thus among my boyish sports,
> On caves and trees, upon the woods and hills,
> Impressed upon all forms the characters
> Of danger or desire; and thus did make
> *The surface of the universal earth*
> With triumph and delight, with hope and fear,
> Work like a sea?[9]

Whitehead continues:

In thus citing Wordsworth the point which I wish to make is that we forget how strained and paradoxical is the view of nature which modern science imposes upon our thoughts. Wordsworth, to the height

[8] *Science and the Modern World* (New York, 1925), pp. 120-122. This passage has been commented upon by Melvin M. Rader in his *Presiding Ideas in Wordsworth's Poetry*, University of Washington Publications in Language and Literature, Vol. VIII, No. 2, pp. 121-216 (Seattle, 1931), pp. 264 ff.

[9] *The Prelude* (1850), Bk. I, ll. 464 ff. (A, ll. 490 ff.). Italics mine.

of genius, *expresses the concrete facts of our apprehension*, facts which are distorted in scientific analysis. . . .[10]

Whitehead briefly comments upon Wordsworth's criticism of science: "In this respect, his characteristic thought can be summed up in his phrase, 'We murder to dissect'. . . . [Wordsworth] alleges against science its absorption in abstractions. His consistent theme is that the important facts of Nature elude the scientific method."[11] With this I should agree most heartily, adding that for Wordsworth the most important "fact" of Nature is the "unity of all," or "the one life within us and abroad."

Despite all this, we must not forget that for Dewey and Whitehead, apprehension of the concrete envelope is only one stage in the growth of our acquaintance with and knowledge of the world. For Wordsworth, apprehension of the togetherness of things in their primordial beauty is presented rather as the culmination of the poet's insight. Hence Wordsworth dwells upon his sentiment of Being and cherishes its content more persistently and with greater enthusiasm than do the philosophers. For Wordsworth, this sentiment is a talent which it is death to hide, and its expression in palpable imagery is the first duty of the lover of Nature. Thus it is not surprising that his account of the unity of things is richer, not only in tone, but in actual content, than anything to be found in philosophical literature. Wordsworth's insistence upon panpsychism is bold and unqualified, a full and uncompromising vision rather than, as in Whitehead's mention of the "brooding presence of the hills," an adumbration of something to be understood only as the outcome of long philosophical research. The best description of the sentiment of Being written by a critic or theorist lies not in the writings of Dewey or Whitehead but in an essay by the late A. C. Bradley. Bradley is purposely vague in order to avoid "theorizing" Wordsworth, but he speaks of the contrast—he even goes so far as to use the word "hostility" between the sensuously perceived object and a spiritual or suprasensuous order to which, after all, the

[10] *Ibid.*, p. 122.   [11] *Ibid.*, p. 121.

object belongs. Bradley speaks of this suprasensuous entity as a background. This background is never something
that could be perceived by the senses: "Sometimes it is an
intimation of boundlessness, contradicting or abolishing the
fixed limits of our habitual view. . . . Always, openly or
covertly, it is the intimation of something illimitable, over-
arching or breaking into the customary 'reality.' Its character
varies; and so sometimes at its touch the soul, suddenly conscious of its own infinity, melts in rapture into that infinite
being; while at other times the 'mortal nature' stands dumb,
incapable of thought, or shrinking from some presence. . . ."[12]

It is noteworthy, in the light of what is to follow in later
chapters, that both Whitehead and Bradley find it significant
to mention Spinoza's monism in connection with their interpretations of Wordsworth.

Let us return to Mr. Whitehead's interpretation. How,
then, does Wordsworth perceive *"the concrete facts of our
apprehension"?* On the surface, at least, the passage from
The Prelude which Whitehead quotes is obscure enough, and
we may well understand that its true import has been long
passed over. But the expansion of the idea in Book XIII of
The Prelude, in the Mt. Snowdon passage, is more explicit,
and by reference to it we can dispel obscurity and learn what
Wordsworth means when he says that the "surface of the universal earth works like a sea." Here is a point interesting for
its own sake, quite aside from interpretation of Wordsworth's
thought; for it bears significantly upon the problem of esthetic
vision. When the artist tells us that he does not add to Nature,
that he "paints what he sees," he raises in our minds questions
which Wordsworth's comments may help to answer.

We must remember that Wordsworth is describing the
immediate aspect of Nature as presented in his own experience.
When he says that the world works "like a sea," he is not
formulating a theory of physics nor even of metaphysics but
reporting directly what appears to his spontaneous perception.
He is describing the world in its full and immediate or esthetic

<hr />

[12] *Oxford Lectures on Poetry* (2d ed., London, 1909), pp. 131, 134.

concreteness. Describing this aspect of things seems to have given Wordsworth much difficulty. The manuscripts of *The Prelude* indicate that in the Mt. Snowdon passage he was a long time groping for the happy expression of this obvious and yet unfamiliar appearance.[13]

The forms or objects of Nature are interfused, they exercise a mutual domination,[14] one object swaying another,[15] or, better, diffusing itself over others,[16] with an interchangeable supremacy,[17] so that each object is at once active and passive in a dynamic intercourse. This mutual interpenetration Wordsworth calls a power[18] of Nature, through which objects work upon one another, each exercising a "subtle reach and comprehensive sway." In the presence of Nature, we must acknowledge this power: we "cannot choose but feel."[19]

The sudden vision of a fresh unity in variety which recognizes this interpenetration affords a new and profoundly satisfying wealth of organized detail where the whole "reflects upon" its elements. Coleridge's distinction between fancy and imagination seems to be implicit here, since Wordsworth tells us that the objects so united "sway" one another. The interfusion seems to be imaginative and not fanciful.[20]

Wordsworth is quite certain that this interpenetration of natural forms does not appear as a static pattern. Interfused objects work one upon another, and Wordsworth insists that this energy is Nature's. When we witness this dynamic inter-

---

[13] See De Selincourt's apparatus criticus on *The Prelude*, A, Bk. XIII, ll. 66 ff. (1850, Bk. XIV, ll. 63 ff.), and his notes to the same section.

[14] *Ibid.* (1850), Bk. XIV, l. 81.   [15] *Ibid.*, W, Bk. XIII, l. 82.

[16] *Ibid.*, A₂, Bk. XII, l. 81.   [17] *Ibid.* (1850), Bk. XIV, l. 84.

[18] *Ibid.*, A, Bk. XIII, l. 84; (1850), Bk. XIV, l. 86.

[19] *Ibid.*

[20] *Table Talk*, June 23; 1834; also *Bibiographia Literaria*, end of chap. xiii. See Rader, *op. cit.*, p. 166. Compare Professor Mather's statement: "If (the artist) puts nature first, he will look at his own position as ambassadorial; he has the proud function of representing and extolling her. If he puts himself first, his duty is solely that of self-expression with such aid or hindrance as inferior nature may provide. In the former case, while he thinks he is imitating nature, he will instinctively so transform the appearance that he will find a style that is his own; in the latter case, he will consciously exploit his own idiosyncracies, and the result will be not style but mannerism" (*Concerning Beauty*, pp. 204-205). Thus for Coleridge, fancy involves *choice*, while imagination is a repetition of a higher power.

penetration, we are aware of the power with which Nature dominates the "outward face of things," the surface where beauty takes shape. We may interpret this as follows: In the apprehension of beauty, we witness the birth of beauty. We see, or we feel, the mutual influence of elements which produces or sustains esthetic value. For Wordsworth, this production seems, somehow, an act embodied in the tissue of the concrete world.

Let us call this esthetic aspect of Nature, which Wordsworth describes, *objective metaphor*. Let us refrain from thinking of it as *objectified metaphor*, lest we find ourselves hastily substituting the concept of pathetic fallacy for something quite different and much more significant. To be sure, in the realms of discourse open to the science of physics or geology, mountains do not "upheave their dusky backs"[21] through seas of mist; but in the realm of objectivity open to the esthetic experience such is sometimes the case. We have just heard Professor Whitehead assert that Wordsworth apprehends the truly concrete. We might venture, on such authority, to suggest that the esthetic object is the genuinely concrete, and the scientific object an abstraction, withdrawn from the fullness of real things and their concrete fusion of interrelations. Thus we do not *pretend* that the mountains are alive. *As concrete, esthetic objects* the mountains have embodied in them characteristics which, in other realms of discourse, belong only to certain quadrupeds. As esthetic objects, the mountains and the animals embody one another. They share an "ideal form" whose presence in both is their interfusion.

We have seen that Wordsworth's experience helped him to think of Nature as a plastic power. Nature and not our

[21] See *The Prelude*, A, Bk. XIII, l. 45 (1850); Bk. XIV, l. 43. While completing this study of Wordsworth's theory of "objective metaphor," I have been fascinated by Professor Mather's theory of correspondences of rhythm which he has presented in his recent volume, *Concerning Beauty*, mentioned in previous notes. His contribution must be studied as a whole. But let me quote these striking sentences: "Everything (the artist) experiences tends to organize itself by analogy and correspondence into groups, and these groups generally develop unexpected interrelations. He lives in constant expectation of the extensions of such correlations in a world that, being always open and flexible, is progressively becoming of a wider and richer orderliness" (p. 187).

faculty of comparison makes one object suffuse another. Nor
is this sheer fancy. After all, no matter how acute one's taste,
natural beauty does appear to be a gift, not a creation of our
own. Nature seems to be the artist, we the spectator. Wordsworth insists that Nature, "unaided by the human mind"
thrusts beauty upon our notice.[22] This is not an arbitrary
statement, but a recording of vivid experience. Toward this
Eolian influence, Wordsworth has advised us to maintain a
"wise passiveness" and to restrain the "meddling intellect."
If we confront Nature with a preconceived classification and
hold to it throughout our observation, we withdraw ourselves
from the fullness of the concrete. We tend to ignore all
aspects of things but those pertinent to the classification. To
overcome this, "to come forth into the light of things," we
must be wisely passive, inviting Nature by withholding our
minds from consciously planned division and analysis. This
does not mean merely that we must be impartial, unprejudiced
observers; there lies a great difference between John Locke on
the one hand and Wordsworth on the other. Wordsworth is
not talking about faithful scientific observation, he is trying to
tell us how to invite inspiration. He seems convinced that the
power which conducts from sense to ideal form, which brings
us into the presence of significant images, i.e., of objects'
"mutual domination," obeys suprapersonal laws of its own.
Wordsworth seems to have felt that this power is animate,
and that its action is often a welling up into our consciousness
of another mind, somewhat like the "intellectual breeze" of
Coleridge's conversation poem.

Imagination is an "element of Nature's inner self."[23]
Wordsworth seems convinced that in genuine love of beauty,
we put away our old self altogether:

> . . . Then will come
> Another soul, spring, centre of his being,
> And that is Nature.[24]

---

[22] *Ibid.*, W. See De Selincourt's notes, p. 602; also A, Bk. II, ll. 347-348.
[23] *The Prelude*, Bk. VIII, l. 513.
[24] *Ibid.*, Y. See De Selincourt's notes, p. 556.

Now, there can be no doubt that Wordsworth was profoundly impressed by what we might call the passivity of the creative mind. We have noticed this doctrine in Boehme. It seems also to have impressed Blake and Shelley. Indeed, according to Professor Gingerich's interpretation, this had much to do with Shelley's disposition toward necessitarianism. Certainly, the "Hymn to Intellectual Beauty" reflects such an attitude:

> The awful shadow of some unseen Power
> Floats—though unseen among us.

Yet Shelley, like Wordsworth, seems to transcend this belief. We need not always be wholly dependent upon an unseen power. "Make me thy lyre even as the forest is" is only the beginning of a supplication which culminates with the words "Be thou me, impetuous one." If this prayer is at all significant, i.e., if Shelley believes in the possibility of its realization, he clearly transcends necessitarian doctrine. And for Wordsworth, the enjoyment of beauty is not always the soul's involuntary submission to usurpation.

It is perhaps true that the marked moral individualism of Wordsworth's early thinking—the individualism of *The Prelude*—withholds him from obeying completely the inspiration which engendered the theory of imagination above described. At any rate, there are for Wordsworth "higher minds" whose creative power seems to resemble Nature's own domination. These minds can initiate creative activity. They are Powers, concerning whom Wordsworth makes some of his boldest assertions. These minds participate in a most intimate manner with the Spirit that rolls through all things. They actively participate in the "active universe." They are "natural beings in the strength of Nature,"[25] creators and receivers both.

The "active" mind receives from without, as does the lower, but also gives in return. In the lower forms of inspiration Nature works upon the mind through the medium of landscape and panoramic beauty, in the higher the mind is united with Nature, or the World-Soul. Inspired men realize

---

[25] *Ibid.*, A, Bk. III, l. 194; (1850), Bk. III, l. 196.

this truth. They possess "consciousness of Whom they are."[26]
The capitalization of *Whom* in the 1850 version leaves no
doubt concerning the meaning.

In the enjoyment of natural beauty—of mountain and
woodland scenery—the passivity of esthetic awareness may be
manifest. To enjoy such objects it is not necessary for us to
master a set of conventions or to study the history of certain
art forms, or even to inquire into the "intent of the artist."
In this sense, the beauty of Nature surprises us or overtakes
us, and yet as our sensibility awakens, we do begin to recognize and to "respect" what Nature offers—if only by singling
out and attending to the "scheme" of mass and line which
constitutes the view we admire. Then an almost involuntary,
at least an unpremeditated, activity breaks in upon our receptive passiveness. This activity carries with it a lively emotional tone; yet we encounter it as we encounter an unexpected
sensation. Certainly this activity is not "ours" in the sense
that we have deliberately planned it. We have come upon it.
Insofar as our immediate consciousness is concerned, it seems
to "belong to" the scene contemplated as much as to ourselves.
The feeling then that mountains and lakes speak to us, so to
say, with our own voices, is a lively one. Combine this feeling with a philosophy of the sort suggested by the sentiment
of Being, and we may come to believe that Nature speaks to us.

Most people will insist that this is no more than a "poetic"
way of putting things. "I sometimes feel *as if* Nature spoke
to me." With this "as if" we need find no quarrel, unless
someone adds "Of course, Nature does no such thing. This
panpsychism is sheer poetry. The truth in these matters lies
entirely with science." Of course, "Nature speaks to me" is
metaphorical, but it may be a more adequate metaphor than
many that are derived from a scientific background. Wordsworth himself uses an "as if" occasionally in connection with
panpsychism. But I know of no passage where he goes on
definitely to prefer another philosophy as more adequate. He
is very far from believing his philosophical animism to be

[26] *Ibid.*, A, Bk. XII, ll. 108-109; (1850), Bk. XIV, l. 115.

merely a "beautiful" or a "vital" falsehood. But, unlike some philosophers, he has moments of humility when he considers the "strange seas of thought" which his philosophy surveys.

The considerations which lead Wordsworth to this panpsychism are not primarily rational. He goes so far as to say that for the most part they lie "far hidden from the reach of words." Such awareness is, for those who feel it, a consciousness "not to be subdued." But this is not quite all; Wordsworth also speaks of "deep analogies by thought supplied."[27] And it is concerning such analogies that I wish here to offer a tentative suggestion, which may help the student to sympathize more fully with Wordsworth's insight. But first let us comment further on the sentiment of Being.

The cultivation of such intuition is a character of romantic art and is hardly to be found among the neoclassicists who immediately precede the romantics in the history of literature. This is because the classicist tends rather more than the romanticist to consider his object as torn from the texture of a concrete environment. He does this, as Dr. Johnson once pointed out, by accepting what he considers to be typical or valuable moments in the life of his object and by concentrating attention upon them. Most neoclassic art is too sophisticated, too much subject to a highly disciplined and premeditated control, to reveal the great intuitions which constitute man's primary orientation in the world. One who is wont to pursue his artistic ends almost wholly by manipulation and rearrangement of material may come to think of Nature as an aggregate of things or as a principle governing these things. But he will not be given to thinking of Nature as the indispensable and inescapable milieu of the concrete object, or even as the object itself with its full margins. The unity of Nature is not intuited as standing simply by itself. There is always a concrete object appearing as a core or center; and we are vividly aware of Nature only insofar as we are aware of its immanence in the finite object. Thus we may "see a world in a grain of sand." This the romantic poet often does, since he respects all concrete objects and accepts them with "natural piety."

[27] *The Prelude*, Bk. III, l. 122.

Thus Walt Whitman in "Starting from Paumanock" writes:

And I will thread a thread through my poems that time and events are compact,
And that all the things of the universe are perfect miracles, each as profound as any.
I will not make poems with reference to parts,
But I will make poems, songs, thoughts, with reference to ensemble. . . .

I suspect that Whitehead and Whitman express philosophies that are essentially similar. Compare the lines just quoted with Mr. Whitehead's statement: "Remembering the poetic rendering of our concrete experience, we see at once that the element of value, of being valuable, of having value, of being an end in itself, of being something which is for its own sake, must not be omitted in any account of an event as the most concrete actual something. 'Value' is the word I use for the intrinsic reality of an event. Value is an element which permeates the poetic view of Nature."[28]

Wordsworth, I think, goes somewhat further than Mr. Whitehead has gone in this passage. But I have little doubt that when Wordsworth speaks of the "life of *things*" it is, at least partially, owing to a feeling that even *things* have a value in themselves. For Wordsworth the "Universe of Death, the falsest of all worlds" is the world as inadequately comprehended by reason, working alone with the materials offered to the sense organs. This is the world of scientific materialism. As Mr. Whitehead points out, it is composed of "bits of matter, bare of intrinsic value."[29]

This romantic intuition includes a sense, upon which our theories of space, time and causality largely depend, that no actual finite thing can stand by itself, that there is nothing wholly self-sufficient or permanent within our environment. Each object, although a concrete individual, owes something to the others and, in turn, it conditions the others. The concrete world is a world of reciprocity or, to quote Wordsworth once more, of the "mutual domination" of things. Hence no

[28] *Op. cit.*, p. 136.   [29] *Loc. cit.*, p. 230.

object is adequately represented if it is shown as standing clear
of its natural setting.　Nature appears as the community of
mutually dependent objects.　Now, if we "take time seriously"
we will recognize that this community is at no moment complete.　No object can remain as permanent, but its successors
cannot, even so, wholly escape its transtemporal *actio ad distans*.
So the instability of every object does not involve the possibility of its total eradication.　No object can disappear without
leaving traces of itself and the omnipresence of such persistence
is open to intuition.　Thus we are aware that there has been a
past and that there will be a future even when we possess
virtually no memory of the one and when we are incapable of
foreseeing the detail of the other.　The sentiment of Being is
transtemporal.

Thus the world that encompasses every object reaches into
an unlimited past and opens upon an unfinished future and we
feel these to be indispensable elements in the full setting of
every event.　It is to the transtemporal aspect of the sentiment
of Being that we must look for explanation of the pantheism
and panpsychism which so often accompanies it in literature.
Indeed, it seems almost impossible to put the content of this
intuition into words without using phrases which most strongly
suggest panpsychism.　I suspect that this is one of the causes
of the animism and panpsychism so prevalent in romantic
poetry.　After all, the immanence of a "remote" past and of
an "unfinished" future in the present moment is likely to appear to us as mental in form.　Indeed, mention of such transtemporal characters might seem to many people a satisfactory
way of defining mind, which, as Wordsworth knew, is "not a
punctual Presence."　The reciprocity of things in space, their
continuity of surface texture, may be compared to the waves
of a sea; but the fact that the present is somehow solidary with
a vanished past and with a nonexistent future—as Whitman
puts it, that "time and events are compact"—all this is much
harder to express.　Common figures of time as "in flight" or
"on the march" are quite incapable of making this clear to our
imagination.　But the poet who writes of the "soul of the wide

world dreaming on things to come" makes this sentiment some-what more explicit. And the poet whose consciousness has once been overwhelmed by the sentiment of Being will often turn toward some sort of panpsychism and will incline to dismiss other philosophies as being unable to do justice to his experi-ence. Thus the sentiment of Being constitutes apprehension of an eternal or infinite mind. This is its final and most im-portant contribution.

The sentiment of Being includes apprehension of two dis-tinct but closely related "facts," the mutual interpenetration of objects and the eternal universe within which these transi-tory objects subsist. Both of these facts point toward pan-psychism. The first is emphasized perhaps rather more heavily in *The Prelude*, and the second rather more heavily in later poems. But we must not generalize too hastily upon this con-trast, as some critics have been tempted to do, for *The Prelude* is by no means without a profound recognition of eternal Being, as in Book III, and *The Excursion* contains some mention of interpenetration, as in the beginning of Book IX. Most prob-ably these two aspects of reality are inseparable in experience. Emphasis shifts from one to the other as the temper of the poet's religion gradually changes. Interpenetration, certainly at least in its earlier appearances, is joined with pantheism. The eternity of Being, however, is more amenable to orthodoxy since it suggests or resembles the doctrine of an eternally trans-cendent God more closely than does the notion of the inter-penetration of things.[30]

Furthermore, I suspect that some form of the sentiment of

[30] But lest the reader be tempted to dismiss our poet as an idle dreamer, let him consider S. Alexander's interesting essay "Spinoza and Time." Alexander is here concerned with the problem of reconciling the "persistence of Time which we experience, with its habit of dying from one moment to another" (p. 24). In answer to this problem Alexander offers the following (p. 46): "We arrive also at a conclusion which seems to repeat Spinoza's view that thought is a universal feature of things, only with a difference. All things for him are in a sense animated, they are all in their degree thinking things. For us things which are not minds, which are merely alive or are inanimate, are not longer minds, but they do bear an aspect, or contain in themselves an element, which cor-responds to the aspect or element of mind in a thinking thing. That aspect or element is Time." Cf. Charles Hartshorne, *Beyond Humanism* (Chicago, 1937), p. 174.

Being lies behind the doctrine, which Mr. Lovejoy has recently described, the theory of the "plenitude of Being" or the "great chain of Being," whose fortunes he has followed from ancient times. To be sure, the plenitude of Being does not necessarily involve panpsychism and it frequently appears in high places very much opposed to pantheism. But, even so, it closely approaches the notion of the compactness and interpenetration of things. I surmise that behind such doctrine there lies, perhaps some distance up the stream of history, an intuition not unlike Wordsworth's. Throughout the eighteenth century in England, however, I opine that this doctrine existed mostly in conceptual form without much direct intuitive support until the rising tide of romanticism established the sentiment of Being in its full power—or, perhaps we should say, until the sentiment of Being established romanticism at the close of the eighteenth century.

* * *

There is another order of being besides that of the concrete world open to intuition, the Platonic realm of pure form, in very recent years explored by Santayana and described by Whitehead as the order of "eternal objects." The poet may be keenly aware of this order also. Thus Wordsworth's enthusiasm in the pursuit of mathematics and his brilliant comments upon "poetry and geometric truth" complement his vivid sense of nature as a concrete togetherness. Wordsworth seems to have recognized clearly enough that we are faced with two distinct types of objectivity, for he raises the question: How do these two come to be related? It is interesting, although perhaps not entirely pertinent to our present discussion, that Wordsworth thought of the independent realm of sheer form as created out of pure intelligence—the intelligence of God:

> Yet must I not entirely overlook
> The pleasure gather'd from the elements
> Of geometric science. I had stepp'd
> In these inquiries but a little way,
> No farther than the threshold; with regret
> Sincere I mention this; but there I found

Enough to exalt, to chear me and compose.
With Indian awe and wonder, ignorance
Which even was cherish'd, did I meditate
Upon the alliance of those simple, pure
Proportions and relations with the frame
And Laws of Nature, how they would become
Herein a leader to the human mind,
And made endeavours frequent to detect
The process by dark guesses of my own.
Yet from this source more frequently I drew
A pleasure calm and deeper, a still sense
Of permanent and universal sway
And paramount endowment in the mind,
An image not unworthy of the one
Surpassing Life, which out of space and time,
Nor touched by welterings of passion, is
And hath the name of God.   Transcendent peace
And silence did await upon these thoughts
That were a frequent comfort to my youth.[31]

One who, like Wordsworth, is so intensely aware of the
concrete order of things and furthermore acquainted with
mathematical argument will, almost inevitably, notice that man
is placed between two orders, the concrete and the formal, and
the contrast between the two will heighten his comprehension
of the primary characters of both; of the interpenetration,
instability, and urgency of concrete things, and of the eternal
and definitive pattern of the forms.

The sense of universal concrete texture is important, not
only in interpreting Nature as an esthetic object, but also in
understanding human affairs and in appreciating the meaning
of history.   And in this connection also a tendency toward panpsychism appears.   The concrete interpenetration of human
events suggests that human nature is no "punctual spirit" but a
Zeitgeist diffused throughout the web of human intercourse
and of historical occurrence.   This intuition closely resembles
its more strictly esthetic counterpart in that it centers upon a
given "capacious" object that is seen to stand against a vast

[31] *The Prelude*, Bk. VI, ll. 135 ff.

background with which it is in organic relation. Thus, after describing his "sight-seeing" in London, Wordsworth writes:

> With strong sensations, teeming as it did
> Of past and present, such a place must needs
> Have pleas'd me, in those times; I sought not then
> Knowledge; but craved for power, and power I found
> In all things; nothing had a circumscribed
> And narrow influence; but all objects, being
> Themselves capacious, also found in me
> Capaciousness and amplitude of mind;
> Such is the strength and glory of our youth.
> The Human Nature unto which I felt
> That I belong'd, and which I lov'd and reverenc'd,
> Was not a punctual Presence, but a Spirit
> Living in time and space, and far diffus'd.
> In this my joy, in this my dignity
> Consisted; the external universe,
> By striking upon what is found within,
> Had given me this conception, with the help
> Of Books, and what they picture and record.[32]

It is interesting to notice that in this passage, as so often elsewhere, Wordsworth combines a panpsychist sense of unity with a suggestion of Eolian inspiration.

This vision of history, as revealing a plastic power in things that live and grow, may free us from the acceptance of a rigid determinism. Human history is presented as a growth, the growth and expansion of a spirit. It is not then primarily a matter of causal sequences linked together by a blind necessity; or what some of the ancients called Chance. Thus the hard and fast determinism, invoked by Oswald in *The Borderers*, is here avoided. Godwinian necessity, so desperately uncongenial to Wordsworth, is later to disturb him and bring with it the moral perplexities of determinism. Thus Oswald's speech in Act III represents an entirely different conception of history, one that Wordsworth did not entertain at the time described in the above quotation.

[32] *Ibid.*, Bk. VIII, ll. 751 ff.

> . . . Remorse—
> It cannot live with thought; think on, think on,
> And it will die. What! in this universe,
> Where the least things control the greatest, where
> The faintest breath that breathes can move a world;
> What! feel remorse, where if a cat had sneezed,
> A leaf had fallen, the thing had never been
> Whose very shadow gnaws us to the vitals.[33]

For the brief period that Godwinian notions dominated his thought, Wordsworth was unable to envisage human history as he had done, if only for a short time, while in London. Oswald's philosophy of history describes man as helplessly in the grip of senseless events. This is quite inconsistent with the notions which Wordsworth was, by disposition and insight, inclined to favor.

*   *   *

In passing, let us suggest that the noblest expression of the sentiment of Being, both in its spatial and its temporal aspects, is Wordsworth's poem "The Solitary Reaper." The girl singing in the fields becomes for a moment the center of the universe. All history and all geography are seen to exist only as the vast margins of her momentary and yet eternal presence. It seems to the poet that her song and the world which it reveals can have no ending. The reaper's song is a symbol of the eternity which encompasses her life, of that unity and fullness of Being which "lies far hidden from the reach of words."

Another and less brilliant expression of the sentiment of Being, but one which shows how pervasive was its influence in Wordsworth's life, appears in the following lines of *The Recluse* fragment:

> —'Tis, but I cannot name it, 't is the sense
> Of majesty, and beauty and repose,
> A blended holiness of earth and sky,
> Something that makes this individual spot,
> The small abiding-place of many men,

[33] Act III, scene v.

A termination and a last retreat,
A centre, come from wheresoe'er you will,
A whole without dependence or defect,
Made for itself and happy in itself,
Perfect contentment, Unity entire.

Like Blake, Wordsworth feels the quality of eternity as the setting or atmosphere of the concrete object that is known in love and imagination.

Perhaps this is the place to call to mind a wonderful passage of Thoreau, a description of the sense of Being which presents experience similar to Wordsworth's and yet rendered in a tempo which is peculiar to Thoreau himself. The passage is in places a masterpiece of softened statement which can be best appreciated by one who has just studied its Wordsworthian analogues:

Far in the night, as we were falling asleep on the bank of the Merrimack, we heard some tyro beating a drum incessantly, in preparation for a country muster, as we learned, and we thought of the line,

"When the drum beat at dead of night."

We could have assured him that his beat would be answered, and the forces be mustered. Fear not, thou drummer of the night, we too will be there. And still he drummed on in the silence of the dark. This stray sound from a far-off sphere came to our ears from time to time, far, sweet, and significant, and we listened with such an unprejudiced sense as if for the first time we heard at all. No doubt he was an insignificant drummer enough, but his music afforded us a prime and leisure hour, and we felt that we were in season wholly. These simple sounds related us to the stars. Aye, there was a logic in them so convincing that the combined sense of mankind could never make me doubt their conclusions. I stop my habitual thinking, as if the plow had suddenly run deeper in its furrow through the crust of the world. How can I go on, who have just stepped over such a bottomless skylight in the bog of my life. Suddenly old Time winked at me,—Ah, you know me, you rogue,—and news had come that IT was well. That ancient universe is in such capital health, I think undoubtedly it will never die. Heal yourselves, doctors; by God I live.—

> Then idle Time ran gadding by
> And left me with Eternity alone;
> I hear beyond the range of sound,
> I see beyond the verge of sight,—

I see, smell, taste, hear, feel, that everlasting Something to which we are allied, at once our maker, our abode, our destiny, our very Selves; the one historic truth, the most remarkable fact which can become the distinct and uninvited subject of our thought, the actual glory of the universe; the only fact which a human being cannot avoid recognizing, or in some way forget or dispense with.—

> It doth expand my privacies
> To all, and leave me single in the crowd.

I have seen how the foundations of the world are laid, and I have not the least doubt that it will stand a good while.[34]

We may raise the question: Why does Wordsworth find the beauty of landscape the most satisfactory approach to mystical awareness? Why should he not include equally all beauty and its apprehension? There are two answers. Wordsworth's taste was more sensitive to natural beauty than to other forms. But I think that we may go somewhat further than this. The beauty of Nature not only prepares the mystic for his vision, but, in its detail, it often symbolizes or expresses the object or content of the mystical insight which it furthers. The vast and all-inclusive permanence of the hills suggests an eternal framework that endures throughout all the phases of the "changeful earth" and the more hurried sequences of light and shadow and darkness. Even more is the turmoil of human consciousness in spectacular contrast with the steady self-assertion of a hillside; and, when we are lost in the beauty of such a scene, we steep our consciousness in the permanence of its object.

Any object of great beauty may echo or reflect the eternal. But few objects of beauty seem so completely to *contain* or to coincide with eternity as does the bold and solid permanence

---

[34] *A Week on the Concord and Merrimack Rivers* (New York, 1921), pp. 125-126.

of the mountains, that silently press in upon the observer and engulf his consciousness. Here space and time, themselves, in their uncertain multiplicity, seem only to be tolerated; they do not dominate or characterize the Presence that awaits us in the mountains, where the "unity of all" is simply and majestically unfolded.

CHAPTER IV

Imagination and the Mind's Abyss

WE HAVE already insisted upon the importance of Jakob Boehme for the student of Wordsworth. Let us examine this influence in greater detail, paying special attention to the many verbal echoes of Boehme which appear in Wordsworth's phraseology.

The student of romanticism who comes upon Boehme for the first time will be delighted and amazed by the German philosopher's emphasis upon creative imagination and upon his interpretation of Nature as the outward semblance and product of a creative spirit. Such a student may at first overlook the fact that Boehme's center of interest is religious whereas that of the romantic poet is esthetic. But as he corrects this omission, he may well come to recognize that for Boehme religion is interpreted as a life of imagination, of sensitivity and creative will; whereas for the romantic poet art and the enjoyment of beauty take on a definitely religious significance.

To be sure, Boehme's writings are steeped in theological language. Fallen angels, days of judgment, the persons of the Trinity, and other theological entities abound in his prose. Of these, Wordsworth will accept but few. But despite such obvious differences, the Behmenist philosophy is more congenial to a romantic poet than is most theology. For Boehme often emphasizes the meaning of theology in the life of the individual and he is impatient with all discourse which leads away from this. Furthermore, his tendency toward pantheism goes so far that even his treatment of the persons of the Trinity, amounts to a study of the human mind and its conditions.

Both Boehme and the romantic poet find in imagination the very heart of the moral life. And for both of them the concept of freedom, the inner freedom of the spirit, which is the true dominion of the imaginative will, is essential to any

ethical evaluation of human life. These similarities of belief
and of feeling justify us in speaking of Boehme as a precursor
of romanticism and they explain how Boehme, despite his
almost barbarous obscurity, became in many instances the
teacher of the great romantics. Thus Tieck, Novalis, Fried-
rich Schlegel, Blake, and the philosopher Schelling—to say
nothing of Coleridge himself—are known to have stood under
the spell of Boehme's inspiration. Indeed, Blake's theory of
imagination is clearly Behmenistic. For that matter, so is
Coleridge's. But Coleridge develops his ideas with greater
respect for philosophical system, an ideal which Blake scorned.
Coleridge, be it remembered, found Boehme a "pillar of fire
by night," but by daylight a "dark cloud."

Boehme's thought and that of his eighteenth-century English follower, William Law, who was responsible for the
handsome and justly famous edition of Boehme translations
published from 1764 to 1781, offer a transition between the
biblical notion of divine creation and the romantic idea of
artistic or esthetic creation, thus bestowing upon the romantic
idea something of a religious significance. For Boehme and
Law, God's act of creation is not limited to an original
"making" of the world. Nature is a constant creation, a
constant "birth" of created being and a manifestation of God.
". . . Whatever God creates is not created immediately by
himself, but in and by, and out of that Nature in which it is
to live, and move and have its Being."[1]

There never was a creation of the world out of nothing.
The world is the body of divine creation, the constant and
continuous product of God's creative *fiat*, which takes place always. We live and move in an "out-breathing" of divine
power. This out-breathing is the world of living things. The
act of creation is not a pseudohistorical event in the dim past
but the life-giving atmosphere in which we live. This whole
world is alive with God's power. Even "inanimate" objects
possess a congealed and submerged vitality, which, according

[1] William Law, *An Appeal to All that Doubt or Disbelieve the Truths of the
Gospel*, in *Works* (London, 1893), VI, 126.

to Law, will be set free at the sound of the last trump. God creates through Nature in order to reveal or manifest himself.

The following excerpt from Law's *The Spirit of Prayer* well illustrates the Behmenistic doctrine of creation and of Nature. In the dialogue, Theophilus denies the opinion "that all Worlds, and all Things, are created out of nothing":

Show me now, Academicus, I do not say a Text, but the least Hint of Scripture, that by all the Art of commenting, can so much as be drawn to look that way. It is a Fiction, big with the grossest Absurdities, and contrary to everything that we know, either from Nature or Scripture, concerning the Rise and Birth, and Nature of Things, that have begun to be. Adam was not created out of nothing; for the Letter of Moses tells us in the plainest Words, out of what he was created or formed, both as to his inward, and his outward Nature. It tells us also as expressly out of what, Eve, the next Creature, was created. But from the Time of Adam and Eve, the Creation of every human Creature is a Birth out of its Parents' Body and Soul, or whole Nature. And to show us how all things, or Worlds, as well as all living Creatures, are not created out of nothing, St. Paul appeals to this very Account, that Moses gives of the Woman's being formed out of the Man; But "all things" (says he) "are out of God."* Here this Fiction of a Creation out of nothing, is by the plain and open Letter of Scripture, absolutely removed from the whole System of created things, or things which begin to be; for St. Paul's Doctrine is, that all things come into Being, out of God, in the same Reality, as the Woman was formed or created out of Man. So again, "There is to us but one God, out of whom are all things";† for so you know the Greek should be translated, not of, but out of God; not of, but out of Man. The Fiction therefore, which I speak of, is not only without, but expressly contrary to, the plain Letter of Scripture. For everything that we see, every Creature that has Life, is by the Scripture-account, a Birth from something else. And here, Sir, you are to take Notice of a Maxim that is not deniable, that the Reason why any thing proceeds, from a Birth, is the Reason why every thing must do so. *For a Birth would not be in Nature, but because Birth is the only Procedure of Nature. Nature itself is a Birth from God, the first Manifestation of the hidden, inconceivable God, and is so far from being out of nothing, that it is the Manifestation of all that is God, which was before* *unmanifest.* As Nature is the first Birth, or Manifestation of God, or Discovery of the Divine Powers, so all Creatures are the Manifestation of the Powers of Nature, brought into a Variety of Births, by the Will of God, out of Nature.

But the Fiction of the Creation out of nothing, is not only contrary to the Letter and Spirit of the Scripture-account of the Rise and Birth of Things, but is in itself full of the grossest Absurdities, and horrid Consequences. It separates everything from God, it leaves no Relation between God and the Creature, nor any Possibility for any Power, Virtue, Quality, or Perfection of God, to be in the Creature: For if it is created out of nothing, it cannot have something of God in it. But I here stop: For, as you know, we have agreed, if God permit, to have hereafter one Day's entire Conversation on the Nature and End of the Writings of Jacob Behmen, and the right Use and Manner of reading them, as preparatory to a New Edition of his Works, so this and some other Points shall be adjourned to that Time. In the Afternoon, we will proceed only on such Matters, as may further set the Christian Redemption in its true and proper Light before your Friend Humanus.[2]

Strictly speaking, man is not merely a creature. He partakes of the essence of his Creator. From this there follows a theory of immortality which involves, as in Wordsworth's "Ode," a doctrine of preëxistence in God. We quote from Law's *An Appeal to All that Doubt or Disbelieve the Truths of the Gospel:*

Herein also appears the High Dignity, and never-ceasing Perpetuity of our Nature. The Essences of our Souls can never cease to be, because they never began to be:[3] and nothing can live eternally, but that which hath lived from all Eternity. The Essences of our Soul were a Breath in God before they became a Living Soul, they lived in God before they lived in the created Soul, and therefore the Soul is a Partaker of the Eternity of God, and can never cease to be. Here, O Man, behold the great Original, and the high State of thy Birth; Here let all that is within thee praise thy God, who has brought Thee into so high a State of Being, who has given Thee Powers as eternal, and boundless as his own Attributes, that there might be no End or Limits of thy Happiness in Him. Thou begannest as *Time*

---

[2] Law, *Works*, VII, 75 ff. Italics mine.
[3] Cf. *The Prelude*, Bk. II, ll. 234 ff., where Wordsworth says of the individual mind that it "hath no beginning."

began, but as Time was in Eternity before it became *Days* and *Years*, so Thou wast in God before Thou wast brought into the Creation: And as Time is neither a *Part* of Eternity, nor *broken* off from it, yet come out of it; so thou art not a Part of God, nor broken off from Him, yet born out of Him.   Thou shouldst only will that which God willeth, only love that which He loveth, cooperate, and unite with Him in the whole Form of thy Life; because all that Thou art, all that Thou hast, is only a Spark of his own Life and Spirit derived into Thee.   If thou desirest, inclinest, and turnest to God, as the *Flowers* of the Field desire, and turn towards the Sun, all the Blessings of the Deity will spring up in Thee; Father, Son, and Holy Ghost, will make their Abode with Thee.   If thou turnest in towards thyself, to live to thyself, to be happy in the Workings of an *own Will*, to be rich in the Sharpness and Acuteness of thy *own Reason*, thou choosest to be a Weed, and canst only have such a Life, Spirit and Blessing from God, as a *Thistle* has from the Sun.[4]

Shawcross has well summarized the general aspect of Cole-ridge's early thinking by pointing out that he tended to consider the world of everyday experience as no more than a shadow or resemblance of a spiritual reality.   "Life is a vision shadowy of truth."   This attitude, while in itself derivable from any number of philosophical sources, would tend to render Cole-ridge sympathetic to the Behmenistic view of Nature.   For Boehme, all natural substances are "signatures" or outer mani-festations of divine power, for the world at once conceals and reveals God's activity.   Such a philosophy would appear even more congenial to Coleridge when he discovered that the inner core of reality which the signatures but darkly manifest is described as "self-hood" (*ichts*, or "something" as opposed to *nichts* and compared with the pronoun *ich*).

For, the Will of the Eternal One is unperceptible, without inclina-tion to any thing; for, it hath nothing to which it can incline itself, *but only* in itself; therefore thus it bringeth it self forth out of it self, and *bringeth* the Efflux of its Unity into Multiplicity, and into Recep-tion to SELF-HOOD, *viz:* to a Place of a Nature out of which properties arise originally.[5]

[4] VI, 61 ff.   [5] Sparrow (tr.), *Theoscopia*, 3: 13.

Here is the very heart of Boehme's ontology. The process of cosmic creation is directed toward finite centers where "properties" may "arise originally." These centers are best described by the term *selfhood*. They are agents or centers of origination. That Coleridge was prepared to offer this ontology a cordial reception, or perhaps that he had already embraced this view, is apparent from the following statement contained in a letter to Thelwall (December, 1796), which has recently been emphasized by Mr. Lawrence Hanson, to the effect that human personality is "a mere *apparition*, a naked spirit, and that life is, I myself I."[6] Certainly such a notion could be rendered consistent enough with Boehme's belief that God embodies himself in the world through his act of creation, that, in William Blake's words "God becomes as we are that we may be as he is." According to this view, the great end of creation is the reproduction of creative mind.

But we may indicate the extent of Coleridge's debt to Boehme more definitely. In the *Signature of All Things*,[7] Boehme asserts that the finite soul may stand to God as a musical instrument to the artist who plays upon it. Let us add that the artist may be thought to have fashioned the instrument himself. The reader may study the following excerpts from the *Signature* and compare them with the analogy of the "Eolian Harp" (composed in 1795):

For God has not brought forth the creation, that he should be thereby perfect, but for his own manifestation, viz. for the great joy and glory; not that this joy first began with the creation, no, for it was from eternity in the great mystery, yet only as a spiritual melody and sport in itself.

The creation is the same sport out of himself, viz. a platform or instrument of the Eternal Spirit, with which he melodises: and it is even as a great harmony of manifold instruments which are all tuned into one harmony; for the eternal word, or divine sound or voice, which is a spirit, has introduced itself with the generation of the great mystery into formings, viz. into an expressed word or *sound:* And as

---

[6] Lawrence Hanson, *The Life of S. T. Coleridge: The Early Years* (London, 1939), p. 311.
[7] It is interesting to notice that a copy of this work appeared in Wordsworth's library after his death.

the joyful melody is in itself in the spirit of the eternal generation, so likewise is the instrument, viz. the expressed form in itself, which the living eternal voice guides, and strikes with his own eternal will-spirit, that it sounds and melodises; as an organ of divers and various sounds or notes is moved with one only air, so that each note, yea every pipe has its peculiar tune, and yet there is but one manner of air or breath in all notes, which sounds in each note or pipe according as the instrument or organ is made.

Thus in the eternity there is only one spirit in the whole work of the divine manifestation, which is the manifestator in the expressed voice and also in the speaking voice of God, which is the life of the grand mystery, and of all that is generated from thence; he is the manifestator of all the works of God.[8]

The voice (or breath) of God continually and eternally brings forth its joy through the creature, as through an instrument; the creature is the manifestation of the voice of God: What God is in the ternal generation of his eternal word out of the great mystery of the Father's property, that the creature is in the image as a joyful harmony, wherewith the Eternal Spirit plays or melodises.[9]

And then secondly we understand, that the signature or form is no spirit, but the receptacle, container, or cabinet of the spirit, wherein it lies; for the signature stands in the essence, and is as a lute that liest still, and is indeed a dumb thing that is neither heard or understood; but if it be played upon, then its form is understood, in what form and tune it stands, and according to what note it is set. Thus likewise the signature of nature in its form is a dumb essence; it is as a prepared instrument of music, upon which the will's spirit plays; what strings he touches, they sound according to their property.[10]

Perhaps we should not limit our study of the background of the "Eolian Harp" to Boehme's work. A student of Berkeley might well find the notion attractive and quite consistent with his master's thought. But there is nothing in Berkeley's writings that would force the idea upon such a student, as there seems to be in Boehme's.

Mr. Hanson has noticed that the "pantheism first suggested tentatively in Coleridge's *Eolian Harp* . . . appears in full bloom in his friend's *Lines Written in Early Spring*"[11]

---

[8] Law trans. (Everyman ed., London, 1926), p. 210.
[9] *Ibid.*, p. 213.
[10] *Ibid.*, p. 10.   [11] Hanson, *op. cit.*, p. 195.

after an interval of more than two years. This is very true, and it is interesting to notice that the ultimate origin again seems to be Boehme.

Like the Wordsworth of 1798, Boehme is suspicious of scholarship and urges a student of the mysterious not to burden himself with book-learning. (Like Wordsworth, Boehme seems to have been better acquainted with written wisdom than this might suggest. He was, for example, well acquainted with Paracelsus and, of course, he knew his Bible intimately. But his attitude was never that of the commentator.) In fact, Wordsworth's attitude toward Nature as expressed in the lyrics of 1798: "Lines Written in Early Spring," "To My Sister," "Expostulation and Reply" and "The Tables Turned" are steeped in Behmenism. They celebrate in Boehme's language a spontaneous feeling of love and harmony in Nature, which requires no scholarship as its background. This feeling may be recognized as a guide of life.

Boehme insists that "a very simple man will be able to see and comprehend, or apprehend the Being of God":

The reader should not make himself blind through his Unbelief, and dull apprehension, for here I bring in the whole or total Nature, with all her children, for a Witness and Demonstration. And if thou art rational, then look round about thee, and view thyself; also consider thyself aright, and then thou wilt soon find from, or out of what Spirit I write. . . .

Before the Looking-Glass I will not invite all Lovers of the holy and highly to be esteemed Arts of Philosophy, Astrology and Theology, wherein I will lay open the root and ground of them.

And though I have not studied nor learned their arts, neither do I know how to go about to measure Circles, and use their mathematical instruments and Compasses, I take no great Care about that. . . .

For I use not their Tables, Formulae, or Schemes, Rules and Ways, for I have not learned from them, but I have another Teacher or School-master, which is the whole or total *Nature*.

From that *whole Nature*, together with its innate, instant Birth or Geniture, have I studied and learned my Philosophy, Astrology, and Theology, and not from Men, or by Men. . . .[12]

[12] Law (tr.), *Aurora*, 22: 1, 2, 8-11.

For Wordsworth and for Boehme it is Nature as a whole, total Nature, or the "sum of things," that teaches. Let us compare the following quotations from Boehme with Wordsworth's lines from "To My Sister":

> Love now, a universal birth,
>   From heart to heart is stealing
> From earth to man, from man to earth,
>   It is the hour of feeling.

The highly sensuous yet mystical pantheism of these lines finds an important analogy in *Aurora* under the title "Of the friendly Love, gracious, amiable, Blessedness and Unity, of the Five Qualifying or Fountain-Spirits of God":

Though it is impossible for the Hands of Men to describe this sufficiently, yet the enlightened Spirit of Man sees it, for it rises up just in such a Form and Birth, as the Light in the Divine Power, and also in the Qualities which are in God. . . .

Now observe, as the Members of Man's Body love one another, so do the Spirits also in the Divine Power; there is nothing else but a mere longing, desiring, and well liking Acceptation, as also a triumphing and rejoicing the one in the other: For through these Spirits come the Understanding and Distinction in God, in Angels, Men, Beasts, and Fowls, and in every thing that lives. . . .[13]

For in these Five Qualities rise up the Seeing, Smelling, Tasting and Feeling, and so a Rational Spirit comes to be.

As when the Light rises up, then one Spirit sees the other.

And when the sweet Spring or Fountain-water rises up in the Light, through all the Spirits, then the one tastes the other, and then the Spirits become living, and the Power of Life penetrates through all.

And in that Power the one smells the other; and through this qualifying Influence and Penetration, the one feels the other.

And so there is nothing else but a hearty loving and friendly Aspect or Seeing, curious Smelling, a good Relishing or Tasting and lovely Feeling, a gracious, amiable blessed Kissing, a Feeding upon

---

[13] Compare Wordsworth's "It is my faith that every flower enjoys the air it breathes." It is true, as Professor Beach has pointed out, that Erasmus Darwin taught at this time a somewhat similar doctrine in which he attributed an element of feeling even to the life of the plant. But Darwin presents his belief as the result of rationally apprehended analogies; Wordsworth, more like Boehme, as the content of an intuitive insight.

and Drinking of one another, and lovely Walking and conversing together.

And this for ever without End! How can a Creature sufficiently rejoice therein? O dear love and gracious amiable Blessedness! Surely thou hast no End. No Man can see any End in thee, thy profound Deep is unsearchable, thou art every where all over thus. . . .

> And from that blessed power that rolls
> About, below, above,
> We'll take the temper of our souls
> They shall be turned to love.

For both Wordsworth and Boehme, the senses are not to be scorned by the mystic and the nature-lover. The senses link the human mind to the world around it, and it is in large measure through the senses that the activity and power of things come home to the mind. Thus were man without his senses, the beauty of the world would be wholly lost to him, and with it much of the meaning and purpose of Nature. Boehme is here describing what he calls a "form" or level of Nature, a stage in the manifestation of God, in which the beauty, freedom, and exuberant power of Nature embody or symbolize the Divine Spirit.[14]

But more striking still are the echoes of Boehme which appear in *The Prelude*. Let us first consider a famous passage from Book VI (ll. 525 ff.). We must consider both versions, that of 1805 and that of 1850.

> Imagination—here the Power so called
> Through sad incompetence of human speech,

[14] But the following passage from William Law's own work, *The Spirit of Prayer*, indicates clearly the Behmenistic conception of the *ultimate* relation of God to man. Here the senses appear as superficial: ". . . though God be everywhere present, yet He is only present to thee in the deepest and most central part of thy soul. Thy natural *senses* cannot possess God, or unite thee to him, nay thy inward faculties of *understanding*, *will*, and *memory*, can only reach after God, but cannot be the *place* of his habitation in thee. But there is a *root*, or *depth* in thee, from whom all these faculties come forth, as lines from a *center*, or as branches from the body of a tree. This depth is called the *center*, the *fund* or *bottom* of the soul. This depth is the *unity*, the *eternity*, I had almost said, *infinity* of thy soul; for it is so infinite that nothing can satisfy it, or give it any rest, but the infinity of God. In this depth of the soul, the Holy Trinity brought forth his own living image in the first created man, bearing in himself a living representation of Father, Son, and Holy Ghost, and this was his indwelling in God and God in him . . ." (VII, 28-29).

That awful Power rose from the mind's abyss
Like an unfathered vapour that enwraps,
At once, some lonely traveller.   I was lost;
Halted without an effort to break through;
But to my conscious soul I now can say—
"I recognise thy glory:" in such strength
Of usurpation, when the light of sense
Goes out, but with a flash that has revealed
The invisible world, doth greatness make abode,
There harbours; whether we be young or old,
Our destiny, our being's heart and home,
Is with infinitude, and only there;
With hope it is, hope that can never die,
Effort, and expectation, and desire.
And something evermore about to be.
Under such banners militant, the soul
Seeks for no trophies, struggles for no spoils
That may attest her prowess, blest in thoughts
That are their own perfection and reward,
Strong in herself and in beatitude
That hides her, like the mighty flood of Nile
Poured from her fount of Abyssinian clouds
To fertilise the whole Egyptian plain.[15]

The figure of *imagination* arising from the *abyss*[16] and the
mention of *desire* and of *something evermore about to be*,
linked as they are with the notion of infinitude, must be considered with reference to the following passages (*A Treatise
of Christ's Testament*, Chapter I):

3.   For if there be a Formability to a Figure, then there must also
have been a Cause from whence the Form were arisen, and God were
not one only God, who were without Ground, Time, and Place; for
all that hath a Beginning hath a Ground; but that which hath no
Beginning, is without Ground and Form.[17]

[15] *The Prelude* (1850), Bk. VI, ll. 593 ff.; compare A, Bk. VI, ll. 525 ff.
[16] Here it seems to me that the human soul, considered as human, *suffers*
usurpation.   Its powers are usurped by the influx of divine power.   Imagination
does the usurping, but imagination is itself a cosmic power not limited to the
human mind, which is but the surface of the "abyss" of divine being.
[17] Recall *The Prelude*, Bk. II, ll. 236-237, where Wordsworth recognizes
that the human soul "hath no Beginning."

4. Every Beginning goeth out of the Eternal ONE through the Exhalation of the Eternal ONE, whereby the Eternal ONE bringing itself into Self-viewing, Perceptibility, and Findingness, to the moving and forming of itself. Every visible and invisible Being, spiritual and corporeal, have taken their Original in the Exhalation of the Eternal ONE, and stand with their Ground therein, for the Beginning of every Being is nothing else but an *Imagination* of the *Abyss*, that the same bring itself by its own Longing into an Imagination, and modelleth and imageth itself, and apprehendeth the Image-likeness, and breatheth it (or, exhaleth it) forth from the Eternal One to a viewing of itself.[18]

One further passage will make this clearer. We quote from Boehme's *Earthly and Heavenly Mystery*, the Fourth Text, where Boehme is writing of the spirit of God:

8. *The Word is its centre or seat, and is in the midst as a heart;* and the spirit of the Word, which takes its origin in the primal eternal will, reveals the wonders of the essential life. There are, then, two mysteries: one in the spirit-life, and one in the essential life. The spirit-life is acknowledged as God, and is rightly so called; and the essential life is acknowledged as the Nature-life, which would have no understanding if the *Spirit or the spirit-life were not desirous. In this desire the divine Being, as the eternal word or heart of God, is continually and from eternity generated;* from which the desiring will as Spirit eternally goes out into the Nature-life, and reveals therein the mystery in essences. So that there are two lives and also two beings, from and in a single, eternal, unfathomable origin.

9. And thus we apprehend what God and Nature is: how the one and the other is from eternity without any ground or beginning. *For it is an everlasting beginning. It begins itself perpetually* and from eternity to eternity, where there is no number; for it is the unground.[19]

I have come upon another passage in *The Prelude* that seems to be an echo of Boehme. It is the famous

> Wisdom and Spirit of the universe!
> Thou Soul that art the eternity of thought!
> That giv'st to forms and images a breath
> And everlasting motion![20]

[18] Law's ed. Italics mine.
[19] Earle's trans. Italics mine.   [20] A, Bk. I, ll. 427 ff.

Compare this with the following from Boehme's *Clavis:*

40. The Holy Scripture says, the wisdom is the breathing of the Divine Power, a ray and breath of the Almighty; also it says, God has made all things by his wisdom; which we understand as follows:

41. The Wisdom is the outflown word of the Divine Power, Virtue, Knowledge, and Holiness; a Subject and Resemblance of the infinite and unsearchable Unity; a Substance wherein the Holy Ghost works, forms, and models; I mean, he forms and models the Divine understanding in the Wisdom; *for the Wisdom is the Passive, and the Spirit of God is the Active,* or Life in her, as the Soul in the Body.

42. The Wisdom is the Great Mystery of the Divine Nature; for in her, the Powers, Colours, and Virtues are made manifest; in her is the variation of the power and virtue, *viz.* the understanding, that is, the Divine vision (or contemplation) wherein the Unity is manifest.

43. She is the true Divine Chaos, wherein all things lie. *Viz.* a Divine Imagination, in which the Ideas (Forms, or *Images*) of Angels and Souls *have been seen from Eternity,* in a Divine Type and Resemblance; yet not then as Creatures, but in resemblance, as when a man beholds his face in a Glass; therefore the Angelical and human Idea flowed forth from the wisdom, and was formed into an Image, as Moses says, *God created Man in his Image, that is, he created the body, and breathed into it the breath of the Divine Effluence,* of Divine Knowledge, from all the Three Principles of the Divine Manifestation. . . .

54. By the word Center *(Centrum),* we understand the first beginning to Nature, *viz.* the most Inward ground, wherein the self-raised will brings itself, by a reception, into something (Egoity, or own propriety), *viz.* into a Natural working; for Nature is but a Tool and Instrument of God, which God's Power and Virtue works with, and *yet it has its own Motion* (or Mobility), *from the outflown will of God:* thus the Center is the Point or Ground of the self-reception to something; from whence something comes to be, and from thence the seven Properties proceed.[21]

Some years ago I suggested that Wordsworth's "Wisdom and Spirit of the Universe" may have been inspired by a study of Berkeley's *Siris,* but Boehme's passage is so much closer to

[21] Law's ed. Italics mine.

Wordsworth's wording that I now consider it a more likely source.

We shall find further echoes of Boehme in the last book of *The Prelude*, in the great meditation upon Mt. Snowdon to which we have already referred. This is at once one of the most magnificent and also one of the most obscure passages to be found in Wordsworth's philosophical poetry. Both its power and its conceptual obscurity are, at least, partially, owing to the Behmenistic concepts and images which are woven into the text, although, as we shall see later on, there are other influences prominent in the last book of *The Prelude*. Again both versions must be considered, as well as the many variant readings which Mr. de Selincourt has noted. The text of 1850 is somewhat clearer and contains more "Behmenisms." Let us quote this version, while asking the reader to study the lines as they stand in Mr. de Selincourt's variorum edition:

> . . . as I looked up,
> The Moon hung naked in a firmament
> Of azure without cloud, and at my feet
> Rested a silent sea of hoary mist.
> A hundred hills their dusky backs upheaved
> All over this still ocean; and beyond,
> Far, far beyond, the solid vapours stretched
> In headlands, tongues, and promontory shapes,
> Into the main Atlantic, that appeared
> To dwindle, and give up his majesty,
> Usurped upon far as the sight could reach.
> Not so the ethereal vault; encroachment none
> Was there, nor loss; only the inferior stars
> Had disappeared, or shed a fainter light
> In the clear presence of the full-orbed Moon,
> Who, from her sovereign elevation, gazed
> Upon the billowy ocean, as it lay
> All meek and silent, save that through a rift—
> Not distant from the shore whereon we stood,
> A fixed, abysmal, gloomy, breathing-place—
> Mounted the roar of waters, torrents, streams
> Innumerable, roaring with one voice!

Heard over earth and sea, and, in that hour,
For so it seemed, felt by the starry heavens.

　　When into air had partially dissolved
That vision, given to spirits of the night
And three chance human wanderers, in calm thought
Reflected, it appeared to me the type
Of a majestic intellect, its acts
And its possessions, what it has and craves,
What in itself it is, and would become.
There I beheld the emblem of a mind
That feeds upon infinity, that broods
Over the dark abyss, intent to hear
Its voices issuing forth to silent light
In one continuous stream; a mind sustained
By recognitions of transcendent power,
In sense conducting to ideal form,
In soul of more than mortal privilege.
One function, above all, of such a mind
Had Nature shadowed there, by putting forth,
'Mid circumstances awful and sublime
That mutual domination which she loves
To exert upon the face of outward things,
So moulded, joined, abstracted, so endowed
With interchangeable supremacy,
That men, least sensitive, see, hear, perceive,
And cannot choose but feel.　The power, which all
Acknowledge when thus moved, which Nature thus
To bodily sense exhibits, is the express
Resemblance of that glorious faculty
That higher minds bear with them as their own.
This is the very spirit in which they deal
With the whole compass of the universe:
They from their native selves can send abroad
Kindred mutations; for themselves create
A like existence; and, whene'er it dawns
Created for them, catch it, or are caught
By its inevitable mastery,
Like angels stopped upon the wing by sound
Of harmony from Heaven's remotest spheres.[22]

[22] *The Prelude* (1850), Bk. XIV, ll. 39-99.

The passage is a curious mixture of landscape, symbolism, and conceptual doctrine, and, of course more than one interpretation is possible. I shall try to interpret it as literally as I can. The Boehme parallels help one to do this. The mountain scene induces a "meditation." The description of this meditation is enriched by concepts with which Wordsworth was, in all probability, unacquainted at the time of his actual ascent of Snowdon. The broad outlines of the moonlit panorama symbolize or represent a metaphysical situation, the metaphysical situation of most interest to a poet and nature-mystic, viz., the creative mind and its mode of activity. The moon, serene and clear above the sea of shifting vapour, represents intelligence, a necessary element in all creation, human or divine. Far below lies the restless surface of cloud-shapes, brilliantly illuminated; and through a rift in this rises the sound of waters from the vast world beneath the mountaintop. Here, according to the 1805 version,

> . . . had Nature lodg'd
> The soul, the Imagination of the whole.[23]

Wordsworth thinks of creative power arising from the dark abyss and taking shape in the world of light and of form. Such an image symbolizes the creative process of Nature and of the human mind.

As we shall see, at the beginning of the third paragraph of the 1805 version, Wordsworth seems to be thinking rather more of the human mind; at the same point in the 1850 text he seems to refer to the cosmic forces of creation. But we know already that the two are intimately related. And in both accounts he speaks of Nature's power of causing finite objects to unite in interfusion, so that one object pervades another, somewhat as Mr. Whitehead has described it in his account of the romantic feeling for the concrete surface of things. So Wordsworth writes of the domination which Nature loves to exert upon the face of outward things, comparing it, as "express resemblance" or "genuine counterpart," with the glorious faculty possessed by human genius. He does not

[23] Bk. XIV, ll. 64-65.

intend us to suppose that this domination is to be interpreted merely as the physical play of light and air upon a bank of clouds. The mystical tone of the passage as a whole makes clear that Wordsworth's intention is not so limited. He is not thinking of the weather; he is thinking rather more of the spirit that moves upon the face of the waters. Notice that in Book VI he uses similar imagery to describe the extrahuman origin of imagination,

> Like an unfather'd vapour that bestows
> Its presence on some solitary place.[24]

Nature exhibits or shadows forth a function of creative mind as it appears in human and divine life. This is still Boehme:

God, by his breathing forth of his eternal wisdom and knowledge, *has revealed himself by Nature and creation*, . . . by the life of angels and men . . . *as also by Nature and its rebreathing forth of the creatures of the visible world*.[25]

Even without the aid of the Boehme parallel, we can be sure that Wordsworth did not mean to identify the power or dominion of Nature with the physical features of the scene that he had just witnessed, for in that case he could hardly have called this power the genuine counterpart and express resemblance of human genius, unless, indeed, he were ready to describe the "vision and faculty divine" as a mere rearrangement of molecules.

The description of the majestic intellect is introduced as a topic to which the poet's mind turns after he has surveyed the spectacular scene from the summit of Mt. Snowdon. The scene is an emblem of the function of the majestic intellect and also of Nature's power which she "loves to exert." Why should this particular scene call this piece of philosophy to mind? I think the answer is to be found by comparing Wordsworth's description of the Mt. Snowdon scene with the following passage from Boehme's *Mysterium Magnum*, Chapter

[24] Bk. VI, ll. 527-528.
[25] *Divine Intuition*, 2: 22. Italics mine.

II.   The presence together of "vapours," "breathing-place," and "imagination" then becomes very significant, particularly if we consider lines 56-65 of the 1805 text.

6.   When I take up a Stone, or Clod of Earth, and look upon it, then I see that which is above, and that which is below, yea, the Whole World therein; only that in each thing one Property happenth to be the Chiefest and Manifest, according to which it is named. All the other Properties are jointly therein, only in distinct Degrees and Centers, and yet all the Degrees and Centers are but one only Center.   There is but one only Root whence all things proceed; it only separates itself in the Compaction, where it is coagulated: *its Original is as a smoke or vaporous breath from the great mystery of the expressed Word,* which stands in All Places in the re-expressing, that is, in the *re-breathing* (or echoing forth) a Likeness according to itself; an Essence according to the Spirit.[26]

For a very similar passage see *Six Theosophic Points,* Chapter II:

19.   And thus we give you to understand what this world's existence is.   *Nothing else than a coagulated smoke from the eternal aether,* which thus had a fulfilment like the Eternal.   It shuts itself in a centrum of a substance, and finally consumes itself again; and returns again into the eternal Magic, and is but for a while a wonder *as a revelation of the Eternal,* whereby the Eternal, which is manifest in itself, manifests itself also out of itself, and *pours out its imagination;* and thus renews that which was seized or made by the motion in desire, that the end may again enter into the beginning.[27]

Whether Wordsworth was influenced by Boehme in the description of the way in which Nature makes one object impress itself upon others so that they work together with "interchangeable supremacy," I cannot say.   There are no verbal echoes to guide us here.   But some such notion is not foreign to Boehme's philosophy.   Consider the following from his *Aurora,* Chapter I:

4.   Now here we must consider, what the word Quality meaneth, or is.   A Quality is the Mobility, boiling springing, and driving of a thing.

[26] Law's ed.   Italics mine.   [27] Earle's trans.   Italics mine.

5. As for example, Heat, which burneth, consumeth and driveth forth all, whatsoever cometh into it which is not of the same property: and again it enlighteneth and warmeth all cold, wet, and dark things, it compacteth and hardeneth soft things.[28]

The following passages are from Chapter VIII of the same work:

64. Now these qualities are mixed in the Body, as if they were all but *one* quality; and yet each quality moveth or boileth in its own power, and so goeth forth.

65. Each quality goes forth from itself into the other, that is, it affecteth the other whereby the same qualities get the will of this; that is, they prove the sharpness and spirit of this quality, as to what is in it, and always mix with it continually.[29]

We must remember that for both Boehme and Wordsworth imagination is not limited to the life of a human being. It is a power deep-rooted in the world's existence which at times arises and possesses a human mind. It is the "best spirit" both of the object seen and of the eye that sees. But we shall find even more of Boehme in this passage.

Let us look once more into Boehme's *Theoscopia or Divine Intuition*. The first passage which I shall quote contains mention of the abyss, of God or the cosmic mind speaking through his creatures, of the part played by sense and soul in this operation, and finally of the fact that Nature reveals the activity of this cosmic mind, which is also revealed in the lives of angels and of human beings. Thus this order of topics parallels lines 67 and following of the 1850 version in a truly striking fashion:

18. For as little as the life's own will can, in selfness and will turned away from God, stand still in Nature a moment from its working, unless it sink down beyond all Nature; so little also can the divine speaking, in the life resigned to the ground, stand still from its working.

19. For if the life stand still from its own will, it is in the *abyss of Nature and creation, in the eternal, divine utterance; and hence God speaks therein.*

[28] John Sparrow (ed.), *The Aurora* (London, 1914), p. 40.
[29] *Ibid.*, p. 160.

20. For from God's speaking the life has proceeded and come into body, and is nothing else than an image-like will of God. Now if its own imagination and will stand still, the divine imagination and will arises. For whatever is will-less is with the Nothing but one thing, and is out of or beyond all Nature, which ungroundedness is God himself.

21. Seeing then the Unground or God is an *eternal speaking,* viz. *a breathing forth of himself,* the Unground accordingly is inspoken into the resigned life; for the breathing of the Unground speaks through the stationary ground of the life. For the life has arisen from the divine breathing, and *is a likeness of the divine breathing, therefore one likeness seizes the other.* As we understand in the case of the *life's senses,* which are such an issue from the breathing of the *soul,* as *the soul is an issue and counterstroke from the divine soul of the divine knowledge.*

22. Now as God, by his breathing forth of his eternal wisdom and knowledge, *has revealed himself by Nature* and creation, both by the inward holy life, *by the life of angels and men,* and has introduced his will of knowledge into form by re-utterance through a formed divulged mode; as also *by Nature and its re-breathing forth of the creatures of the visible world,* and has always made the external, uttered by Nature, subject to the inward principle, so that the inward should rule through the external corporeal, and be a spirit of the external.[30]

There are certain images and figures of speech in Wordsworth's text which can be explained by reference to other passages from Boehme. These include:

1.   a majestic intellect, its acts
And its possessions. . . .

2.   what it has and craves,
What in itself it is, and would become.

3. Voices issuing forth to silent light.

4.   a mind
That feeds upon infinity.

[30] Italics mine. In paragraph 21 "one likeness seizes the other" is probably the origin of Wordsworth's "recognitions of transcendent power." I am quoting from Earle's translation (*Six Theosophic Points and Other Writings by Jacob Böhme,* London, 1919, pp. 185-187). An English translation of the *Theoscopia or Divine Intuition* was published as early as 1661 by John Sparrow. It is included in his *Several Treatises by Jacob Behme,* 1661, of which there is a copy in the British Museum. The *Theoscopia* is not included in the Law edition.

As regards (1) the term "majesty" is often used by Boehme when he is referring to the Deity, particularly when he emphasizes the doctrine that God can exist independently of his manifestation in the world.[31]   This interpretation of the "majestic intellect" is strengthened by the fact that in the glossary of Edward Taylor's *Jacob Behmen's Theosophick Philosophy Unfolded* (1691), a copy of which was in Wordsworth's library, *majesty* is defined as follows: "*Majesty*, the light of the glorious Son of God, the second Principle, according to which only God is called God, for according to the first, *viz.*, the Father's Property, he is not called God, but a consuming fire."   The "Father's Property" is sometimes identified with the "abyss," the restless reservoir of divine, creative energy from which, under the guidance of intelligence, finite creatures issue forth.   Boehme sometimes uses "abyss" to signify "God, the Father," the sheer power of "groundless will" of deity, the primal energy of creation which in contact with divine intelligence, "God, the Son," or the "conceived will," makes creation of a world possible.[32]   The Holy Ghost, which may enter the heart of man, is the outcome of this joint activity.

Consider also along with (1) the following paragraph from Boehme's *Of Election*, Chapter I:

34.   The bottomless unfathomable Will, which is the Father and Beginning of all Beings, *generates* in itself a place of comprehensibility, or, as may be said, *possesses* the Place and the Place is the ground and Beginning of every Being, and *repossesses the unfathomable Will again*, which is the Father of Beginning to be a Ground.[33]

We are told that the will repossesses itself.   This merges with (2), where we find mention of what the mind *has and craves*, what *in itself it is and would become*.   Consider in connection with this the following passage from the *Theoscopia*, Chapter I, which is typical of Boehme's thought:

---

[31] *Threefold Life of Man*, 4: 87-88. See also *Six Theosophic Points*, 1: 31-33, 60; *Six Mystical Points*, 5: 7, 8.
[32] *Of Election*, I, 5-12. See Brinton, *op. cit.*, pp. 181 ff.
[33] Law's ed. Italics mine.

17. God, so far as he is called God, can will nothing but himself; for he has nothing before or after him that he can will. But if he will anything, that very same has emanated from him, and is a counter-stroke of himself, wherein the eternal will wills in its something. Now if the something were only a one, the will could have no exercise therein. And therefore the unfathomable will has separated itself into beginnings and carried itself into being, that it might work in something, as we have a similitude in the soul of man.[34]

The word "craves" in this connection should be compared with the "desire" of Book VI, discussed above.[35]

(3) The voices issued forth to the silent *light*. Boehme uses the word *light* for contemplation and spiritual illumination in contrast with the "fire" of the self-centered aggressiveness which hides the spiritual world from man's vision.[36]

(4) The mind that "feeds upon infinity" has many parallels in Boehme. Sometimes this mind is identified with the Holy Ghost, which enters the finite mind and makes possible its communion with Deity. Boehme's doctrine on this point is very difficult. It is usually a mixture of Christian trinitarianism and gnosticism and pantheism. It is also complicated by reference to the maze of doctrine surrounding transubstantiation. We shall see that the Holy Ghost, entering into the human soul, makes possible the soul's divine nourishment. If the Holy Ghost has deeply penetrated a human soul, the soul enjoys divine inspiration in this way. The following passages will make this difficult doctrine somewhat clearer. We must remember that the Holy Ghost is a member of the Trinity and hence is God himself, who enters creaturely life and makes possible its divine inspiration and nourishment. Wordsworth probably learned something of this doctrine from Coleridge and then proceeded to extract from it what seemed to him consistent with his own point of view.

The next quotation is from *Forty Questions Concerning the Soul: The Twelfth Question Answered.*

[34] Earle's trans.   [35] See pp. 110-111.
[36] See *Six Theosophic Points*, 7: 3-5; also Rufus Jones, *Spiritual Reformers in the Sixteenth and Seventeenth Centuries* (London, 1914), pp. 181-182.

30. And the Holy Ghost sitteth in the Heart of the Image, and proceedeth from the Image with voices, languages, wonders, sounds and songs. . . .

37. Thus the Soul and the Image in the Spirit are all three in one another for they are one essence according to the Holy Trinity.

38. The Soul is in the world and also in God. . . .

The Thirteenth Question Answered.

1. If the Soul enters thus (as above mentioned) . . . into the Light of God, then it has wholly a longing and lusting, and *continually attracts in its Desire the Divine Power, viz. the Divine Body into itself;* and the Holy Ghost is the Power of God's spirit, and so it obtains the Body and Spirit of God, and *eats at God's Table:* all that the Father hath is the son's, and whatever the Son hath, that belongs to his Image.

2. It *eateth God's Flesh,* Christ's Flesh, and by this eating the Divine Body does also grow in it (or from, or out of it, or as a Chicken grows in an Egg) so that it thus gets the Divine Body, and so becomes God's Child, not only a Similitude, but a Child born in God out of his Essence, and lives in God.[37]

In the above quotation the term *Image* refers to man, or the image of God.

When the soul is nourished by God, God is nourishing the Holy Spirit, "who sits in the heart of the image," and thus the majestic intellect itself may be described as feeding upon infinity.   This tendency to unite God and his creatures is characteristic of Boehme's almost pantheistic Christianity. And it seems to appear in Wordsworth's poetry at this place. It is possible, of course, to construe the "mighty mind" of the 1805 version as no more than the finite mind of a poet which is supported by the idea of God as an "underpresence."   We might even argue that the "underpresence" is *nothing more* than an *idea,* belonging with other ideas in the depths of the poet's mind.   So Jung has spoken of the feeling of a presence, still frequent in modern life, which is apprehended "as a sort of creative background, a life-producing sun in the depths of the unconscious mind."[38]   This feeling the psychological

---

[37] Law's ed. Italics mine.
[38] C. G. Jung, *Psychology and Religion* (New Haven, 1938), p. 72.

analyst does not evaluate as true or false. But this is not like Wordsworth. The "mighty mind" of the 1805 version which feeds upon infinity may very likely refer to the divine mind (as the Holy Ghost) embodying itself in its creatures, although this is not so clear as in the 1850 version, where the majestic intellect's participation in the production of a creaturely world is made slightly more explicit. The difference between the 1805 treatment of the "mighty mind" and the 1850 treatment of the "majestic intellect" is simply that in the former version Wordsworth does not emphasize as heavily the fact of human participation in divinity. Recall Wordsworth's early

> . . . the one interior life
> That lives in all things. . . .
> In which all beings live with God, themselves
> Are God. . . .[39]

and compare with Boehme's statement, "God is the Being of all Beings and we are gods in him through which he reveals himself."[40] In general the 1850 version contains less emphasis upon the participation of human and divine. As Mr. de Selincourt has pointed out, Wordsworth seemed in later life eager to remove from his poems any too obvious pantheism. This does not seem to be the case in the Mt. Snowdon passage, I suspect, because the trinitarian character of Boehme's thinking gave it in Wordsworth's eyes a more orthodox appearance than it perhaps deserves.

In the 1850 version the relation of the majestic intellect to the finite mind is made somewhat clearer by mention of the way in which this intellect presides over voices issuing forth from the abyss into finite sense and soul. There remains the curious term "underpresence" in the 1805 text. I have been unable to find any term of Boehme's of which "underpresence" may safely be called a verbal echo. This is not surprising, as terms compounded with "under" as a prefix are favorites with

---

[39] De Selincourt (ed.), *The Prelude*, p. 512.
[40] *Three-fold Life of Man*, 6: 5.

Wordsworth[41] and hence very probably his own.[42]   But the concept involved here is quite in harmony with Boehme's philosophy.   Let me quote from Professor Brinton's study of Boehme:

The "abysmal will" in Boehme's philosophy is the ultimate inner nature of being.   It is known immediately, and so, as pure subjectivity, all distinction of subject and object in the act of knowing it disappears. Boehme's explanations are all historico-genetic.   Things develop and grow, inspired by irrational wills and do not move along fixed logical lines.   Will, as *substratum of nature,* manifests itself in all things— stones, vegetables, animals, men. . . .   It becomes conscious life in actualizing an idea.[43]

In *A Treatise on Christ's Testaments* (1: 7), we are told that lost souls "can in no wise come to this center or ground out of which they are existed [*sic*], and *fall again* into the eternal speaking word, and give their own wills into the speaking word."[44]   The soul may gain assistance from an extra-human source which underlies its being.   In Boehme this source may be called by one of several names: "unground," "abyss," "abysmal will," "*Mysterium magnum*," "God."   According to this doctrine the soul must sink down into God to realize its full power.   But God is always there beneath it as its underpresence.   The line between God and soul is not a real barrier.   Thus even the finite soul, considered as finite, may recognize God as what is "dim or vast in its own being," for God is always present so to speak, at the root of every soul.   (It is a temptation to read *dim or vast* as Wordsworth's poetic rendering of Boehme's *Mysterium magnum*, a term by which the theosopher often speaks of the source whence all creatures proceed, and which occurs as the title of one of his works.)

We must apologize for the complexity of the foregoing Boehme set to Wordsworth's blank verse is no easier than the German theosopher's own prose.   Wordsworth's blank verse is studded with Behmenistic phrases which, when woven into

---

[41] De Selincourt (ed.), *The Prelude,* p. 600.
[42] But see below, p. 180, where Herder's use of "underpower" is noted.
[43] *Op. cit.,* p. 106. Italics mine.   [44] Law's ed. Italics mine.

the poet's argument, do not always quite retain their original meaning. We may suppose that Wordsworth gathered many of these echoes while listening to Coleridge, who, fresh from a perusal of Boehme, freely employed the theosopher's vocabulary. Whether Wordsworth ever intended to "accept" Behmenism as a whole is very doubtful. But he absorbed a great deal of it and often found its vocabulary congenial. Thus there can now be little doubt concerning Wordsworth's belief that imagination is a natural or cosmic or even divine power which unites the finite mind with its environment. This power "rises" into human consciousness. It is latent in Nature because it has been at work in the very creation of Nature. As Boehme says, "All things are created out of imagination."[45]

Just as God creates man in his own image, and fashions even the whole world as a vast semblance of himself; so the poet expresses or embodies the quality of his own mind in the medium of words. This notion was, to be sure, common in the Renascence and appears in later writers, as for instance in Shaftesbury.[46] Both divine and human creation evoke conscious and unconscious powers. Here Boehme is hardly orthodox, standing closer in the history of thought to Schopenhauer and to von Hartmann[47] than to most theologians. For him creation is a passage from an indeterminate and subconscious potentiality to a fully realized and determinate consciousness. Coleridge was not wholly free of Behmenism when he said of Shakespeare that he possessed "a genial understanding, directing self-consciously a power and an implicit wisdom deeper than consciousness." Here we seem to encounter a faint reference to the majestic intellect standing like the moon, serene and silent, above the plastic turmoil of the abyss, which it enlightens and to which it grants significance.

Whether we describe human or divine creation, we speak of the "abyss," the chaos which is the matrix of imagination. At this level all minds, divine, cosmic, or finite, are one. This is the "one interior life" from which all definitely realized

[45] *The Signature of All Things*, Everyman ed., p. 207.
[46] *Characteristicks*, Part III, sec. 3, "Advice to an Author."
[47] See above, pp. 17-18.

consciousness must emerge.   Here the analogy of the "Eolian
Harp" seems to be inverted.   Inspiration does not come upon
us from "without" and "above," but from "within" and "below."   Boehme uses both figures and Wordsworth and Coleridge follow him.   Coleridge at first preferred the symbol of
the harp, while Wordsworth seemed to have inclined more
toward the figure of the "abyss."   But Wordsworth mentions
"Eolian visitations" and Coleridge speaks of an "implicit wisdom deeper than consciousness."

   The feeling that creative energy arises from below, that,
so to speak, the dark roots of the plant are as important as
warmth and sunlight, or that a dimly conscious tendency is
as important as a clearly conceived program appears in late
eighteenth-century English criticism more than once.   Thus
the Behmenistic Blake scorns "number, weight, and measure"
and celebrates the expansive energy of spontaneous inspiration.
And Blake likes to mention the abyss.   Again Edward Young
and even Alexander Gerard tend toward this position, but
employing the simile of the plant.   Young writes: "An original may be said to be of a vegetable nature: it arises spontaneously from the vital root of genius; it grows, it is not
made. . . ."[48]   And Gerard compares poetic genius to a plant
that draws it sustenance from the earth beneath it.[49]

   So a premium is put by some thinkers upon a spontaneity
of growth at the expense of formal patterns and rules.   Wordsworth, in a sonnet published as late as 1842, the date of whose
composition is however uncertain, writes to similar effect, here
employing the simile of the plant:

> A POET!—He hath put his heart to school,
> Nor dares to move unpropped upon the staff
> Which Art hath lodged within his hand—must laugh
> By precept only, and shed tears by rule.
> Thy Art be Nature; the live current quaff,
> And let the groveller sip his stagnant pool,

[48] Edward Young's *Conjectures on Original Composition*, ed. Steinke (New
York, 1917), pp. 45-46.
[49] Alexander Gerard, *Essay on Genius* (London, 1774), Part I, sec. 3.   My
attention has been called to Young and Gerard by Dr. James Benziger.

In fear that else, when Critics grave and cool
Have killed him, Scorn would write his epitaph.
How does the Meadow-flower its bloom unfold?
Because the lovely little flower is free
Down to its root, and, in that freedom, bold;
And so the grandeur of the Forest-tree
Comes not by casting in a formal mould,
But from its *own* divine vitality.[50]

But in the Mt. Snowdon meditation creative activity is represented as involving both intelligence and a spontaneous fertility of suggestion. Intelligence presides watchfully over the restless but unorganized tendencies whose ultimate source is the abyss. Just as God may be conceived as God the Father, the source of energy and desire, and also as God the Son, the *logos* or Majestic Wisdom, surveying chaos and creation, so the poet's mind may be said to include both intelligence and a source of unorganized intimation, the one always standing in the full light of consciousness, the other, in a sort of twilight, eluding consciousness again and again, only suddenly to arise and possess it.

*   *   *

In general, the later drafts of *The Prelude* contain less pantheism than the earlier. But, strangely enough, some of the later versions are the more highly charged wtih Behmenistic imagery and vocabulary. Thus it is not surprising to find some Boehme parallels in poems that follow after the first version of *The Prelude*. I have discovered two of these, one in the "Ode to Duty" and the other in *The Excursion*. We shall examine the former at once, postponing discussion of the latter until we have described Boehme's philosophy as a whole

The "Ode to Duty" very likely owes something to Boehme, although here, as we shall see later, other influences may be said fairly to jostle one another for possession of the poem. There appears at times in Boehme a curious symbol, the Virgin Wisdom or Virgin *Sophia*. She is presented as the virgin mother of God, i.e., of God the Son, the *logos* or wisdom of the

---

[50] Sonnet XXVII of "Miscellaneous Sonnets" was published in 1842 in *Poems, Chiefly of Early and Late Years.*

triune God. Indeed, she herself is wisdom in its first innocent emergence from the "fiery" energy of God the Father. She seems to represent a primordial apprehension of value which is somehow prior to the *logos* or second person of the Trinity. Perhaps she stands for the feminine or appreciative aspect of wisdom, as distinct from its more masculine or constructive form, the "eternal feminine" of Boehme's philosophy. She exercises powers of mediation and appears, in some ways, to be not unlike the "Daughter of the Voice," the *Bath-Kol* of Talmudic lore. As Brinton says, ". . . she knocks inwardly at the door of man's soul, or hovers outwardly before him in a constellation, or some awful aspect of Nature. In the beauty of fruits and the fragrance of flowers she inspires in him a yearning for the paradise whence he fell."[51] She is the incarnation of Duty, at once sweetly beautiful and sternly sublime. In Law's translation under the heading "The Gate of the Syderial, or Starry Spirit" Boehme writes:

. . . Because the Spirit of the soul is out of the Eternal, and had the Virgin, before the Fall, the therefore now the Spirit of the great World continually seeks the Virgin in the Spirit of the Soul, and supposes that she is there still, as before the Fall, where the Spirit of the great World appeared to Adam's Virgin with very great Joy and desired also to live in the Virgin and to be eternal. Because he felt his Corruptibility, and that he was so rough in himself, therefore he would fain partake of the loving Kindness and Sweetness of the Virgin, and live in her, that so he might live eternally, and not break again.

For by the great Longing of the Darkness after the Light and Virtue of God, this World has been generated out of the Darkness, when the holy Virtue of God (shone, or) beheld itself in the Darkness; and therefore *this great Desiring and Longing after the divine Virtue, continues in the Spirit of the Sun, Stars, and Elements, and in all Things.* . . .[52]

We learn a few lines below (14: 39) that the Virgin sometimes manifests her power in the "Smell of the Lily" which can call the scholar from behind the "curtain of Antichrist,"

[51] *Op. cit.,* p. 200.
[52] *The Three Principles,* tr. Law, 14: 32-33. Italics mine.

where he has practiced his narrow and rationalist theory of good and evil.

That the Virgin Sophia has something to do with the personification of Duty in the "Ode," seems more than merely possible, once we admit that Wordsworth was acquainted with Boehme. And I think that by now we should be ready to make this admission. But perhaps the most available of possible sources for Wordsworth's personification of Duty lies in the biblical *Wisdom of Solomon,* in particular the following passage:

> Wisdom, which is the worker of all things, taught me: for in her is an understanding spirit, holy, one only, manifold, subtil, lively, clear, undefiled, plain, not subject to hurt, loving the thing that is good, quick, which cannot be letted, ready to do good, kind to man, steadfast, sure, free from care, having all power, overseeing all things, and going through all understanding, pure, and most subtil, spirits.
>
> For wisdom is more moving than any motion: she passeth and goeth through all things by reason of her pureness. For she is the breath of the power of God, and a pure influence flowing from the glory of the Almighty: therefore can no defiled thing fall into her. For she is the brightness of the everlasting light, the unspotted mirror of the power of God, and the image of his goodness. And being but one, she can do all things: and remaining in herself, she *maketh all things new:* and in all ages entering into holy souls, she maketh them friends of God, and prophets. For God loveth none but him that dwelleth with wisdom. For she is more beautiful than the sun, and above all the order of stars: being compared with the light, she is found before it. For after this cometh night: but vice shall not prevail against wisdom. Wisdom reacheth from one end to another mightily: and sweetly doth she order all things.[53]

This passage, combined with Boehme's Virgin Sophia and the Talmudic notion of the daughter of the voice can explain much in the "Ode to Duty."

* * *

Book IX of *The Excursion* opens with a passage which is frequently commented upon by students of Wordsworth's philosophy. Much of it will seem to be in harmony with

[53] *The Wisdom of Solomon,* chap. vii.

Wordsworthian doctrine which we have already discussed.   In this passage, to quote from Wordsworth's "argument," the "Wanderer asserts that an active principle pervades the Universe, its noblest seat the human soul."   The "argument" continues with the following phrases: "How lively this principle is in Childhood—Hence the delight in Old Age of looking back upon Childhood."   The passage itself is as follows:

> "To every Form of being is assigned,"
> Thus calmly spake the venerable Sage,
> "An *active* Principle:—howe'er removed
> From sense and observation, it subsists
> In all things, in all natures; in the stars
> Of azure heaven, the unenduring clouds,
> In flower and tree, in every pebbly stone
> That paves the brooks, the stationary rocks,
> The moving waters, and the invisible air.
> Whate'er exists hath properties that spread
> Beyond itself, communicating good,
> A simple blessing, or with evil mixed;
> Spirit that knows no insulated spot,
> No chasm, no solitude; from link to link
> It circulates, the Soul of all the worlds.
> This is the freedom of the universe;
> Unfolded still the more, more visible,
> The more we know; and yet is reverenced least,
> And least respected in the human Mind,
> Its most apparent home.   The food of hope
> Is meditated action; robbed of this
> Her sole support, she languishes and dies.
> We perish also; for we live by hope
> And by desire; we see by the glad light
> And breathe the sweet air of futurity;
> And so we live, or else we have no life.
> To-morrow—may perchance this very hour
> (For every moment hath its own to-morrow!)
> Those blooming Boys, whose hearts are almost sick
> With present triumph, will be sure to find
> A field before them freshened with the dew
> Of other expectations;—in which course

Their happy year spins round. The youth obeys
A like glad impulse; and so moves the man
'Mid all his apprehensions, cares, and fears,—
Or so he ought to move. Ah! why in age
Do we revert so fondly to the walks
Of childhood—but that there the Soul discerns
The dear memorial footsteps unimpaired
Of her own native vigour; thence can hear
Reverberations; and a choral song
Commingling with the incense that ascends,
Undaunted, toward the imperishable heavens,
From her own lonely altar? [54]

The philosophical content of the opening lines of this passage has aroused considerable comment. The "active principle" here described has been attributed to several different sources. Newton has been mentioned and Matthew Hale. I think that, as we shall see, a good case may be made for Shaftesbury, who . is in this my favorite candidate.

Again, the passage (ll. 13-15) contains an echo of a notion widespread throughout the history of philosophy, viz., what Mr. Lovejoy has called the "plenitude of being." For the student of Wordsworth these lines are, however, perhaps nothing more than another and powerful expression of the sentiment of Being. We shall consider all this very shortly. But for the moment let our attention rest upon line 16: "This is the freedom of the universe." We are told that this freedom is most at home in the human mind. Whatever the active principle may be, its primary manifestation is freedom and a freedom which is not limited to human beings but, insofar as this world is concerned, most completely realized in their lives. This freedom is intimately connected with the influence which every being spreads about itself.

Such a concept of freedom is prominent in Boehme's philosophy. It has to do with the relation of God to the world. This doctrine culminates in the following passage: "The will which is called Father, which has freedom in itself, so gen-

[54] Bk. IX, ll. 1-44.

erates itself in Nature, that it is susceptible of Nature, and that it is the universal power of Nature."[55]

God, conceived as freedom, "enters" the physical world which he has "already" created and brings into that world an order which the three physical "laws" or "forms" of attraction, expansion, and rotation cannot by themselves produce. The embodiment of freedom in the swirling, "wrathful" world of physical Nature makes possible a spiritual order with laws or forms of its own. It is in this order that the human soul develops.

The purely physical or "dark" world, conceived as independent and without freedom, is itself a manifestation of God. Boehme succeeds even in finding therein embodiments of the persons of the Trinity. But it is only after this lower world has "returned" to God and once again issued forth as the higher or "light" world, that spiritual life, of which "freedom" or creaturely identity and autonomy is the foundation, may become even remotely possible. To be sure, the highest creaturely expression or development of freedom is the human soul, whose spiritual life is enriched by moral insight and religious vision; but freedom pervades and is the "universal power" of Nature, as Nature rises above the purely physical level toward life, consciousness, and love.[56]

In Wordsworth's account, the "freedom of the universe" is concentrated in every existent as an "active principle." The presence of this principle seems to constitute each finite entity as an agent exercising an influence upon the world. At least, in its higher manifestations, freedom involves the possibility of choice and the pursuit of ends. Boehme emphasizes this latter point. It is owing to the embodiment of freedom that choice between good and evil is possible. Certainly nothing of the sort exists in the "dark" world.

[55] *Six Theosophic Points*, 1: 56; see also *Aurora*, 8: 64 ff.
[56] A philosophy very similar to this teaching of Boehme's was published by Schelling in the year 1809, under the title *Philosophical Inquiries into the Nature of Human Freedom and Matters Connected Therewith*. This work occupies pages 333-416 of Volume VII of Schelling's collected works. Pages 404-405 should be of interest to the student of Boehme and Wordsworth. There is an English translation by James Gutmann, *Schelling: Of Human Freedom* (Chicago, 1936).

The passage from *The Excursion* which we have been considering has, in all probability, origins besides those in the works of Boehme. Thus *Essays and Studies* for 1932 contains an essay entitled "A Note on Wordsworth's Metaphysical System," by Mr. S. G. Dunn, who presents interesting and unexpected conclusions concerning Wordsworth and Sir Isaac Newton's concept of the "active principle" in God's omnipresent will, which, as the cause of *actio ad distans*, holds the heavenly bodies on their courses and maintains the order of the physical universe. Newton is willing to accept the doctrine that in God "are all things contained and moved" and he quotes many classical and biblical texts in defense of his position. Mr. Dunn has made the connection between Newton's *Scholium* on God and Wordsworth's "active principle" seem a plausible one. But there is certainly more here than Newton could have supplied, for we are told that the agency of the active principle is *felt* by the human mind, and most keenly in childhood. This teaching is then at most a very free adaptation of Newton's thought rather than an acceptance. But when we recall Wordsworth's deep respect for Newton, we will be inclined to grant that Newton's thought is very likely echoed in this passage, i.e., we may suspect that Wordsworth was aware of a certain Newtonian quality present in this teaching. After all, as Mr. Beach has pointed out, Wordsworth's interest in physics or "natural philosophy" was well represented in his library.

No discussion of this passage from *The Excursion* can be complete without reference to one of Shaftesbury's meditations which is included in his work *The Moralists*. We shall quote first the two paragraphs which introduce the meditation itself. I have, in quoting, ignored Shaftesbury's italics and inserted those which help to emphasize the parallel with Wordsworth's statement in *The Excursion:*

. . . For were there in Nature Two or more Principles, either they must agree, or not. If they agree not, all must be Confusion, till one be predominant. If they agree, there must be some natural Reason for their Agreement; and this natural Reason cannot be from Chance, but from some particular Design, Contrivance, or Thought: which brings us up again to ONE Principle, and makes the other two to be subordinate. And thus when we have compar'd each of the Three Opinions, viz. "That there is no designing *active Principle*; That there is more than one"; or, "That finally there is but ONE:" we shall perceive, that the only consistent Opinion is the last. And since one or other of these Opinions must of necessity be true; what can we determine, other than that the last is, and must be so, demonstrably? If it be Demonstration, "That in Three Opinions One of which must necessarily be true, Two being plainly absurd, the Third must be the Truth."

Enough, said I, Theocles. My Doubts are vanish'd. MALICE and CHANCE (vain Phantoms!) have yielded to that all-prevalent WISDOM which you have establish'd. You are Conqueror in the cool way of Reason, and may with Honour now grow warm again, in your Poetick Vein. *Return therefore, I intreat you, once more, to that Perfection of Being; and address your self to It as before, on our Approaches to these Silvan Scenes, where first It seem'd to inspire you.* I shall now no longer be in danger of imagining either Magick or Superstition in the case; since you invoke no other POWER than that single ONE, *which seems so natural.*[57]

The meditation itself follows. The reader will notice that the third paragraph is rich with Newtonian echoes. Therefore, we may accept most of Mr. Dunn's argument, only insisting that Wordsworth borrowed, at least in this instance, indirectly from Newton:

THUS I continue then, said THEOCLES, addressing myself, as you wou'd have me, to that Guardian-DEITY and Inspirer, whom we are to imagine present here; but not here only. For, "O Mighty GENIUS! *Sole Animating and Inspiring Power!* Author and Subject of these Thoughts! *Thy influence is universal: and in all Things thou art inmost.* From Thee depend their secret Springs of Action. Thou mov'st them with an irresistible unweary'd Force, by sacred and inviolable Laws, *fram'd for the Good of each particular Being;* as best may sute with the Perfection, Life, and Vigour of the Whole. *The vital Principle is widely shar'd, and infinitely vary'd: Dispers'd throughout; no where extinct.* All lives: and by Succession still revives. The Temporary Beings quit their borrow'd Forms, and yield their Elementary Substance to New-Comers. Call'd in their several turns, to Life,

[57] *The Moralists* (1732), Part III, sec. 1, p. 365.

they view the Light, and viewing pass; that others too may be Spectators of the goodly Scene, and greater numbers still enjoy the Privilege of NATURE. Munificent and Great, she imparts her-self to most; and makes the Subjects of her Bounty infinite. Nought stays her hastning Hand. *No Time nor Substance is lost or unimprov'd.* New Forms arise: and when the old dissolve, the Matter whence they were compos'd is not left useless, but wrought with equal Management and Art, even in Corruption, Nature's seeming Waste, and vile Abhorrence. *The abject State appears merely as the Way or Passage to some better.* But cou'd we nearly view it, and with Indifference, remote from the Antipathy of Sense; we then perhaps shou'd highest raise our Admiration: convinc'd that even the Way itself was equal to the End. Nor can we judg less favourably of that consummate Art exhibited thro all the Works of Nature; since our weak Eyes, help'd by mechanick Art, discover in these Works a hidden Scene of Wonders; Worlds within Worlds, of infinite Minuteness, tho as to Art still equal to the greatest, and pregnant with more Wonders than the most discerning Sense, join'd with the greatest Art, or the acutest Reason, can penetrate or unfold.

"But 'tis in vain for us to search the bulky Mass of MATTER: seeking to know its Nature; how great the Whole it-self, or even how small its Parts.

"If knowing only some of the Rules of MOTION, we seek to trace it further, 'tis in vain we follow it into the Bodys it has reach'd. Our tardy Apprehensions fail us, and can reach nothing beyond the Body it-self, thro which it is diffus'd. Wonderful Being! (if we may call it so) which Bodys never receive, except from others which lose it; nor ever lose, unless by imparting it to others. Even without Change of Place it has its Force: and Bodys big with Motion labour to move, yet stir not; whilst they express an Energy beyond our Comprehension.

"In vain too we pursue that Phantom TIME, too small, and yet too mighty for our Grasp; when shrinking to a narrow point, it scapes our Hold, or mocks our scanty Thought by swelling to Eternity: an Object unproportion'd to our Capacity, as is thy Being, O thou Antient Cause! older than Time, yet young with fresh Eternity.

"In vain we try to fathom the Abyss of SPACE, the Seat of thy extensive Being; *of which no Place is empty, no Void which is not full.*

"In vain we labour to understand that Principle of SENSE and THOUGHT, which seeming in us to depend so much on Motion, yet differs so much from it, and from Matter it-self, as not to suffer us to conceive how Thought can more result from this, than this arise from Thought. But Thought we own pre-eminent, and confess the reallest of Beings; the only Existence of which we are made sure, by being conscious. All else may be only dream and Shadow. All which even Sense suggests may be deceitful. The SENSE it-self remains still: REASON subsists: and THOUGHT maintains its Eldership of Being. *Thus are we in a manner conscious of that originally and externally existent* THOUGHT *whence we derive our own.* And thus the Assurance we have of the Existence of Beings above our Sense, and of THEE (the Great Exemplar of thy Works) comes from Thee, the ALL TRUE, and Perfect, who hast thus communicated Thyself more immediately to us, so as in some manner to inhabit within our Souls; Thou who are Original SOUL, *diffusive, vital in all, inspiriting the Whole!*

"All Nature's Wonders serve to excite and perfect this Idea of their Author. 'Tis here he suffers us to see, and even converse with him, in a manner sutable to our Frailty. How glorious is it to contemplate Him, in this noblest of his Works apparent to us, The System of the bigger World?"[58]

Not only is the Shaftesbury parallel more complete than the Newtonian, but the spirit and atmosphere of Shaftesbury's work are far more in harmony with Wordsworth's insight than is that of Newton. In fact, the above excerpts from *The Moralists* seem quite adequately to explain the philosophical points made in the first lines of *The Excursion,* Book IX, with the exception of the "freedom of the universe" which can be explained, I think, only by reference to Boehme.

There are other indications of Shaftesbury's influence upon *The Excursion.*[59] Wordsworth's insistence upon the social character of much animal life assumes considerable significance in this connection. Shaftesbury in his eagerness to refute Hobbes's conception of the "state of nature" as one of constant

---

[58] *Ibid.,* pp. 366-370.
[59] I hesitate to follow Mr. Beach (*op. cit.,* pp. 90 ff.) in his suggestion that there is an influence of Shaftesbury upon the "Tintern Abbey" lines. The evidence which he offers could, I think, be made to point toward Berkeley equally well, particularly when we consider such a passage as that from the *Siris,* quoted above (p. 35). Nor is there evidence that, in the period when the "Tintern Abbey" lines were written either Wordsworth or Coleridge was reading Shaftesbury.

conflict and unrelieved competition, the "war of all against all," pointed to the sociable habits of animals and the fact that they seem frequently to need one another's companionship. Thus Shaftesbury, in commenting upon the cynical argument that man is a wolf to man, insists that among themselves wolves are not without their amiable and sociable characteristics. Shaftesbury has been speaking of the "Oeconomy of the Beaver, the Ant and the Bee." His attention then returns to the human race:

. . . to say in disparagement of Man, "That he is *to Man a Wolf*, appears somewhat absurd, when one considers that Wolves are to Wolves very kind and loving Creatures. The Sexes strictly *join* in the Care and Nurture of the Young: and this *Union* is continu'd still between 'em. They howl to one another, to bring Company; whether to hunt, or invade their Prey, or assemble on the Discovery of a good Carcase. Even the Swinish Kinds want not *common Affection*, and run in Herds to the Assistance of their distress'd Fellows."[60]

This theme appears in Book IV (ll. 427-459) of *The Excursion:*

> These craggy regions, these chaotic wilds,
> Does that benignity pervade, that warms
> The mole contented with her darksome walk
> In the cold ground; and to the emmet gives
> Her foresight, and intelligence that makes
> The tiny creatures strong by social league;
> Supports the generations, multiplies
> Their tribes, till we behold a spacious plain
> Or grassy bottom, all, with little hills—
> Their labour, covered, as a lake with waves;
> Thousands of cities, in the desert place
> Built up of life, and food, and means of life!
> Nor wanting here, to entertain the thought,
> Creatures that in communities exist
> Less, as might seem, for general guardianship
> Or through dependence upon mutual aid,
> Than by participation of delight
> And a strict love of fellowship, combined.

[60] Part II, sec. 4, p. 320.

What other spirit can it be that prompts
The gilded summer flies to mix and weave
Their sports together in the solar beam,
Or in the gloom of twilight hum their joy?
More obviously the self-same influence rules
The feathered kinds; the fieldfare's pensive flock,
The cawing rooks, and sea-mews from afar,
Hovering above these inland solitudes,
By the rough wind unscattered, at whose call
Up through the trenches of the long-drawn vales
Their voyage was begun: nor is its power
Unfelt among the sedentary fowl
That seek yon pool, and there prolong their stay
In silent congress; or together roused
Take flight. . . .

Benevolent Nature teaches animals not only to care for themselves but implants in them a social sense both as a means of protection and as a source of enjoyment. This thesis is advanced by the Wanderer, as he endeavors to correct the despondency of the Solitary who has found in human life far too little of such sympathy.

We might also add—although on this point so many sources are available that nothing conclusive may be hoped for —that the argument of *The Excursion* parallels Shaftesbury's theory of good and evil in their relation to God. This is the belief common to Shaftesbury, Leibnitz, and Pope that whatever evil exists is woven into the full context of the world where good overbalances evil, and that world, if once seen as a whole, contains a full justification of all its apparent imperfections. This point of view appears in the Wanderer's discourse, especially at the beginning of the fourth book. It is prominent in Shaftesbury's *The Moralists:* "For 't was impossible, you thought that Heaven should have acted otherwise than for the best. So that even for this misery and Ill of Man there was undoubtedly some good arising; something which overbalanced all, and made full amends."[61] This amounts to the Wanderer's

---

[61] *Ibid.*, Part I, sec. 2, p. 204.

> . . . assured belief
> That the procession of our fate, howe'er
> Sad or disturbed, is ordered by a Being
> Of infinite benevolence and power;
> Whose everlasting purposes embrace
> All accidents, converting them to good.[62]

If it stood by itself, this last parallel would be of very little significance. But when it is considered along with the other passages mentioned, it becomes somewhat more noteworthy.

Authors like Newton and Shaftesbury may be considered as exercising *minor* influences upon Wordsworth's thought. By this we mean chiefly that these writers supply the poet with concepts and terminology helpful to him but not central in a description of his distinctive attitude toward the world or of his characteristic method of reflection.

[62] Bk. IV, ll. 12 ff.

CHAPTER V

The Moral of the Ancient Mariner

THERE IS AMPLE evidence that from 1796 to 1805 or thereabouts Wordsworth and Coleridge shared one another's thought about as completely as it is possible for two men of intellectual independence to do. This does not mean, of course, that they always agreed. But upon investigation we shall find a very substantial agreement on fundamentals, although we shall always have to allow for Coleridge's greater inclination toward orthodoxy and greater fear of pantheism and for his less vivid and much less persistent mysticism. The grounds of the two poets' greatest agreement, as well as a hint concerning possible differences, becomes apparent when we examine certain passages in *The Prelude* which are directly and especially addressed to Coleridge.

Let us quote these passages:

> . . . But who shall parcel out
> His intellect, by geometric rules,
> Split, like a province, into round and square?
> Who knows the individual hour in which
> His habits were first sown, even as a seed,
> Who that shall point, as with a wand, and say,
> "This portion of the river of my mind
> Came from yon fountain?" Thou, my Friend! art one
> More deeply read in thy own thoughts; to thee
> Science appears but, what in truth she is,
> Not as our glory and our absolute boast,
> But as a succedaneum, and a prop
> To our infirmity. Thou art no slave
> Of that false secondary power, by which,
> In weakness, we create distinctions, then
> Deem that our puny boundaries are things
> Which we perceive, and not which we have made.
> To thee, unblinded by these outward shows,

The unity of all has been reveal'd
And thou wilt doubt with me, less aptly skill'd
Than many are to class the cabinet
Of their sensations, and, in voluble phrase,
Run through the history and birth of each,
As of a single independent thing.
Hard task to analyse a soul, in which,
Not only general habits and desires,
But each most obvious and particular thought,
Not in a mystical and idle sense,
But in the words of reason deeply weigh'd,
Hath no beginning.[1]
                        With such a theme,
Coleridge! with this my argument, of thee
Shall I be silent?   O most loving soul!
Placed on this earth to love and understand,
And from thy presence shed the light of love,
Shall I be mute ere thou be spoken of?
Thy gentle Spirit to my heart of hearts
Did also find its way; and thus the life
Of all things and the mighty unity
In all which we behold, and feel, and are,
Admitted more habitually a mild
Interposition, and closelier gathering thoughts
Of man and his concerns, such as become
A human Creature, be he who he may!
Poet, or destined for a humbler name;
And so the deep enthusiastic joy,
The rapture of the Hallelujah sent
From all that breathes and is, was chasten'd, stemm'd
And balanced by a Reason which indeed
Is reason; duty and pathetic truth;
And God and Man divided, as they ought,
Between them the great system of the world
Where Man is sphered, and which God animates.[2]

We may summarize Wordsworth's account of his intellectual debt to Coleridge as follows:

   _1_) Repudiation of strict sensationalism and associationism.

[1] _The Prelude_, Bk. II, ll. 203-232.   [2] _Ibid._, Bk. XIV, ll. 275-300.

2) Repudiation of an atomistic pluralism and advocacy of an idealism expressing the "one life within us and abroad."

3) Emphasis upon the importance of reason as a valuable counter for mystical enthusiasm.

4) Emphasis upon a proper distinction between *human* and *divine*.

With reference to points 1 and 2 Coleridge's influence corresponds with that of Boehme; with reference to points 3 and 4 it diverges from Boehme. Whether topics 2 and 4 are mutually inconsistent is a matter to which we shall occasionally return. Coleridge seems to have advocated a type of monistic idealism in some way freed from pantheism. We know from *Biographia Literaria* that, even as late as 1815, he thought such a combination not impossible. He even expresses doubt that Spinoza need be considered a pantheist. Such a comment raises the endless and rather tiresome dispute concerning the proper use of the term *pantheism*. If one adheres without compromise to an extreme form of pantheism, he must insist that God's being *contains* the human soul along with every other finite entity in the universe. In its idealistic form, such a theory would invoke the statement, which should not, of course, be attributed to Berkeley, that every finite entity, including the human soul, is no more than an idea in the unity of God's mind. Such a theory certainly deserves the label "pantheistic," but, like solipsism, it is very rarely maintained. Such a view, if persistently developed, would clearly pulverize ethical theory, for all moral action would issue directly from God, who would be the one moral agent in the universe. A thinker may, however, stop short of this extreme and grant finite being some ultimate distinction, arguing that only under certain circumstances may the finite mind transcend its usual limitations and possess its birthright of divinity. When the human soul is, so to speak, "true to itself," God acts within it and, for a moment, there is no essential difference between human activity and divine agency, insofar as it is concentrated in the life of the finite soul. In this case, "identity" of human and divine becomes an ideal, rarely realized, rather than a necessary and universal order of things. If we limit pantheism, as some do, to the notion that all human souls constantly manifest deity in equal measure, then we must decline to classify Wordsworth as a pantheist. But, by these tokens, Spinoza himself is no pantheist.

The Coleridge of *Religious Musings* and the "Eolian Harp" approached pantheism of an extreme type. As time passed, he seems to have grown more and more cautious in these matters, although we must remember that even in the "Eolian Harp" itself he voices some hesitation concerning his speculation.

To judge by the passage from *The Prelude* above quoted, we may surmise that Coleridge was inclined to caution Wordsworth against an extreme statement of pantheism of the sort which we have just described and to urge upon him recognition of a division of powers, divine and human. There are times, however, when Wordsworth may have disappointed his friend. But, at any rate, in his personal tribute to Coleridge at the close of *The Prelude*, Wordsworth graciously thanks him for advice which was not perhaps always too closely followed. In all probability Wordsworth found such advice difficult to follow in the light of experience which, for him, admitted of no denial.

*   *   *

The early thinking of Wordsworth and Coleridge actually coincided more closely than the above suggests. It centered about one idea which was, if not the psychological origin, at least the logical culmination of their humanitarian, esthetic, and religious doctrines. This notion we may designate as the theory of imaginative love. We find this hidden in the allegory of the *Ancient Mariner* and more clearly stated in the philosophical passages of *The Prelude*. It contains the explanation which Wordsworth offers of the spiritual efficacy of "natural piety" and of his mystical love of beauty. It is, in short, the keystone of that heroic system of natural religion which the two poets constructed during the period of mutually inspiring companionship when they walked together upon

"Quantock's airy ridge." They believed that creative and appreciative imagination engenders a love of Nature and a love of man, and they did not hesitate to affirm that this love is a profoundly religious experience which owes its power to the mystical communion with a cosmic spirit. This last belief was essentially a faith in an animate Nature, and it served them both as the justification of their almost worshipful love of woodlands and hillsides from which they drew spiritual strength. This idea, however, was not by any means a mere doctrine with which they defended their peculiar religious position; it hovered over their thinking, "a master o'er a slave," and found expression again and again in their most successful utterances.

After Professor J. L. Lowes's monumental study of the *Ancient Mariner* as a work of pure imagination, it may seem futile to search the poem for any didactic meaning or philosophical message. Professor Lowes has written that "to interpret the drift of the *Ancient Mariner* as didactic in its intention is to stultify both Coleridge and one's self!"[3] But I trust that this essay will not result in verification of Professor Lowes's dictum. We must not be too quick to class even slightly obscure poems of Coleridge's as being no more than works of pure imagination. When we recall his philosophical disposition and the great fame which his metaphysical speculation brought him during his own lifetime, the danger involved in such procedure should seem obvious.

Nonetheless, owing to the fact that no moral except perhaps the apparent platitude in the last stanzas is really very obvious to the reader or demonstrable to the scholar, I should hesitate to present any theory concerning a meaning buried in the poem, were it not that Coleridge himself has admitted the presence of such a moral. He seems to have thought this moral forced upon the reader, and indeed he feared that there was *too much* moral. The latter is probably true: the moral is not woven very closely into the narrative, it may even be superfluous in the esthetic structure; but it is there nonetheless,

[3] *The Road to Xanadu* (New York, 1927), p. 299.

although not so obvious to the reader as Coleridge may have supposed:

Mrs. Barbauld once told me that she admired the *Ancient Mariner* very much, but that there were two faults in it—it was improbable, and had no moral. As for the probability, I owned that that might admit some question; but as to the want of a moral, I told her that in my judgment the poem had too much; and that the only, or chief fault, if I might say so, was the obtrusion of the moral sentiment so openly on the reader as a principle or cause of action in a work of such pure imagination.[4]

Now, it is true enough that moralizing or the use of allegory in a ballad in which an imaginative use is made of the supernatural for its own sake is apt to seem out of place or even mechanical. But, even so, may we interpret this expression of Coleridge's regret as referring to the brief expression of piety at the close of the poem? This Professor Lowes seems to have done.[5] To be sure, the last stanzas may seem to some a trite and an unnecessary conclusion of the vivid tale of supernatural melodrama which the body of the poem contains. But we have no right to suppose that the philosophical Coleridge, who at the period during which he wrote the *Ancient Mariner* was deeply engrossed in metaphysical and religious speculation, cared to tag so lengthy a work with a religious platitude:

> He prayeth best, who loveth best
> All things both great and small;
> For the dear God that loveth us
> He made and loveth all.[6]

Could Coleridge have considered this stanza as *too much* moral? He might well have thought so, if the lines in question were merely a pious recognition of the Mariner's sin in killing an albatross. But certainly Coleridge had a sense of the ridiculous which would have withheld him from writing a phantasy of some six hundred lines on the dangers of cruelty to animals. Furthermore, if the lines are to stand by themselves as the full moral sentiment attached to the poem, they

---

[4] *Table Talk*, May 31, 1830.   [5] *Op. cit.*, p. 302.
[6] *The Rime of the Ancient Mariner*, Part VII, ll. 614-617.

can be no more than a superstitious sailor's comment on his own
miraculous adventures, a natural comment and one quite in
keeping with the poem as a whole and surely not to be regretted by the author.

Hence we may be sure that a consideration of the moral is
incomplete without reference to earlier passages of other than
purely narrative significance. When we make such a study, we
shall find that the poem is heavily laden with an ethical philosophy and contains a "vision of the best" as well as a profound
insight into the depths to which a human soul may be driven.

That *The Rime of the Ancient Mariner* of all poems should
embody a philosophical meaning, may seem utterly outlandish
to many students. And there are critics who feel that Coleridge was a poet only insofar as he escaped being a philosopher.[7] In the *Ancient Mariner*, such critics tell us, "The
swift and unerring flight of imagination frees itself from the
snares of contemplation so obviously present in *Religious Musings* and *The Destiny of Nations*." But philosophy once freed
from pedantry is a very common subject matter of poetry and
indeed a suitable one—particularly the romantic philosophy in
which Wordsworth and Coleridge delighted during those days
of intellectual and creative exhilaration which they spent together by the Quantock Hills. Here was a time when they
were both intensely happy, overwhelmed with a realization of
what they thought most precious in life—what Coleridge called
"the benignant touch of Love and Beauty."[8]

It is then not surprising that their faith in their newly
found *summum bonum* should appear in this poem. The
glorious sense of a new way of life and a new happiness—the
secret of which the poets believed they possessed—may well
have hovered on the threshold of Coleridge's creative consciousness as he wrote the *Ancient Mariner*. This ethical notion
existed in Coleridge's mind along with the great mass of
imagery drawn from the writings of the English voyagers and
from legends of the sea, which, Professor Lowes has shown us,
lay in Coleridge's mind, awaiting creative transmutation. This

[7] Lowes, *op. cit.*, p. 299.   [8] "The Dungeon" (1797), l. 30.

doctrine of the highest happiness constitutes the ethical philosophy embodied by Wordsworth in the last books of *The Prelude*.

The *Ancient Mariner* is a narrative poem. There is a fine dramatic use of incident.in the verse and much description of nature to which most of the simple and lively imagery is devoted. Neither of these elements is held in check for the sake of the philosophical allegory; so we must not expect to find the poem entirely dominated by a subtlc moral. We now know that Coleridge drew much of the tale and the description from legends and from the accounts of voyages made by the British explorers with which he was intimately acquainted. Nonetheless, there are incidents and characters in the poem which do not, apparently, spring from such sources; and it is these which we shall find most significant in the allegory.

The philosophy of the last books of *The Prelude* centers about Wordsworth's faith in the vital importance of imagination or the faculty of esthetic enjoyment and creation by which the poet may "love whate'er he sees." This faculty seems to be of greatest value eudaemonistically when it apprehends the forms of Nature as beautiful. Then there may arise in the soul a profound love of man and a sense of communion with Nature or with the spirit that enlivens Nature. Thus the habitual use and the development of this faculty amplifies and strengthens the human spirit, raising it also to a life of moral freedom and happiness.

Wordsworth really knew such a life only after escaping from the spiritual lethargy and despair to which an orgy of analytical reasoning upon moral matters had reduced him. Analysis, both because of the desperate results it secured and the habit of mind it engendered, for a time deprived the poet of the very faculties upon which his happiness depended. He was withheld from his strengthening spiritual intercourse with Nature and was even reduced to an indifference concerning matters humane.[9]

Here we find in the two poems very similar experience.

<hr>

[9] *The Prelude* (1805), Bk. XI, ll. 75 ff. and 133 ff.

The horrible loneliness of the Ancient Mariner and the bitter despair which undermined Wordsworth's love of Nature and of man were similar experiences and, so to say, ran a similar course. In neither poem do we learn that the suffering was *overcome*. Coleridge speaks of the Mariner's suffering as penance done for a sin, and Wordsworth tells us that he, living in the company of dear friends and being continually close to Nature, found at last a happier way of life which led him in turn to dispel his intellectual doubts.

The world which we apprehend solely through the lower faculty of reason is a "universe of death," and if we devote ourselves exclusively to the study of this universe, as Coleridge has put it, we bring "death into our own souls."[10]   In such a world, living beings are reduced to a passive automatism, when any spiritual freedom and initiative is unthinkable, and where all things are subject to a determinism of mechanical cause and effect. Thus human beings are not free agents: they are mere vehicles of causation. Accordingly, what we describe as personality appears as nothing substantial but as a mere flux or chain or psychological determinism. Spiritual freedom is ruled quite out of the picture. Such a philosophy might almost be compared with what the great mystics have sometimes called the "dark night of the soul," when illumination is withdrawn and the devotee is driven in despair to doubt the validity of the experience that once supported his spiritual life. Wordsworth, however, seems to have felt a perverse satisfaction in cultivating a type of thought which, for one of his disposition, makes illumination impossible. Like the Ancient Mariner, he was at one time rather proud of having shot the albatross "that made the breeze to blow."

The final recovery of happiness is symbolized in the *Ancient Mariner* by the sailor's return to his home port. That Wordsworth was probably aware of this allegorical meaning, and that he very likely had it in mind while writing *The Prelude* is evident from the lines in Book XI, addressed to Coleridge, in which he describes the state of moral helplessness

[10] See above, p. 66.

into which he had fallen. Here Wordsworth seems to refer
to the symbolism of the *Ancient Mariner:*

> This History, my Friend, hath chiefly told
> Of intellectual power, from stage to stage
> Advancing, hand in hand with love and joy,
> And of imagination teaching truth
> Until that natural graciousness of mind
> Gave way to over-pressure from the times
> And their disastrous issues. What avail'd,
> *When Spells forbade the voyager to land,*
> The fragrance which did ever and anon
> Give notice of the Shore, from arbours breathed
> Of blessed sentiment and fearless love?
> What did such sweet remembrances avail,
> Perfidious then, as seem'd, what serv'd they then?[11]

Any attempt to determine the value of this as a reference
to Coleridge's poem is complicated by Wordsworth's note on
the *Ancient Mariner* which appears in the 1800 edition of
Lyrical Ballads. Here Wordsworth censures the poem, hold-
ing, among other things, that it lacks that unity of thought
which makes one event "produce another." But this does not
mean that Wordsworth was unaware of the presence of a moral
in the poem. It may only mean that he considered the poem
lacking in continuity of meaning. And this fault is all the
more obvious when we consider the precarious position which
the moral holds. Coleridge gives us no inkling of a possible
allegorical interpretation until we reach the middle of Part
III and encounter the character *Life-in-Death.*

At any rate, in the lines from *The Prelude* above quoted
we find the moral summarized, save of course for the reference in line 46 to the "over-pressure" of the times which
refers to the political origin of Wordsworth's moral meditations springing from his intimate acquaintance with the French
Revolution. Let us proceed then to interpret Coleridge's
poem in terms of the philosophy of *The Prelude.*

The earlier stanzas of the *Ancient Mariner* are not ob-

[11] *The Prelude*, Bk. XI, ll. 42 ff. Italics mine.

viously conformable with our interpretation. They seem by
themselves quite remote from allegory. It is indeed possible,
particularly so, when we consider Coleridge's account[12] of the
imaginative plan entertained at the very outset, that Coleridge
began the work without any didactic intention at all, only realizing the poem's philosophical possibilities when he reached
the third and fourth parts. This theory is to some measure
substantiated by the fact that Coleridge at first had not intended that the Mariner commit any sin. Without some such
explanation of the Mariner's misfortune the philosophy of *The
Prelude* could not have been foreshadowed, for there would
have been no symbol of the abuse of reason which is the source
of the suffering recorded in *The Prelude*. In fact, the introduction of the sin was Wordsworth's suggestion made, according to his remark to Miss Fenwick, at the very beginning,
probably quite without any allegorical intent.

That composition of the poem should have been actually
begun before the allegorical intention took shape may seem to
many students a very unlikely supposition. In defense of it
I shall only say that composition is not always a matter of fulfilling a predetermined pattern and that the possibilities of a
theme may actually be discovered while the theme is being
worked out. After all, any story that includes supernatural
elements has allegorical possibilities, especially when the notion of supernatural punishment has been introduced.

For the sake of clarity, then, let us emphasize that the
prime foundations of our argument are limited to: (1) the
incident of Part IV where the spell begins to break owing to
the awakening of esthetic love which rescues the Mariner from
his spiritual isolation, and (2) the last stanzas, wherein the
Mariner is rewarded with a deep sense of human love and
sympathy. Both these moments are clearly paralleled by *The
Prelude*. Arguing from this similarity, we shall indicate further possible correspondences in the interpretation of the
Guardian Saint and the Hermit. For our purpose, we *must*
interpret the shooting of the albatross as the symbol of reason's

[12] *Biographia Literaria*, chap. xiv.

conquest of feeling. The obscurity of this symbol may be owing to the fact that Coleridge very likely wrote the earlier stanzas without any didactic purpose. Again, we repeat that the precise significance of the death and revival of the crew is obscure and may not be entirely allegorical.

Let us now present the allegory as it appears after a reading of the poem as a whole, but keeping in mind the scheme of our argument. The Mariner through a sin of his own has endured the most horrible loneliness, living quite apart from man and God, in spiritual agony, yet unable to pray for aid. He has endured a life-in-death and realized—here his suffering was perhaps acuter than Wordsworth's—that he has brought similar agony upon his companions, who have hung the dead albatross about his neck as a mark of his sin. Their sullen enmity is the cause of his greatest agony, and he cannot forget that he has caused their suffering and finally their death.

Although he cannot save himself, he realizes the beauty of what he has destroyed and this is only cause for greater horror:

> Alone, alone, all, all alone,
> Alone on a wide wide sea!
> And never a saint took pity on
> My soul in agony.
>
> The many men, so beautiful!
> And they all dead did lie:
> And a thousand thousand slimy things
> Lived on; and so did I.[13]

He shuts his eyes, turning away from the face of Nature, in disgust and weariness:

> For the sky and the sea, and the sea and the sky
> Lay like a load on my weary eye,
> And the dead were at my feet.[14]

There is no consolation but only the "weary weight of this unintelligible world." The same spiritual isolation and help-

---

[13] *The Rime of the Ancient Mariner*, Part IV, ll. 232-239.
[14] *Ibid.*, Part IV, ll. 250-253.

lessness also overcame Wordsworth. A too robust and hasty indulgence in analytical reasoning separated him from the humanizing influence of the poets and of communion with Nature. Such an employment of reason Coleridge seems to have symbolized in the killing of the playful and innocent albatross that "made the breeze to blow."

Wordsworth speaks of this exercise of reason as lacking in warmth of feeling. It is rather the analytical pondering of a skeptic than the triumphant synthesis of an inspired philosopher:

> . . . suffice it here
> To hint that danger cannot but attend
> Upon a Function rather proud to be
> The enemy of falsehood, than the friend
> Of truth, to sit in judgment than to feel.[15]

But Wordsworth was too well protected by what Coleridge called the "Guardian spirit," i.e., imaginative love of Nature and communion with her which—

> . . . howe'er impaired or damp'd,
> Yet having once been born can never die.[16]

Wordsworth says of himself:

> . . . I had felt
> Too forcibly, too early in my life,
> Visitings of imaginative power
> For this to last: I shook the habit off
> Entirely and forever, and again
> In Nature's presence stood, as I stand now,
> A sensitive and a creative soul.[17]

Coleridge describes the first breaking of the spell in a way which reveals the real similarity of meaning in the two poems. The guardian saint takes pity upon the Mariner: the quiet beauty of the rising moon, softly going up into the heaven and spreading the sea with an "April hoar-frost," reawakens a love of Nature and brings with it a new ability to feel.

[15] *The Prelude*, Bk. XI, ll. 133 ff.
[16] *Ibid.*, Bk. XI, ll. 106-107. [17] *Ibid.*, Bk. XI, ll. 251 ff.

Coleridge added in the *Sybilline Leaves* marginalia a beautiful note to this passage. Here is the mystical sense of the deep animation which the forms of Nature bear within themselves. The stars come into their natural home in the blue heaven, "which they enter unannounced as Lords which are certainly expected and yet there is a silent joy at their arrival."

This passage in the marginalia marks the turning point of the poem. The punishment loses its full severity; the Mariner rejoices in the beauty about him and, "unaware" and spontaneously, blesses the *beautiful* water-snakes which but a short time before he had heartily despised as "slimy things." Then he finds himself at last capable of prayer. Nature is no longer a barren waste, unsupportably dreary, for a sense of communion with some spiritual power has returned. (Recall that at the period when the poem was written Coleridge spoke of the Almighty Spirit as veiled in the "hues of the wide landscape.")[18] Thus an esthetic or imaginative love is reawakened, and the dead albatross, the mark of his sin, falls from the Mariner's neck.

Some students may feel that the Mariner's blessing the water-snakes has no hidden significance: It is easily to be explained by the humanitarian ideas common to many advanced thinkers at the close of the eighteenth century. But the point is not that the Mariner suddenly becomes a humanitarian, but that his renewed sympathy with "man and bird and beast," even with all "*things,* both great and small" is the result of imagination and of esthetic sensitivity.

The Mariner's penance and suffering are not at once over, for he has not as yet fully recovered his love and understanding of *man.* Thus he is unable to speak with the bodies of his companions who for a time work the ship:

> The body of my brother's son
> Stood by me, knee to knee:
> The body and I pulled at one rope,
> But he said nought to me.[19]

[18] "Lime Tree Bower," ll. 38 ff.
[19] *The Rime of the Ancient Mariner*, Part V, ll. 341-344.

The pious Hermit alone has the power to shrive the Mariner and free him from the heavy consequences of his sin, the good Hermit who

> . . . loves to talk with marineres
> That come from a far countree.[20]

We may find a possible interpretation of the Hermit in the idea of an enlightened religion which is acquainted with the life of the spirit and aware of the difficulties which beset it.

Even the worthy Hermit is, with good reason, terrified by the Mariner's plight. But the Mariner has reached home at last and a deep sense of human fellowship and love return to him with a strengthened religion.

> O Wedding-guest! this soul hath been
> Alone on a wide wide sea:
> So lonely 'twas that God himself
> Scarce seeméd there to be.

> O sweeter than the marriage feast,
> 'Tis sweeter far to me,
> To walk together to the kirk
> With a goodly company!—

> To walk together to the kirk,
> And altogether pray,
> While each to his great Father bends,
> Old men, and babes, and loving friends
> And youths and maidens gay![21]

The meaning of the moral in the lines "He prayeth best . . ." should now be obvious. *Love* has its romantic meaning, depending as it does upon the presence of imagination in the soul, the imagination for which the water-snakes were beautiful, although, as also in Wordsworth, this love must widen into a more humane and a more religious sentiment. To this the "flow of love" which burst from the Mariner's heart when first he was aware of Nature's beauty was only a prelude. The final development is something more similar to St. Paul's *charity* in that it extends toward human beings and is sustained

[20] *Ibid.*, Part VII, ll. 517-518.   [21] *Ibid.*, Part VII, ll. 597-609.

by a mystical sense of communion which in this case is engendered by the presence of imagination and delight in Nature.
The element of communion may seem lacking in the Ancient
Mariner until one recalls that before the rebirth of love the
Mariner was unable to pray, being, as we may interpret, quite
"alone," and spiritually isolated. This gives us the meaning
of "He prayeth best who loveth best" not only man and bird
and beast but as well "all *things* both great and small."

Coleridge's account of the return to happiness is paralleled
by the story in *The Prelude*. Reference to a rationally considered religion as a final stage is made by Wordsworth:

> And so the deep enthusiastic joy,
> The rapture of the Hallelujah sent
> From all that breathes and is, was chasten'd, stemm'd
> And balanced by a Reason which indeed
> Is reason. . . .[22]

This, we suggest, is symbolized by Coleridge in the person of
the Hermit.

In *The Prelude* great emphasis is placed upon the gentle-
ness and the profound human kindliness which the imaginative
life of the Nature lover engenders in the soul:

> But joy to him,
> Oh, joy to him who here hath sown, hath laid
> Here the foundations of his future years!
> For all that friendship, all that love can do,
> All that a darling countenance can look
> Or dear voice utter to complete the man,
> Perfect him, made imperfect in himself,
> All shall be his: and he whose soul hath risen
> Up to the height of feeling intellect
> Shall want no humbler tenderness, his heart
> Be tender as a nursing Mother's heart;
> Of female softness shall his life be full,
> Of little loves and delicate desires,
> Mild interests and gentlest sympathies.[23]

---

[22] *The Prelude*, Bk. XIII, ll. 261 ff.   [23] *Ibid.*, Bk. XIII, ll. 197 ff.

This state of beatitude followed upon a first reawakening of human interest when Nature brought again "a wiser mood" first teaching the poet

> To look with feelings of fraternal love
> Upon those unassuming things, that hold
> A silent station in this beauteous world.
> Thus moderated, thus composed, I found
> Once more in Man an object of delight
> Of pure imagination, and of love. . . .[24]

This brought Wordsworth to the final stage when he took again "the intellectual eye"

> . . . studious more to see
> Great truths, than touch and handle little ones.[25]

But there is a difference, despite all the similarity we have suggested, between the two accounts of regained happiness. The Mariner is still haunted by the memory of the spiritual crisis through which he has passed and must at times recount it to others. As Professor Lowes mentions, the Mariner is not altogether free from his sin. Now, although Wordsworth states that, after attaining his new balance of reason and emotion, he still recalled his past confusion, he says nothing to imply that he lived at times under a spell of horror. It is perhaps significant in this connection to recall that Coleridge was destined to undergo later another period of spiritual depression which he has recorded in "Dejection." Coleridge was perhaps never as free from such difficulty as was Wordsworth when he wrote *The Prelude*. Recall Coleridge's comment on himself and Wordsworth, published in *Anima Poetae* and dated 1805:

The *thinking* disease is that in which the feelings, instead of embodying themselves in acts, ascend and become materials of general reasoning and intellectual pride. The dreadful consequences of this perversion (may be) instanced in Germany, e.g., in Fichte *versus*

[24] *Ibid.*, Bk. XIII, ll. 45-50.
[25] *Ibid.*, Bk. XII, ll. 44 ff. (with omissions).

Kant, Schelling *versus* Fichte, and in Verbidigno (Wordsworth) *versus* S.T.C.[26]

Further, the reader will observe that Coleridge has throughout rendered his account in semblance more Christian than did Wordsworth. One reason for this is, of course, the setting of the allegory. The Mariner is a medieval sailor and naturally speaks in Christian and even in Roman terms. We may also ascribe this Christian attitude to Coleridge's usual habit of suffusing a semi-orthodox cloud over all the philosophy which he originated or adapted from other thinkers.[27] Wordsworth was slower to accept Christian thinking. But since at this period the Christianity of Coleridge seems to have been, like Blake's later faith, more romantic than truly orthodox, we need not consider this a ground of any profound difference of thought between Wordsworth and his friend.

Nor is it essential to ponder (from our present point of view) whether or not Coleridge had ever, before he wrote the *Ancient Mariner,* been quite "alone on a wide, wide sea" and suffered as intensely as did his character, the Mariner. Suffice it to say that he had passed through a period of religious and spiritual confusion and even despair, as one of his restless mental energy might well do. Consider his lines to Godwin, published in 1795:

> Nor will I not thy holy guidance bless,
> And hymn thee, Godwin! with an ardent lay;
> For that thy voice, in Passion's stormy day,
> *When wild I roam'd the bleak Heath of Distress,*
> Bade the bright form of Justice meet my way—
> And told her that her name was Happiness.[28]

Coleridge, of course, did not rest satisfied with a Godwinian solution. But the lines to Godwin show us that Coleridge

---

[26] E. H. Coleridge (ed.), *Anima Poetae* (Boston, 1895), p. 143.

[27] Cf. Professor de Selincourt's mention of this fact in his edition of *The Prelude,* p. lvii.

[28] E. H. Coleridge (ed.), *The Poems of Samuel Taylor Coleridge* (Oxford, 1924), p. 86, ll. 9-12. Italics mine.

knew at least something of what he wrote when he described the Mariner's spiritual loneliness.

* * *

No discussion of the moral of the *Ancient Mariner* is complete without a consideration of Coleridge's "Ode to Dejection." Here again is described a loss of sympathy or communion with Nature. But here Coleridge is driven to the point of denying that the communion is ever a really genuine one. The "dark night of the soul" returns and engenders a new philosophy which is not wholly consistent with the view of *The Prelude*. Also Coleridge's uneasiness before the prospect of pantheism becomes manifest and this sharpens the disagreement with Wordsworth.

Coleridge's "Ode to Dejection" is, along with a number of his earlier poems, an expression of the experience which lies behind the doctrine of imaginative love. But it is distinguished from these in that the poet here laments— and here the poem is somewhat similar to the "Intimations Ode" of Wordsworth —the loss of his ability to participate in the enthusiasm and the power which he and his friend had drawn from the imaginative life. It is further unique in that it contains an interpretation of the communion with Nature which certainly seems to be at odds with the many statements of the romantic faith to be found in the earlier poems. The popular notion of Wordsworthian philosophy is certainly violated in the lines:

> Oh, William! we receive but what we give
> And in our lives alone does Nature live.[29]

But the teaching of the "Ode" is subtle and in places inconsistent, so that we must weigh the author's *ipsissima verba* carefully before accepting any interpretation as obvious. To be sure, Coleridge is disagreeing with Wordsworth; but the precise point of disagreement is not easy to state, nor is Coleridge accepting a tenet so foreign to Wordsworth's thinking as we might easily suppose, when he writes:

[29] When Coleridge printed the "Dejection Ode," he disguised this reference to Wordsworth by substituting "Lady" for "William" in line 47.

We may not hope from outward forms to win
The passion and the life whose fountains are within.[30]

We shall find that Wordsworth is not unaware of the subjective elements involved in communion with Nature. Certainly, as we have seen, he is not inclined to make his communion with Nature depend upon sensuous accuracy.

Nonetheless, aside from such difficulties of interpretation, the really fascinating problem which the "Ode" presents arises from the fact that we find Coleridge accusing Wordsworth of what has often been called the "pathetic fallacy." From Coleridge, the companion of Wordsworth's early meditation, this is a startling accusation, as it virtually denies the reality of the communion with Nature. Upon what grounds does Coleridge make this accusation and how far is it justified philosophically?

But before we endeavor to answer these questions we must make as careful a statement as possible of the precise doctrine of the "Ode" itself. We shall find much of this doctrine echoed in Wordsworth's "Intimations Ode" and at least one tenet stoutly denied. The first four stanzas, those written in 1802,[31] seem to agree with "Dejection": "There has passed away a glory from the earth." It is of the greatest importance to recall that these stanzas were, in all probability, in composition from March 26, 1802, until, at the earliest, June 17 of that year, and that the remaining stanzas were written at least two years later.[32] Now, "Dejection" was written on the night of April 4, 1802. These dates supply further evidence for the hypothesis that Wordsworth and Coleridge shared much of their intellectual life with one another. The experience and the doctrine of "Dejection" are restated and more critically interpreted in the later stanzas of the "Intimations Ode." Certainly, the echoes of the terminology of "Dejection" which we

---

[30] E. H. Coleridge (ed.), *op. cit.*, p. 365, ll. 45-46. "The fountains within" is a figure of speech common to Coleridge and to William Law, who writes in his *Spirit of Prayer* "All is fruitless and insignificant, all the means of thy redemption are at a stand, all outward forms are but a dead formality, till this fountain of living water is found within thee. . . ." But Law is closer to Wordsworth than to Coleridge and finds Nature animated by spiritual power.

[31] George M. Harper, *Wordsworth* (New York, 1929), p. 446.

[32] *Ibid.*

shall find in the later stanzas of the "Intimations Ode" give us the right to interpret Wordsworth's poem as in part an answer to "Dejection."

In Stanzas 3, 5, and 6, of Coleridge's "Ode" we find three attitudes or ways of life clearly mentioned, the life of utilitarian action, the life of theory, and the life of imagination. Proper to each of these ways of life a special world-view is indicated.   To the first way of life appears

> . . . that inanimate cold world allowed
> To the poor loveless ever-anxious crowd.[33]

"That cold, inanimate world"—the world which is merely the environment and instrument of human interests—the object of ever-anxious planning and worry.   This is the world as it appears to lust, to ambition, or to an anxiety bred of necessity. It is reflected in Wordsworth's "Intimations Ode":

> The homely Nurse doth all she can
> To make her Foster-child, her Inmate Man,
> Forget the glories he hath known
> And that imperial palace whence he came.

Thus if the "world is too much with us," if we are carried away by "mad endeavor" to satisfy one of our many interests, we forfeit our birthright of spontaneous and joyous response to the multitude of beautiful and interesting things with which we are always surrounded.   The life of imaginative love is then to be distinguished sharply from that of the "practical" man.   This truth Coleridge flashes before us in the brief mention of the "loveless, ever-anxious crowd."

But the life of pure reason is not, as it was for the Greeks, a much better alternative.   Analysis, meditation, speculation suit only a "part" of the spirit.   If allowed full play, they deaden the esthetic sense and engender a "habit of the soul" which seems to dull original and spontaneous perceptions or even to make them impossible.   For Coleridge a sort of philosophical introspection seems to have been the most deadly form of this rationalist disintegration:

[33] E. H. Coleridge (ed.), *op. cit.*, p. 365, ll. 51-52.

And haply by abstruse research to steal
From my own nature all the natural man.
This was my sole resource, my only plan:
Till that which suits a part infects the whole,
And now is almost grown the habit of my soul.[34]

It is a well-known truth that clearly to analyze one's own emotions, or even to make them the objects of investigation, is apt to take the driving power away from them. It is further true that the attitude of rational contemplation is opposed to the imaginative life. Once concepts become the most favored instruments of thought and the chief goal of expression becomes clarity or precision, then the spontaneous joy in words and in images—which is really the life of poetry—is often wholly lost. Ideas may flourish for their own sake and even for the sake of the personal self-assertion of the thinker, for there is often a pride in reason; but neither logic nor self-assertion is easily at home with the imaginative life.

The former point Wordsworth is loath to admit. That reason and imagination are necessarily and ultimately incompatible is quite foreign to the spirit of *The Prelude* and to that of the "Intimations Ode." In fact, he seems to have identified at least one function of imagination with "reason in its most exalted mood."

This explains why in the "Intimations Ode" Wordsworth finds it possible to address the child, whose immortality broods over him, as "best philosopher" and "seer blest." It is, of course, a daring exaggeration; but it is not, as some polemicists will argue, utterly perverse. It shows that Wordsworth at this time saw nothing in spontaneous mysticism that need be at odds with philosophy. It is rather the practical life which is at enmity with joy. In fact, the "years that bring the philosophic mind"—although exiling us from the "imperial palace" where ecstasy was so frequent—add something that is a compensation for its loss; for the lucid moments of insight that do remain are enriched by a comprehension of their full meaning. Of course, reason alone is not a substitute for joyous insight; with-

[34] *Ibid.*, p. 367, ll. 89-93.

out *that* we must ever toil in darkness and with "opinion ever changing." But it remains true that reason and insight are not incompatible. This Wordsworth had already learned.

The third way of life which Coleridge mentions is the *summum bonum* of the romantic faith which he had years before embraced:

> Joy, William! is the spirit and the power,
> Which wedding Nature to us gives in dower,
> A new Earth and new Heaven,
> Undreamt of by the sensual and the proud—[35]

Joy of this type goes hand in hand with the shaping spirit of imagination, and what destroys one seems to destroy the other:

> Nor care I that they rob me of my mirth;
>   But oh! each visitation
> Suspends what nature gave me at my birth,
>   My shaping spirit of Imagination.[36]

In the "Tintern Abbey" lines Wordsworth refers to the "deep power of joy" as a source of sympathy with Nature and in the "Intimations Ode," Wordsworth uses the word "joy" in Coleridge's sense:

> . . . Joy that in our embers
> Is something that doth live.

This Joy seems to be the occasion of a mystical enlightenment. Wordsworth emphasizes the awed amazement with which the soul suffers these illuminations, he being perhaps in this respect a more humble man than his friend.[37]

Joy is free from desire—from passion, anxiety, or pride— and it is free from the conceptual pondering of a conscientious reason. Joy is itself beautiful and is the source of beauty. Without this "music in the soul," this spontaneous acceptance of our environment and creative response to it, there is no beauty visible to man, nor any friendly Nature. Without Joy, the sensitive man is spiritually alone and must suffer the agony

---

[35] *Ibid.*, p. 366, ll. 67-70.   [36] *Ibid.*, p. 366, ll. 83-86.
[37] Joy is mentioned in *The Prelude*, Bk. I, ll. 585; Bk. II, l. 465.

of the *Ancient Mariner*, save that in "Dejection" there seems to be no hope for his ultimate salvation.

> A grief without a pang, void, dark and drear,
> A stifled, drowsy, unimpassioned grief. . . .[38]

> The sky and the sea and the sea and the sky
> Lay like a load on my weary eye.[39]

In the *Ancient Mariner* Coleridge is describing the purgatory through which so many souls must pass. In "Dejection" he describes what for him must have seemed damnation, for he no longer is capable of the life that still seems so precious, paradoxically and tragically precious, since he no longer believes that there is any genuine objectivity in the communion with Nature. To the joyous man, Coleridge realizes, the world seems indeed a friendly place:

> For hope grew round me, like the wining vine,
> And fruits, and foliage, not my own, seemed mine.[40]

But Coleridge can advance no further: he does not describe Joy as a "consciousness of Whom we are."[41] He has lost the mysticism of the conversation poems. He cannot now leap from the experience of Joy to the faith that cries: "There is one life within us and abroad."

Years later, Coleridge linked an interpretation of Plotinus with the doctrine of the "Ode":

The sense of beauty subsists in simultaneous intuitive (sic) of the relation of parts, each to each, and of all to a whole exciting an immediate and absolute complacency, without intervenience, therefore, of any interest sensual or intellectual. . . . The mystics meant the same, when they defined beauty, in and through which the spirit reveals itself; and declare that the most beautiful, where the most obstacles to a full manifestation have been most perfectly overcome. . . .[42]

---

[38] E. H. Coleridge (ed.), *op. cit.*, p. 364, ll. 21-22.
[39] *Ibid.*, p. 197, ll. 250-251.   [40] *Ibid.*, p. 366, ll. 80-81.
[41] *The Prelude* (1805), Bk. XIII, ll. 108 ff. *Whom* is capitalized in the 1850 version (Bk. XIV, ll. 114 ff.).
[42] "Essays on the Fine Arts," No. 3 in *Felix Farley's Journal*, Aug., 1814, quoted from Cottle's *Early Recollections*, Appendix, V, ii, pp. 201-240.

He quotes Plotinus as follows:

When, therefore, sense beholds the form in bodies, at strife with matter, binding and vanquishing its contrary nature, and sees form gracefully shining forth in other forms, it collects together the scattered whole, and introduces it to itself and to the individual form within; and *renders it consonant, congruous, and friendly to its own intimate form.*[43]

This passage, Coleridge asserts, is faintly represented in "Dejection" although he adds that the parallelism is quite contingent. The following passage is also pertinent:

The beautiful arises from the perceived harmony of an object, whether sight or sound, with the inborn and constitutive rules of the judgment and imagination: and it is always intuitive. As light to the eye, even such is beauty to the mind, which cannot but have complacency in whatever is perceived as prefigured to its living faculties. Hence the Greeks called a beautiful object Καλον, quasi Καλοῦν, i.e. calling on the soul, which received instantly and *welcomes it as something connatural.* . . .[44]

The meaning of these passages translated into the terminology of "Dejection" is no more than this: Our "shaping imagination" delights in apprehending the objects about us. It delights in seeing many sensible objects united in a single moment of beauty. This satisfies the inner nature of thinking which always seeks an organization of scattered material. The object so perceived is, because it reflects organizing power, cheering to the mind which loves to contemplate it. This theory, although drawn, at least in part, from the work of the most mystical of philosophers, is, when taken by itself, free

[43] Enn. I, lib. vi, Ch. 3. The translation is Taylor's. Coleridge quotes in the Greek. Italics mine.

[44] Italics mine. Coleridge's borrowings from Plotinus are consistent enough with Wordsworth's description of the activity of imagination as presented in the last book of *The Prelude.* Here also we find an account of elements being drawn together or recognized as belonging together so that a material diversity takes on a unity of form. Thus the human mind participates in the making of what Wordsworth calls "transformations," wherein several elements are maintained together in "mutual domination." But Wordsworth weaves this into the notion of "objective metaphor" which is just the sort of thing which Coleridge opposes in "Dejection."

enough from any mystical corollary in harmony with the doctrine of imaginative love. "Friendship" with Nature is, strangely enough, explained upon what we might well call "epistemological" grounds. No room is left for direct communion of spirit with spirit which, according to Coleridge's earlier belief, might accompany esthetic enjoyment. In fact, Coleridge insists in the "Ode" that "In our lives alone does Nature live." And, although he admits that there seems to the joyous man to be a "life of things" he will not admit that this life exists elsewhere than in our own enthusiasm. We take, Coleridge would seem to say, our feeling of complacency and love which the beautiful object inspires for the recognition of some self beyond us which we believe experiences such emotion.

> Joy lifts thy spirit, joy attunes thy voice,
> To thee do all things live from pole to pole,
> Their life the *eddying* of thy living soul![45]

Thus Coleridge hopes that Wordsworth will remain acutely sensitive and respond in creative activity to a world which must then seem to him consonant and friendly. This world he will spontaneously believe to be animated by a spirit whose love will pulse "From earth to man, from man to earth." But this will be partly an illusion. Here Coleridge's suspicion of pantheism comes again to the fore.

The world is inanimate and cold to him who under affliction, pride, or overmuch thought or, as Wordsworth would say, anything "that is at enmity with Joy" fails to face his environment with imaginative acquiescence and delight. In such a case beauty may be recognized, but its presence is not felt. Coleridge described this as follows:

. . . when we declare an object beautiful, the contemplation or intuition of its beauty precedes the *feeling* of complacency, in order of nature at least; nay in great depression of spirits may even exist without sensibly producing it.[46]

This note, along with the words "I see, not feel, how beautiful they are" may seem to contradict the doctrine of the

[45] E. H. Coleridge (ed.), *op. cit.*, p. 368, ll. 134-136. Italics mine.
[46] *Biographia Literaria*, ed. Shawcross, II, 241.

"Ode" itself. For we are told that affliction robs one of Joy and of the shaping spirit of imagination. (How without imagination we can recognize beauty is, at least against the background of Coleridge's philosophy, difficult to understand. After all, imagination is the faculty which apprehends unity in variety, and still Coleridge argues that even in great dejection when the imagination is deadened we recognize beauty as an *organization* of various elements.)

According to Coleridge, we may, when living joylessly, recognize beauty without feeling any communion with Nature. Accordingly, we have no right to say that the feeling of communion is a genuine revelation necessarily attendant upon an experience or beauty. Is it not—when it exists at all—only our own joy somehow projected beyond us? The logic of such argument is however extremely doubtful. From the premise that a given state of mind is required for the awakening of a sense of personal unity with Nature it is hardly legitimate to conclude that this sense of communion is *nothing more than* this very state of mind itself. In the same way we might argue that all knowledge is identical with the clarity of mind which is often dependent upon good health. To some extent, "Dejection" rationalizes Coleridge's despair. It produces a philosophy which denies the possibility of the very mysticism whose passing it laments.

Furthermore, we may, as we have seen, challenge Coleridge's doctrine that beauty may be recognized and not felt. That the esthetic experience may ever be wholly devoid of feeling seems to drive us toward a purely "logical" theory of beauty, a theory according to which recognition of beauty is a purely cognitive matter. Now, there are many estheticians who feel that scientific judgment is an afterthought insofar as the appreciation of beauty is concerned. The primary act of appreciation is inseparable from the feeling of pleasure through which the apt organization of the elements announces itself. But such considerations, although tempting us to follow, would carry us far afield into problems that we may not hope to solve. It is now more important to consider Wordsworth's own attitude toward his friend's comment.

We have already indicated a parallelism of "Dejection" and the "Intimations Ode." That Wordsworth is here consciously repudiating Coleridge's teaching is clear enough from the lines:

> . . . truths that wake
> To perish never;
> Which neither listlessness, nor
> Mad endeavor
> Nor Man nor Boy
> Nor all that is at enmity with joy,
> Can utterly abolish or destroy!

And again from the lines:

> In the primal sympathy
> Which having been must ever be.

This is a flat, dogmatic denial of Coleridge's thesis. These are the only passages in Wordsworth with which I am acquainted that seem clearly directed against Coleridge's theory.[47] There are, however, lines in *The Prelude* which are, although perhaps not consciously intended to be so, pertinent to the problems which "Dejection" raises. For we may find very clear evidence that Wordsworth himself believed that certain subjective conditions supply a *sine qua non* of imaginative love.

Even the least sensitive of men are at times aware of the "domination" which Nature, or the Spirit of Nature, exerts upon the face of outward things. When moved by natural beauty, as it seems all men may be, they "cannot choose but feel" and acknowledge Nature's power.[48] Thus Wordsworth's attitude toward the members of the "loveless, ever-anxious crowd" is tempered by the assurance that their blindness belongs to the accidents rather than to the essence of their human nature. But all men are, at least, *capable* of such moments of feeling, and there are many men who are not Wordsworthian nature-mystics. Hence we must expect to find a distinction drawn between the thyrsus-bearers, who are many, and the mystics, who are few, and this distinction Wordsworth actually

---

[47] With the possible exception of *The Prelude* (1805), Bk. XI, ll. 326 ff.
[48] *Ibid.*, Bk. XIII, ll. 84 *et circa*. See also Bk. III, l. 191.

outlines. For there are higher minds who possess a truly active imagination, and who need no spectacular invitation to spiritual life. For them imagination seems to perform a function similar to that of Joy in the "Dejection Ode." They are "wed to Nature" or to Nature's Soul in the

> . . . consciousness
> Of Whom they are, habitually infused
> Through every image and through every thought.[49]

Such consciousness, coupled with the heightened sensitivity and insight into matters humane which an active imagination achieves, constitutes what Coleridge might well have called in the language of "Dejection" "purity of heart":

> Hence sovereignty within and peace at will
> Emotion which best foresight need not fear
> Most worthy then of trust when most intense.
> Hence cheerfulness in every act of life
> Hence truth in moral judgments and delight
> That fails not in the external universe.[50]

Joy is inseparable from the moral freedom and the imaginative activity which thus accompany one another. Therefore even for Wordsworth there is a point of view from which he might exclaim, "The fountains are within!" And, in fact, he does, and quite as emphatically as Coleridge, saying of imagination and love:

> Here must thou be O Man!
> Strength to thyself; no Helper hast thou here;
> Here keepest thou thy individual state:
> No other can divide with thee this work,
> No secondary hand can intervene
> To fashion this ability; it is thine
> (The prime and vital principle is thine)
> In the recesses of thy nature, far
> From any reach of outward fellowship
> Or is not thine at all.[51]

[49] *The Prelude* (1805), Bk. XIII, ll. 114-116.
[50] *Ibid.*, Bk. XIII, ll. 114 ff.
[51] *Ibid.*, Bk. XIII, ll. 185 ff.; also Bk. XI, l. 333.

To be sure, Wordsworth is here emphasizing the fact that man cannot draw this high endowment from his fellows. He is not speaking directly of man's relation to Nature. The emphatic mention of the "prime and vital principle" seems to transcend the context. It is apparently possession of this prime principle which constitutes a "higher mind" capable of esthetic creation and of response to subtle, hidden beauty. It is this principle which enables the mind to transcend merely sensuous experience and "To hold communion with the invisible world."[52] We shall find later that the concept of the "higher mind" must be considered also in connection with Wordsworth's political philosophy. We may summarize Wordsworth's attitude toward the philosophy of "Dejection" as follows:

1. Wordsworth, feeling secure in the intensity of his own experience, flatly denies that imaginative love, the primal sympathy with the life that pulses at the heart of things can, once aroused, ever be wholly lost. But he agrees with Coleridge that life of practical care and mad endeavor is an enemy of joy and hence of love. Again, unlike Coleridge, he does not consider reason as essentially opposed to imaginative love.

2. Wordsworth believes that all men when moved by natural beauty cannot choose but acknowledge some faint monition of this richer sympathy. This Coleridge does not, apparently, admit.

3. Wordsworth does, however, realize that full communion with the soul of the world—with God—is a privilege of a few higher minds. These minds are endowed with an active imagination which needs very little to arouse it.[53] This imagination is of moral as well as of mystical power and produces a harmony of spirit which makes joyous communion possible. But he does not follow Coleridge through the doubtful "argument" that, because such a state of character and happy emotion is a necessary condition of mystical insight, such insight itself is nothing but this emotion somehow objectified.

[52] Ibid., Bk. XIII, l. 105.
[53] This latter point is made by Mark Akenside in his Pleasures of Imagination in fashion quite similar to Wordsworth's. (See the fragment of Book IV added by Akenside in the edition of 1768, ll. 58 ff.)

From all this we may conclude that Coleridge's rebuke of Wordsworth's idealism which he administered so gently in the "Dejection Ode" is not a very weighty one. And, whatever our prejudices or loyalties in the difficult question of the validity of mysticism, we surely have no reason to believe that Coleridge has contributed anything of weight to the case against Wordsworth. In fact, when we examine Wordsworth's teaching with the problem of "Dejection" in mind, we realize anew the subtlety and insight with which he explored his spiritual experience.

In fact, Coleridge himself in *Biographia Literaria* turned again in a happier mood toward a philosophy of idealism in which mind and its object are considered as complementary moments of one and the same process. This later speculation belongs, however, to another phase of Coleridge's development and has little to do with the emotional and spiritual problems which we have been discussing. It does, however, owe much to Boehme, as Coleridge himself asserts, and it parallels the thought of the last books of *The Prelude*. Furthermore, Coleridge is inclined to condone the pantheistic tendency which this thought contains.[54]

[54] See above, p. 66, and below, p. 261.

CHAPTER VI

Of Human Freedom

A. C. BRADLEY once remarked in passing that Wordsworth and Spinoza have something in common. And, on the other hand, students of Spinoza like Mr. A. C. Wolf have made similar, although more qualified, comments. Among recent writers on Wordsworth we may mention Mr. Melvin M. Rader, who touches several times upon the Spinozian aspect of Wordsworth's thought. To me the similarity has always seemed to be both obvious and significant, although I have always felt that the same may be said of the differences that, so to speak, qualify and condition this resemblance.

Once we have come to appreciate the sentiment of Being we cannot deny that the Wordsworthian awareness of the world is *sub specie aeternitatis*. The sentiment of Being is as essential to Spinozism as it is to Wordsworth's thought. It points directly toward a theory of Nature as an all-inclusive unity, apparent to finite observation as *facies totius universi*, the universal presence of the world. To quote the American mystic, Paul Benjamin Blood: "Indeed we may fancy an intelligence which, instead of regarding things as simply owning entity, should regard chiefly their background as affected by the holes which they are making in it."[1] This, after all, is but another and less dogmatic way of stating Spinoza's famous dictum, "All determination is negation."

But let there be no misunderstanding. Neither Wordsworth nor Coleridge should be called faithful followers of Spinoza. Their philosophical background is far too complex for that. But the all-encompassing substance, the *deus sive natura* of Spinoza, which is at once corporeal and imbued with intelligence, and within whose scope all finite beings partake of a universal life so that "all individual things, although in

---

[1] See William James, *Memories and Studies* (New York, 1911), p. 380.

different degrees, are animated"[2]—this unity of Being stands as close to the Nature of Wordsworth as the world of a strict logician can ever stand to the world of a poet—far closer than in most instances, for in this case both the logician and the poet describe an intuitive and deeply religious consciousness of Nature as a whole, of Nature as the eternal matrix of our human life; and this intuition is said to constitute the culmination at once of science and of the life of the spirit.

The similarity is obvious enough nor is external evidence lacking, if we are willing to follow our usual procedure of supposing that Coleridge's conversation was rich enough and vivid enough largely to take the place in Wordsworth's "education" of a more formal study of the philosophers. Certainly Coleridge knew Spinoza[3] and talked of him to Wordsworth,

[2] *Ethics*, Part II, prop. XIII, n.

[3] I append a summary of such evidence. In *Biographia Literaria*, Chapter X, Coleridge writes that while he was living by the Quantock Hills (the time of his closest intimacy with Wordsworth) his head was with Spinoza but his heart with Paul and John. There are also several bits of evidence that refer to a time but little later than this. In 1802 we find Coleridge writing, in a note, communicated to his literary executors by Wordsworth, the following comment on Sir Thomas Brown:

"Strong feeling and an active intellect conjoined, lead almost necessarily, in the first stage of philosophizing, to Spinosism. Sir T. Brown was a Spinosist without knowing it" (T. M. Raysor, *Coleridge's Miscellaneous Criticism*, Cambridge, Mass., 1936, p. 253). Coleridge here speaks with a slight condescension of Spinozism. It belongs to the "first stage" of philosophizing. This is probably because of the pantheism actually present or at least latent in Spinoza's writing, against which we may imagine Coleridge warning Wordsworth with only partial success.

And again we learn that in 1808 Coleridge still tended to find Spinozism in Thomas Brown. There is an interesting note to Part II, section 14. Brown has written:

"God, being all goodnesse, can love nothing but himself; he loves us but for that part which is, as it were, himselfe, and the traduction of his Holy Spirit."

Coleridge comments, "This recalls a sublime thought of Spinosa. Every true virtue is a part of that love, with which God loveth himself."

This is very important. For Spinoza the love "with which God loveth himself" is the "intellectual love," which appears in *The Prelude*, as we shall see below.

In later life Coleridge often spoke of Spinoza, placing his *Ethics*, with the *Novum Organum* and the *Critique of Pure Reason*, as one of the three great works that have appeared since the introduction of Christianity (*Biographia Literaria*, chap. ix, p. 16).

That his conversation was full of Spinoza around 1798 and later is very likely. While in Germany at this period, he conversed frequently of Spinozism,

as any reader of *Biographia Literaria* will recall. In 1814, it
is true, Wordsworth insisted that *The Excursion* was free from
pantheism, and he mentions "spinosistic" as an epithet which
his poetry does not deserve. He is here referring to the
thought of *The Excursion*, and not to *The Prelude* in its original form, where pantheism stands out boldly inviting the more
cautious revisions which were in progress when in 1814 Wordsworth repudiated Spinozism entirely. (Wordsworth had repudiated Spinoza's ethics some seven or eight years earlier.)
Wordsworth's mention of Spinoza follows:

> She talks of my being a worshipper of nature, a passionate expres-
> sion utterd incautiously in the Poem upon the Wye has led her into
> this mistake. She, reading in cold heartedness & substituting the letter
> for the Spirit—Unless I am mistaken (there is nothing?) of this kind
> in the Excursion—There is indeed a passage towards the end of the
> 4th Book where the Wanderer introduces the Simile of the Boy &
> the Shell And what follows—That has something ordinarily but
> absurdly called Spinosistic—But the intelligent reader will easily see
> the *dramatic* propriety of the passage The Wanderer in the begin-
> ning of the book had given vent to his own devotional feelings and
> announced in some degree his own creed. He is here preparing the
> way for more distinct conceptions of the Deity by reminding the Soli-
> tary of such religious feelings as cannot but exist in the minds of those
> who affect Atheism—She condemns me for not distinguishing between
> Nature as the work of God & God himself— But where does she
> find this Doctrine inculcated? Whence does she gather that the
> author of the Excursion looks upon Nature & God as the same? He
> does not indeed consider the Supreme Being as bearing the same rela-
> tion to the Universe as a Watch maker bears to a watch—In fact
> there is nothing in the course of religious education adopted in this
> country & in the use made by us of the Holy Scriptures that appears
> to me so injurious as the perpetually talking about *making* by God—
> Oh! that your Correspondent had heard a conversation which I had
> in bed with my sweet little boy four & a half years old upon this
> subject the other morning "How did God make me? Where is God?

---

giving the following concentrated definition of this philosophy: "Each thing has
a life of its own, and we are all one life" (Clement Carlyon, *Early Years and
Late Reflections*, London, 1856, I, 193 ff.). And then there is the famous anec-
dote, in Chapter X of the *Biographia*, in which Coleridge and Wordsworth are
overheard discussing one *Spy Nozy*, during their sojourn by the Quantock Hills.

How does he speak? He never spoke to *me*" I told him that God was a *spirit*, that he was not like his flesh which he could touch; but more like his thoughts in his mind which he could not touch—The wind was tossing the fir trees and the sky & light were dancing about in their dark branches as seen through the Window Noting these fluctuations he exclaimed eagerly "There is a bit of him—I see it there" This is not meant entirely for Fathers prattle; but for Heaven's sake in your religious talk with children say as little as possible about *making*. One of the main objects of the *Recluse* is to reduce the calculating understanding to its proper level among the human faculties— Therefore my book must be disliked by the Unitarians as their religion rests entirely on that basis & therefore is in fact no religion at all;— but—I won't say what—[4]

As Mr. Rader has pointed out,[5] the latter part of this quotation indicates that Wordsworth was, even in 1814, willing to think of God as immanent in Nature. This is certainly closer to Spinoza than to Deism or to Unitarianism. More important is the observation that the passage following upon the simile of the boy and the shell in *The Excursion* contains something often absurdly mistaken for Spinozism. From this we may draw two conclusions. In the first place, we may infer that Wordsworth knows what Spinozism is and, in the second place, that he knows it to be something different from the sentiments and insights expressed in the passage from *The Excursion* already mentioned. Both these conclusions are consistent with our interpretation of Wordsworth's natural religion and even with our hypothesis that, through Coleridge, Wordsworth owes something to Spinoza.

Even if Wordsworth were clearly conscious of the ultimately Spinozian origin of the concepts which he had discussed with Coleridge years earlier and expressed in *The Prelude*, he might still have quite honestly denied that the passage in question from *The Excursion* is Spinozian in nature. After all, the transcendental consciousness there described is based upon esthetic insight, and Wordsworth also mentions *faith*. Spinoza's intellectual love is based upon noetic or strictly cognitive in-

⁴ Edith J. Morley, *The Correspondence of Crabb Robinson with the Wordsworth Circle* (Oxford, 1927), I, 79-80.   ⁵ *Op. cit.*, pp. 179 and 203-204.

sight and is certainly quite distinct from any act of faith. A difference between *The Prelude* and *The Excursion* here becomes apparent. In 1805, to be sure, Wordsworth was willing to merge esthetic and noetic insight, but the philosophy of *The Prelude,* unlike that of *The Excursion,* has little need of an act of faith as an external support.

Spinoza's thought, owing to certain unresolved conflicts that lie within it, is the forerunner of at least two movements in modern philosophy. It foreshadows the mechanism and determinism of certain eighteenth- and nineteenth-century "philosophies of science" and also that mystical pantheism which appears, at times, in conjunction with and, at times, in opposition to such philosophy. It is, of course, toward the latter movement that Wordsworth and, to a lesser degree, Coleridge were attracted. There was, in their day, a strong tendency to reread Spinoza without emphasizing his tendency toward mechanism. Coleridge's interpretation of Spinoza is epitomized in the sentence, "Each thing has a life of its own, and we are all one life." This is to emphasize the vitalistic pantheism which Spinoza entertained, even though he could find no place for recognition of cosmic purpose, teleology, or final causation in Nature. After all, we must remember that for Spinoza one "attribute," or pervasive aspect, of the world is the system of Cartesian mechanism, the world of physical extension. What Coleridge has done is to minimize, if not to ignore, this Cartesian element in Spinozism. He may be said to extract the Renaissance spirit from Spinoza's work and to ignore the theory of the physical world, the Cartesian mechanism, which is none too successfully combined with it. What he does is virtually to reduce Spinoza to sixteenth-century pantheism, to Bruno or Campanella. Incidentally, this brings one much closer to Boehme, who is in the Romantic period occasionally compared with Spinoza, for instance by Schelling.[6]

We must be ready to admit that Coleridge's philosophy of 1798 and of 1800, along with that of *The Prelude* in its first draft, does not constitute a complete acceptance of Spinoza's

[6] *Works,* 2d division, III, 123-124.

system. As we know, Wordsworth's philosophy turns upon esthetic considerations, and these Spinoza hardly found time to discuss. But Spinozism, as a tradition, has a tendency to overflow its original boundaries and to become the source of an esthetically oriented pantheism, a philosophy of the "one life within us and abroad." This tendency may be observed in the writings of Herder and of Goethe. And it seems to have been such a reconstructed Spinozism that appealed to Coleridge. That a study of Herder's work was the occasion of Coleridge's Neo-Spinozism is by no means unlikely. We know that Coleridge was, or was about to become, acquainted with some of Herder's writing by 1799.[7]

Herder's reconstruction of Spinozism is outlined in the following passages. The reader will notice that Herder dislikes the Cartesian elements in Spinoza:

Philolaus: . . . (Spinoza) cannot often and strongly enough say: "God is an extensum." Yet what applies to time applies equally to space, and if time be entirely incomparable with the idea of eternity, then space is equally incommensurable with the idea of a "simple Substance," which Spinoza however insists upon with rock-like firmness.

Theophron: What you say is very true. But if you note where Spinoza propounds this error, the reason for it will be immediately obvious.

Philolaus: He propounds it when he distinguishes spirit from matter, that is, thought from extension.

Theophron: Are matter and extension then the same? There you see the Cartesian error from which the philosopher could not free himself, and which makes half of his system obscure. Descartes defined matter in terms of extension. It would just as well be defined in terms of time, for both the one and the other are external conditions of its existence in spatial and temporal relations. Thus both become also the necessary conditions of measurement for all thinking minds, which are themselves limited by place and time, but they never become the essence of matter.[8]

---

[7] See his letter to Southey of September 24, 1799.
[8] J. G. Herder, God, Some Conversations (1787), tr. F. H. Burkhardt (New York, 1940), pp. 101-102. (Suphan ed., XVI, 446-449.)

Thus Herder repudiates the strong traces of Cartesian mechanism which stand out in Spinoza's thought.   Before Herder has completed his study of Spinoza, he offers the reader a sort of Neo-Spinozism.   Here the Cartesian *thought* and *extension*, the so-called "attributes" of Spinoza's world-substance, are reconsidered from an organic point of view: "All the forces of nature function organically.   Every organization is nothing else than a system of living forces which serve a principal force in accordance with eternal laws of wisdom, goodness and beauty."[9]

Here is something very similar to Coleridge's vitalism which he expressed in the words, "we are all one life."   Such an interpretation of Spinoza is very free, but it is not an arbitrary one.   According to Spinoza, as Herder emphasizes, every finite entity exerts power to maintain its own being, to persist in its own existence, and this fact constitutes the ultimate motivation of all energy.   All finite beings are to some degree animate; and in each case the degree of animation depends upon the "perfection" or level of organization which the finite being possesses.

When we consider Herder's vitalistic Spinozism so similar to Coleridge's interpretation, and when we recall that Herder was a ready champion of a romantic theory of literature not unlike that of the Lake poets, we come to recognize him as a most important figure in any study of Wordsworth's philosophy.   Consider, for instance, the following:

[If] we weaken ourselves through abstraction, separate and split up our senses, and shred our whole feeling into little threads which no longer feel anything wholly and purely,—[then] naturally the great sense of "God, the Omnipresent in the world" must thereby become weakened and dulled.[10]

Consider in connection with this the following brilliant passage from the *Conversations:*

[9] Burkhardt (tr.), *op. cit.,* p. 190; Suphan ed., XVI, 569.
[10] *Alteste Urkunde des Menschengeschlechts* (Suphan ed.), VI, 273; Burkhardt (tr.), *op. cit.,* pp. 10-11.

Theano: . . . Yesterday, Philolaus, you wished to know the laws of God's regimen in the world, or, as you put it, the symbols expressive of His reality, power, wisdom and goodness.   But how is it possible that Theophron should draw so few drops out of the ocean which flows around us?   Yesterday I heard almost with disgust how you expressed views as if the existence of God were unknowable, and I was astonished Theophron, that you could wish to engage in these petty subtleties.   It seems to me that the existence of a being can be known only through being and the observation of it, and not through arbitrary conceptions and empty words, any more than it can be eliminated by the latter.   There is a saying that we become neither rich nor satisfied through dreams, and just as little do we become so through words.   We are human beings, and as such, it seems to me, we must learn to know God as He has really offered and revealed Himself to us.   Through ideas we apprehend Him only as an idea, through words ,only as a word, but through observations of nature, through the use of our powers, through the enjoyment of life, we enjoy Him as a real Existence full of force and life.   If you call this enthusiasm, then I shall gladly be an enthusiast, for I would rather see and enjoy the real rose than dream with barren racking of my brains, of an imagined or painted rose.

Theophron: Bravo, Theano!   Yet you see the rose which you enjoy and you would not blindfold your eyes because of that enjoyment.   And what are you working at there?   Why, you are embroidering the flower yourself.   You are then imitating the art of nature, which only your seeing eye made visible to you, and which now your mind's eye, your lively memory as it were, is tracing for the needle. Do not, therefore, exclude thought from any feeling or from any enjoyment of the creation. It is as necessary to our observation of God, as the image of the sketch in your mind is necessary to your working needle. He would misunderstand humanity who sought only to taste and feel the Creator without seeing or apprehending Him.[11]

Here surely no comment is necessary to indicate the similarity between Herder on one hand and Wordsworth and Coleridge on the other.   Compare also the thought of the following passage with the refusal of the poets to "parcel out [the] intellect by geometric rules."[12]

[11] Burkhardt (tr.), *op. cit.*, pp. 162-163; Suphan ed., XVI, 532-533.
[12] *The Prelude*, Bk. II, ll. 208-209.

We are accustomed to attribute to the soul a group of *underpowers* *(unter kräfte)* such as imagination and foresight, the gift of poetic composition and memory. . . . We will never unearth the roots of these powers, if we consider them only from above as ideas, which are located in the soul, or if we separate them one from another as special departmentalized activities and conceive of them as independent, particular entities. In imaginative recall, in memory, and in foresight must the *one* God-like power of our soul present itself, the inner reflective power, consciousness or apperception: through this power man possesses understanding, knowledge, will, and freedom. . . .[13]

The term "underpowers" reminds us of *The Prelude,* Book I, line 163.

In his work "On Perception and Feeling," from which the above quotation is taken, Herder sought "to bridge the traditional distinctions between body and soul, emotions and intellect, knowledge and will." He maintained that there are no distinct and isolated soul-faculties, but only grades of a single force. He stresses the relation between perception and feeling, and especially the importance of the latter in human knowledge. The body is a complex of forces of different grades; the soul is a force of the highest grade. Since the connection which it has with the bodily forces is the most intimate possible, there can be, he says, no psychology without a physiology.[14] The little treatise "On Perception and Feeling" closes with a tribute to Spinoza and a brief appreciation of his theory of freedom in its ethical and religious contexts.

It was, indeed, Spinoza's ethical thought which had the profounder influence upon Wordsworth. In Spinoza's system of morality one of the central concepts is that of intuition. Wordsworth seems to have identified this "intuition," at least insofar as its moral power is concerned, with his own term "imagination." This becomes particularly obvious when he tells us that imagination is inseparably united with "intellectual love," which is described as the emotional mainspring of a pantheistic religion.[15] Some students may feel it is arbitrary to insist that Wordsworth's "intellectual love" must be a

[13] Suphan ed., VIII, 195.   [14] Burkhardt (tr.), *op. cit.,* pp. 12-13.
[15] *The Prelude,* Bk. XIII, ll. 53-59.

romantic version of Spinoza's *amor intellectualis dei.* And
still that is just what I am inclined to do. *The Prelude* is
addressed to Coleridge with whom Wordsworth has held discussions of Spinoza. The "intellectual love of God," as any
student of philosophy will readily confirm, constitutes, as a
phrase, virtually the epitome of Spinoza's religion. Now,
when the term appears, in a context quite consistent with
Spinoza's philosophical religion, there seems to be small ground
for doubt that Wordsworth is referring to a Spinozian background, which Coleridge of course would understand at once.
In later versions of *The Prelude* Wordsworth changed "intellectual love" to "spiritual love." For the general public this
is clearer. The *love* of the conclusion of *The Prelude* is certainly a spiritual experience even as Spinoza's *amor intellectualis dei* is spiritual, being directed toward suprasensuous
objects[16] and carrying a religious sentiment. But when writing
for Coleridge, Wordsworth found "intellectual love" a far
more illuminating term, for, as we shall see, this love in its
cognitive aspect is akin to "reason in its most exalted mood";
and this phrase exactly describes the intuitive insight of Spinoza, which we shall mention below:

> This love more intellectual cannot be
> Without Imagination, which, in truth,
> Is but another name for absolute strength
> And clearest insight, amplitude of mind,
> And reason in her most exalted mood.
> This faculty hath been the moving soul
> Of our long labour: we have traced the stream
> From darkness, and the very place of birth
> In its blind cavern, whence is faintly heard
> The sound of waters; follow'd it to light

[16] This does not mean that imagination, or even Spinoza's intuition, would be
possible in isolation from the life of the senses, but that in the final vision which
imagination supports more is revealed than can possibly be included in a philosophy of sensationalism, which is enslaved to "vulgar sense." For Wordsworth
"intellectual" is not a synonym for "rational" but for suprasensuous and spiritual.
See Havens, *op. cit.*, pp. 329 and 563. As Mr. Havens insists, "intellectual"
connotes the German *vernunft* rather than *verstand*. It implies far-reaching
vision. It is prepared to grasp "great truths" rather than to analyze little ones
(*The Prelude*, Bk. XII, ll. 56 ff.).

> And open day, accompanied its course
> Among the ways of Nature, afterwards
> Lost sight of it bewilder'd and engulph'd,
> Then given it greeting, as it rose once more
> With strength, reflecting in its solemn breast
> The works of man and face of human life,
> And lastly, from its progress have we drawn
> The feeling of life endless, the great thought
> By which we live, Infinity and God.
> Imagination having been our theme,
> So also hath that intellectual love,
> For they are each in each, and cannot stand
> Dividually.[17]

We may be reminded that the term "intellectual" appears elsewhere in Wordsworth, notably in Book I, lines 575-585, of *The Prelude,* where sensuously perceived material is said to take on an "intellectual charm" even in the earliest stages of the poet's esthetic development. Even while still close to its earliest sources, imagination contains something of the intellectual love; and at this early time this mode of feeling has a pantheistic tone, a premonition of later insight which even in its primitive form

> ... surely must belong
> To those first-born affinities that fit
> Our new existence to existing things
> And, in our dawn of being, constitute
> The bond of union betwixt life and joy.[18]

In all probability, Wordsworth is describing the awakening of the sense of Being which in its fullest development coincides with many features of Spinoza's pantheism. In fact, he suggests in Book XIII, lines 172 and following, the notion of an almost continuous development.

But there is further very interesting evidence. When in 1808 Coleridge wrote that "every true virtue is a part of that love with which God loveth himself,"[19] he certainly referred

---

[17] *The Prelude,* Bk. XIII, ll. 166 ff.
[18] *Ibid.,* Bk. I, ll. 554-558.   [19] See above, p. 173 n.

to Spinoza's "intellectual love" which, we shall see, is presented by Spinoza as possessing this high dignity.   Thus Coleridge is insisting that the "intellectual love" contains all "true virtue."   This is exactly what Wordsworth asserts in the conclusion of *The Prelude*, although, to be sure, he uses another vocabulary.   He describes the intellectual love and imagination as going hand in hand, inseparable from one another; and, further, imagination is recognized as the central power which supports all virtue.   The life of virtue and genuine freedom thus depends upon the presence of intellectual love.   In 1808 Coleridge is repeating an ethical doctrine which Wordsworth had outlined in the first draft of *The Prelude*, where he was in all probability recording discussions which he and his friend had shared at an even earlier time.   Our line of reasoning will become clearer, once we have presented a full account of Spinoza's doctrine of intuition and the pantheistic love of God which accompanies it.

At any rate, Spinoza's spiritual resemblance to Wordsworth is clearly revealed when he tells us that through the intellectual love of God we become clearly conscious of our true dependence upon God or Nature and, as he puts it, *"sentimus experimurque nos aeternos esse"* ("we feel and experience our immortality").   This is Spinoza's mysticism which sometimes followed upon the concentration of intellectual attention that his philosophy demanded of him.   In Wordsworth's case it is usually an esthetic rather than an intellectual concentration of attention which introduces such awareness.   But the essential experience is the same.

Before we present the detail of Spinoza's doctrine, it will be helpful to consider the background of Wordsworth's thinking which immediately preceded his acceptance of it.   In Spinoza's theory of ethics, Wordsworth found a way of overcoming some of the almost technical difficulties that had troubled him since his study of Godwin, which seems to have taken place shortly after his return from France.   At that time Wordsworth felt the need of an objective and impersonal rationalism as an ethical and political guide.   This need had,

Wordsworth thought, become manifest through the failure of the French Revolution to avoid grave excesses. Wordsworth's earlier and perhaps naïve trust in the efficacy of a popular wisdom, undisciplined by any scientific thinking or recondite philosophical reflection, had been weakened not so much by the Terror as by the willingness of the French people to turn toward foreign conquest. Thus as he tells us in *The Prelude*, Book X, he turned eagerly toward a strict rationalism in ethical and political thought. This rationalism, it is now generally supposed, had its source in Godwin; and the happier philosophy which preceded it in Wordsworth's mind sprang, in outline, from Rousseau's theory of the general will that was so widespread throughout revolutionary thought.

Under the guidance of Godwin, Wordsworth rushed eagerly into ethical speculation, and, true to the spirit of the old Enlightenment, demanded strictly rational proof for everything he sought. In *The Prelude* he describes this inquiry as a pitiless application of reason.[20] Thus it is not surprising that his philosophy soon failed to answer the questions that it raised:

> Thus I fared,
> Dragging all passions, notions, shapes of faith,
> Like culprits to the bar; suspiciously
> Calling the mind to establish in plain day
> Her titles and her honours, now believing,
> Now disbelieving, endlessly perplexed
> With impulse, motive, right and wrong, the ground
> Of moral obligation, what the rule
> And what the sanction, till, demanding *proof*,
> And seeking it in everything, I lost
> All feeling of conviction, and, in fine,
> Sick, wearied out with contrarieties,
> Yielded up moral questions in despair.[21]

In his confusion he asked himself upon what ground and on what authority do we call this action good and that bad? What, after all, is worth while in itself and the standard of

---

[20] Bk. X, ll. 877 ff.   [21] *Ibid.*, Bk. X, ll. 889 ff.

goodness? He had no answers to these questions, and he
feared that there were none.

> "The lordly attributes
> Of will and choice," I bitterly exclaimed,
> "What are they but a mockery of a Being
> Who hath no concern of his a test
> Of good and evil; knows not what to fear
> Or hope for, what to covet or to shun;
> And who, if those could be discerned, would yet
> Be little profited, would see and ask
> Where is the obligation to enforce?"[22]

Perplexed and baffled, Wordsworth doubted man's ability to
obey an acknowledged moral law; he feared that man must
always

> act amiss
> The dupe of folly, or the slave of crime.[23]

All three of these doubts might well have been inspired by
reflection upon Godwin's argument. For Godwin considered
virtue as much a matter of intellectual understanding as of
moral intention. The aim of virtue, he believed, is the pro-
motion of happiness. Thus to be truly virtuous a man must
have a deep understanding of what human happiness is, as well
as the desire to foster it.

Hence it appears, first, that virtue consists in a desire for the benefit
of the species: and, secondly, that the desire can only be denominated
virtuous, which flows from a distinct perception of the value, and
consequently of the nature of the thing desired. But how extensive
must be the capacity that comprehends the full value of that benefit
which is the object of virtue! It must begin with a collective idea of
the human species. It must discriminate, among all the different
causes that produce a pleasurable state of mind, that which produces
the most exquisite and durable pleasure. . . . It [eminent virtue]
demands that I should perceive in what manner social intercourse may
be conducive to virtue and felicity, and imagine the unspeakable ad-
vantages that may arise from a coincidence and succession of generous
efforts.[24]

[22] *Ibid.* (1850), Bk. XI, ll. 309 ff.   [23] *Ibid.*, Bk. XI, ll. 319 ff.
[24] William Godwin, *Enquiry Concerning Political Justice* (Dublin, 1793), VI,

From this it would follow that virtue requires something akin to omniscience. No wonder Wordsworth despaired of human virtue and found Godwinism intolerable. Indeed, he was probably wholly at ease in the acceptance of Godwinian ethics for but a very short time. After all, his opinion of Godwinian philosophy expressed in *The Prelude* is less damning than that which appears by suggestion and implication in *The Borderers,* written in 1795 and 1796, before Wordsworth had, as Mr. dc Selincourt points out, found any philosophy to put in the place of Godwinian rationalism and determinism. In *The Borderers* the ethics of independent reason is presented as a scheme of rationalization cleverly adapted to further the self-justification of an intelligent but uneasy criminal. Oswald, or Rivers as he was first called, has come to accept an ethical rationalism, because of the very weaknesses of this doctrine which enable him to interpret his crime as the beginning of a career of rational "freedom," a life of "enlightenment," free of conventional or sentimental restrictions and even of all conscientious scruples, a life wholly devoted to self-assertion and the exercise of worldly power. The principal support of such a philosophy is the doctrine of determinism, by appeal to which any criminal may attribute the origin of all good and evil actions in himself and in others to the blind workings of a mechanical order of nature, which is quite indifferent to all human standards and quite lacking in any end or purpose of its own.

> *Osw.*   Remorse—
> It cannot live with thought; think on, think on,
> And it will die. What! in this universe,
> Where the least things control the greatest, where
> The faintest breath that breathes can move a world;
> What! feel remorse, where, if a cat had sneezed,
> A leaf had fallen, the thing had never been
> Whose very shadow gnaws us to the vitals.

---

235. For a fuller account of Wordsworth in relation to Godwin, see Emile Legouis, *The Early Life of William Wordsworth,* tr. J. W. Matthews (London, 1921), pp. 259-267.

> *Mar.* Now, whither are you wandering? That a man,
> So used to suit his language to the time,
> Should thus so widely differ from himself—
> It is most strange.[25]

Oswald argues that recognition of this determinism frees us from sentiment and from remorse.

> As time advances either we become
> The prey or masters of our own past deeds.[26]

The denial of all conventional and traditional moral scruples seems to Oswald a preparation through which the hero must pass if he is to realize his independence. Thus Oswald praises Marmaduke, who has broken away, albeit with much misgiving, from convention:

> To-day you have thrown off a tyranny
> That lives but in the torpid acquiescence
> Of our emasculated souls, the tyranny
> Of the world's masters, with the musty rules
> By which they hold their craft from age to age.
> You have obeyed the only law that sense
> Submits to recognise; the immediate law,
> From the clear light of circumstances flashed
> Upon an independent Intellect.[27]

Oswald attempts by drastic methods to educate Marmaduke, the chivalrous Robin Hood of the Border, to share his aspirations and his crimes, for, as he says, fellowship we *must* have, even though the ideal of such rational "enlightenment"

---

[25] *The Borderers*, Act III, ll. 1560-1571. The reader will recall that Spinoza is a determinist as well as Oswald, but his determinism is of another pattern: every being tends to express or to fulfill its own essence. Thus events do not necessarily control moral issues. The control may issue from the very natures of the persons involved. This possible view of determinism is quite ignored by Oswald. It is openly scorned by Godwin, who insists that the theory of self-determinism is only a stopgap. Ultimately the individual is determined from without (*Political Justice*, Bk. IV, chap. v). Godwinian determinism is mechanical. He recognizes nothing comparable to organic systems. His universe is truly a "heap of little things," bound together by abstract law which we can learn slowly to recognize without understanding.

[26] *The Borderers*, Act III, ll. 1521-1522.

[27] *Ibid.*, Act III, ll. 1488-1496.

and indifference to human sentiment seems rather to glorify solitude. Oswald recognizes no moral standards; he praises none of the virtues except in that he asserts that the free man may be proud of his ability to endure suffering.

> *Osw.*   Ay, look up—
> Cast round you your mind's eye, and you will learn
> Fortitude is the child of Enterprise:
> Great actions move our admiration chiefly
> Because they carry in themselves an earnest
> That we can suffer greatly.
> *Mar.*   Very true.
> *Osw.* Action is transitory—a step, a blow,
> The motion of a muscle—this way or that
> 'Tis done, and in the after-vacancy
> We wonder at ourselves like men betrayed:
> Suffering is permanent, obscure and dark,
> And shares the nature of infinity.
> *Mar.* Truth—and I feel it.[28]

How this admiration is compatible with the rigid and mechanical determinism expressed in the same play we are not told. The moral of the play is simple enough, as Wordsworth himself expressed it; it shows the "dangerous use that may be made of reason when a man has committed a great crime." It follows from this that reason is not the final arbiter of right and wrong, as Godwin so eagerly taught.[29]

Wordsworth's later ethics of imagination appeals to the emotions as well as to the reason and even combines both in the notion of "feeling intellect." It offers freedom, but freedom as the realization of the whole personality. Such freedom includes emotional sympathies. The free man need not strive to free himself of any genuine human emotion. Such a philosophy must aim to avoid the lifeless abstractions of the understanding and to grasp ethical situations in their full human setting. It also strives to remain in contact with those sources of emotional energy latent in a natural religion of mystical background.

[28] *Ibid.*, Act III, ll. 1533-1545.
[29] Cf. De Selincourt's note on Godwin in his edition of *The Prelude*, p. 586.

Against the setting of Godwinian ethics the moral theory of Spinoza, as expounded by Coleridge, was to appear most attractive. Its weaknesses, although real, are as nothing compared to the difficulties latent in Godwinism.

Coleridge seems to have translated much of Spinoza's vocabulary into contemporary terms. This may cause some difficulty at first glance. Spinoza uses *imagination* as a synonym for "mere experience" or a vague common-sense apprehension of things; Spinoza's term *intuition* corresponds, insofar as ethical doctrine is concerned, with Wordsworth's imagination.

The phases of Spinoza's philosophy that seem most to have attracted Wordsworth are the accounts of intellectual love and the masterful analysis of the act of knowing, which appears in various forms throughout the philosopher's three original metaphysical works. In these related doctrines, Wordsworth found a further background for his philosophy of imagination, a background which supplemented ideas drawn from Boehme.

We may know objects (and the relations pertaining between them), Spinoza teaches, in one of three ways.[30] We may apprehend them through mere experience without grasping the rationale of their activity or of their relations to other objects. Thus, to use Spinoza's example, if we solve a problem in proportion by applying the rule that the product of the means is equal to the product of the extremes, a rule which we have seen in successful operation without discovering the reason of its validity, we depend upon mere experience. Such knowledge is prone to error and confusion, for it is based upon no insight into the nature of the objects known, and is perforce superficial. But despite this, mere experience possesses a virtue that the second method of knowledge lacks, namely, the warmth and vividness of that which we immediately sense. For the second mode of knowledge, which is called Reason, although infallible, deals only with the common properties of

[30] *Ethics*, II, 40, n. 2; *Short Treatise Concerning God, Man and His Happiness*, tr. A. Wolf (London, 1910), pp. 69 ff. It is only with the *Ethics* that Wordsworth could have been acquainted. The *Short Treatise* existed at the time only in manuscript. It reveals, however, in certain passages so striking a resemblance between the two points of view that the student should not fail to consult it.

objects of which the theorems of geometry and the laws of physics are examples. Thus if we solve the proportion by making use of the nineteenth proposition of the seventh book of Euclid, granted that we understand the demonstration, we employ reason to make use of the common properties of extended objects. Such knowledge is abstract and gives us the rationale without the object, just as mere experience gives us the object without the rationale. Intuition, the third mode of knowledge, combines the good qualities of both mere experience and reason, giving us the object and the rationale inseparably united. Thus, in solving at a glance the proportion 2:4::3:x, we combine the certainty of the rational demonstration with the familiar vividness of experience.

This mode of knowledge Spinoza considered the most excellent of all. The human mind, he tells us, rejoices in it for its own value; for, when intuiting, the mind is most active. The activity of intuition, we might say, stands to that of mere experience, as the activity of a set of tennis to that of languidly shuffling from one room to another.

With reference to the conative side of human nature, Spinoza thought intuition and reason the more powerful forms of knowledge. In fact, they may free a man from the bondage of desire which the life of mere experience engenders. As we come to understand the causes and the effects of possible activities, we cease to follow immediate impulses, and our desires gradually become centered upon lasting goods. And this is true freedom.

In the *Ethics* intuition is further exalted because of its close relation to the intellectual love of God, a phenomenon of the utmost ethical importance, which we must now examine. All thought, Spinoza maintained, is organized in an infinite intellect, the intellect of God,[31] who knows all things, through the third mode of knowledge. Now, when it grasps an object intuitively, the human mind is absolutely identical, insofar as that act of knowing is concerned, with the intellect of God. To know a thing as it really exists, is to know the thing as God knows it, *sub specie aeternitatis* as it exists necessarily in the

---

[31] *Ethics*, I, 17, col. 2, n.

order of things. When we know an object thus, our knowledge and God's knowledge are one and the same, otherwise, when in confusion and error, our knowledge, although depending upon God's, is not identical with it. For when we are in error, God knows that we are wrong and the reason for our being wrong, knowledge from which we are excluded.

Of our identification with the divine mind we become conscious, writes Spinoza,[32] through awakening our power of intuition. We know then that we exist in God, who is the sustaining cause of all our activities. Thus when we rejoice in the intuition we rejoice in God, who is the cause thereof. This ecstatic contemplation of the divinity, the source of our highest joy, Spinoza called the "Intellectual Love of God,"

This intellectual love of the mind toward God is that very love of God whereby God loves himself. When the human mind loves God as the cause of its intuition and the source of its joy, it is really contemplating itself in its strength and realizing that this strength exists in and through God. But the enlightened human mind is in contact with divinity. Thus its love is part of a greater love which God, insofar as he can be explained through the human mind, bears to himself as he contemplates that mind, rejoicing in himself that he is the cause thereof. Or, to put it briefly, the human mind is a part of God's perfection and hence a source of his delight.

This realization that the mind exists in and through God is not, when it is the result of the intellectual love, a product of speculative construction—

although in Part I [writes Spinoza] I showed in general terms that all things (and consequently, also, the human mind) depend as to their essence and existence on God, yet that demonstration, though legitimate and placed beyond the chances of doubt, does not affect our mind so much, as when the same conclusion is derived from the actual essence of some particular thing, which we say depends on God.[33]

This immediate awareness is the fruit of intuitive, even mystical, knowledge which Spinoza considers more powerful than knowledge of the rational type.

[32] *Ibid.*, V, 32 and 36, n.   [33] *Ibid.*, V, 36, n.

The love of God, of which the intellectual love is an intense example based upon a flash of insight, was in Spinoza's eyes of the greatest ethical value. It may become the ruling force of a man's life and may free him from the bondage of desire which the goods of this world arouse. The religious man fixes his love upon a secure object that cannot fail him and is thus well oriented in his universe. In Spinoza's words this is expressed as follows:

We may thus readily conceive the power, which clear and distinct knowledge, and especially that third kind of knowledge, founded on the actual knowledge of God, possesses over the emotions; if it does not absolutely destroy them, in so far as they are passions; at any rate, it causes them to occupy a very small part of the mind. Further, it begets a love toward a thing immutable and eternal, whereof we may really enter into possession; neither can it be defiled with those faults which are inherent in ordinary love; but it may grow from strength to strength, and may engross the greater part of the mind, and deeply penetrate it.[34]

Spinoza's intellectual love of God is recognized among students of philosophy and religion as the expression of a worship almost free of anthropomorphic elements. It is not praise; it is not prayer. It is not an extension of personal or public loyalties. It has nothing to do with family, or with church or nation. Even further, he who feels the intellectual love of God will not ask that God love him in return. Such love asks for nothing. It is complete fulfillment. Spinoza's name for such love is "acquiescence." It is "blessedness itself."

This particular point of strong resemblance between Spinozian and Wordsworthian religion has been remarked by an English philosopher, the late Samuel Alexander, who was an outstanding student of Spinoza and a lover of Wordsworth. Alexander quotes the lines:

> Sound needed none,
> Nor any voice of joy; his spirit drank
> The spectacle; sensation, soul, and form,
> All melted into him; they swallowed up

---

[34] *Ibid.*, V, 20, n.

His animal being; in them did he live;
And by them did he live; they were his life.
In such access of mind, in such high hour,
Of visitation from the living God,
Thought was not; in enjoyment it expired.
No thanks he breathed, he proffered no request;
Rapt into still communion that transcends
The imperfect offices of prayer and praise,
His mind was a thanksgiving to the power
That made him; it was blessedness and love.[35]

You have only to compare the magnificent lines describing the mystical absorption of the youth in the spectacle of nature with Spinoza's scientific account of the "intellectual love of God" in order to recognise that two great men may have like emotions and the one be a poet and the other a philosopher, and the expression of each be perfect in its kind, but that of the one a poet's work, and that of the other a philosopher and scientific man's. In the second case the words only catch fire from the subject matter; in the other the words are themselves on fire.[36]

We need not doubt that this mystical tendency of Spinoza's was quite akin to Wordsworth's. The relation of intuition to the awareness of God, and the belief that we not only know but feel our immortality[37] are the great points of similarity. But Spinoza differed from Wordsworth in that his profaner interest lay in mathematics and science rather than in art. Wordsworth, who had once entertained a passion for mathematics, could see, however, the importance of Spinoza's third mode of knowing as a description of esthetic imagination. Upon this recognition he constructed the moral philosophy with which he closed *The Prelude* and with which he answered the moral problems which had troubled him since his return from France.[38]

---

[35] *The Excursion*, Bk. I, ll. 205 ff.
[36] *Beauty and Other Forms of Value* (London, 1933), p. 60.
[37] *Ethics*, V, 23, n.
[38] Sir Frederick Pollock (*Spinoza, His Life and Philosophy*, London, 1899, p. 376), writing of Spinoza's influence, mentions the possibility of Coleridge's having made a Spinozist of Wordsworth. He is aware of the artistic potentialities of Spinozism, but is inclined to doubt that Wordsworth borrowed doctrines from Spinoza. He even asserts that Wordsworth's more or less systematic views of man and of the world are wholly different from Spinoza's. But he was

Wordsworth considered the highest form of knowledge to be manifest in poetic imagination as well as in intuition employed in other fields. This highest knowledge he describes as

> absolute strength
> And clearest insight, amplitude of mind
> And Reason in her most exalted mood.[39]

In his famous Preface to the *Lyrical Ballads*, Wordsworth writes of the distinction between poetry and science. We may discover here what he meant when he related imagination to reason:

The remotest discoveries of the Chemist, the Botanist or Mineralogist, will be as proper objects of the Poet's art as any upon which it can be employed, if the time should ever come when these things shall be familiar to us, and the relations under which they are contemplated by the followers of these respective sciences shall be manifestly and palpably material to us as enjoying and suffering beings. If the time should ever come when what is now called science, thus familiarized to men, shall be ready to put on, as it were, a form of flesh and blood the Poet will lend his divine spirit to aid the transfiguration, and will welcome the Being thus produced as a dear and genuine inmate of the household of man.

Wordsworth is here referring to the abstract nature of purely rational knowledge, which is opposed to the warmth and intimacy of the intuitive. This, as we have seen, Spinoza emphasizes. In fact, the following statement from the manuscript of the *Short Treatise Concerning God, Man and His Happiness*, which neither Wordsworth nor Coleridge could have known, shows the general similarity of the views of the poet and the philosopher:

The second (mode of knowledge) we call belief because the things we apprehend only with our reason are not seen by us, but are only known to us through the conviction of our understanding that it must be so and not otherwise. But we call that clear knowledge which

---

ignorant of Wordsworth's interest in the intellectual love that casts such a Spinozian color upon one period of his thought.

[39] *The Prelude*, Bk. XIII, ll. 168 ff.

com⌐   ⌐ from our being convinced by reasons, but from our feeling
⌐ enjoying the thing itself, and it surpasses the others by far.[40]

Wordsworth seems to have turned toward Spinoza primarily in search of ethical concepts. The notion of intellectual love, as an outcome of imagination, is woven into his statement of the ideal human existence. This statement follows upon the Mt. Snowdon meditation, where the influence of Boehme is remarkable. In the Mt. Snowdon meditation, the pantheistic theology springs from Boehme, but the detail of the *moral* philosophy which supplements Boehme's theology is Spinozian in quality. Here imagination (Spinoza's intuition) supports not only the intellectual love, which constitutes a spiritual orientation, but is also the surest guide of conduct:

> Imagination having been our theme,
> So also hath that intellectual love,
> For they are each in each, and cannot stand
> Dividually.[41]

This passage,[42] too long to quote in full, sings the praises of a faculty similar to Spinoza's third mode of knowledge. The following quotation contains the essence of the argument. Wordsworth writes of those who possess an awakened faculty of imagination:

> . . . in a world of life they live,
> By sensible impressions not enthrall'd
> But quickened, rouz'd and made thereby more apt
> To hold communion with the invisible world.
> Such minds are truly from the Deity,
> For they are Powers; and hence the highest bliss
> That can be known is theirs, the consciousness[43]

[40] *Short Treatise*, p. 69.
[41] *The Prelude*, Bk. XIII, ll. 185 ff.; see also ll. 166 ff.
[42] *Ibid.*, Bk. XIII, ll. 83-210 (1850, Bk. XIV, ll. 87-231).
[43] This doctrine is somewhat similar to Hartley's conception of the religious life. Hartley speaks of the gradual strengthening through association of the comfortable sense that we live in the presence and under the protection of God. But he denies the life of imagination any eudaemonistic or religious value. This sharply distinguishes him from Wordsworth, who regards imagination as the keystone of his natural religion. (See Hartley, *Observations on Man*, Part II, prop. LXXI and prop. LIX.) It was not until a generation after Hartley that British philosophy of mind grew more kindly disposed toward imagination. So

Of whom they are habitually infused
Through every image, and through every thought
And all impressions, hence religion, faith,
And endless occupation for the soul
Whether discursive or intuitive;
Hence sovereignty within and peace of will
Emotion which best foresight need not fear
Most worthy then of trust when most intense.
Hence cheerfulness in every act of life
Hence truth in moral judgments and delight
That fails not in the external universe.[44]

The life of imagination brings with it, then, freedom from unruly desire and establishes the soul as a Power which recognizes its own nature and origin and is thus oriented in the universe. Hence arises moral sovereignty and peace of will, when a man's emotions may be trusted most when most intense; for a consciousness of his true being guides his moral judgments and welds his desire to unquestionable good.

A few moments' reflection will show us how neatly this ethic answers the problems which Wordsworth's encounter with Godwinism has summoned to his mind. In the first place, he found in the life of the imagination a *summum bonum* by which to judge the value of human actions. Thus he was no

---

we find in Thomas Reid, a psychologist who considers imagination as a faculty valuable alike in morals, religion, and science. But even Reid insists that imagination, to be most beneficial, must be subject to a rational control, based on judgment (*Essays on the Intellectual Powers of Man*, Essay IV, chap. iv).

[44] *The Prelude*, Bk. XIII, ll. 105 ff. The philosophical attitude of these lines is to some extent anticipated by the youthful Wordsworth when he writes in "An Evening Walk" (ll. 80 ff.) of

> A mind that, in calm angelic mood
> Of happy wisdom, meditating good,
> Beholds, of all from his high powers required,
> Much done, and much designed, and more desired,—
> *Harmonious thoughts, a soul by truth refined,*
> *Entire affection for all human kind.*

The lines italicized constitute what we might call a "first state" of the ideal which is expressed later against the backgrounds of subtle and more fully developed philosophies, against the theory of Godwinian "independent intellect" and universal benevolence, and later against the Spinozian theory of moral freedom and intellectual love. This would suggest that Wordsworth's ethical thought developed in the same way as his religious concepts. Original feeling was clarified by the discovery of concepts which conformed with it.

longer baffled in his search for a criterion of good and evil. He could call all actions good that tend to promote the life of imagination, understanding, and freedom.

The problem of obligation was also solved. For coupled with understanding, the desires of the religious man are to be trusted. If he desires a way of life after he understands it, he may call that way of life good; thus his emotions are trustworthy. Considered in this light, moral problems center about the question, "Do I really want to act thus?" rather than about, "Should I act thus?" This naturally leads to the assertion of an emphatic individualism. The human soul becomes the witness and the judge of things,[45] and the supreme arbiter of right and wrong. Such a step as this Wordsworth was eager to take.

In fact, following Godwin as he seems to have done, Wordsworth had already taken this step despite himself. He was committed to a morality both intellectualist and individualist before he reached the position of *The Prelude*. But his intellectualism had bred only despair. For Godwin was unable to bring home to him the intrinsic power of imaginative knowledge, which doctrine forms the very core of the ethics of *The Prelude*. According to this interpretation, it was from the Spinozian point of view that Wordsworth described the human frame as "good and graciously disposed." Perhaps a true Spinozist would be inclined to look upon the human *conatus* or instinctive equipment as quite amoral, for it seems possible to satisfy any phase of man's conative nature either in a good or in an evil manner. But it is easy to grasp what Wordsworth meant. Only give the *conatus* the benefit of clear understanding and it may be trusted.

To be sure, we cannot say that this theory dispels the fear that many men must always live the "dupes of folly and the slaves of crime." But at least it shows us how man may rise from such a state. And this was enough for Wordsworth.

*   *   *

We may remember that Boehme also found in imagination an all-important moral faculty. But, as Boehme describes it,

[45] *The Prelude*, Bk. XII, l. 367.

imagination can damn as well as save. The soul can be poisoned and the power of moral decision misled by an imagination which embraces evil.

Boehme's attitude toward imagination as a moral power is in reality much closer to popular common sense than is Wordsworth's teaching in *The Prelude*. The popular point of view is itself actually presented by Mark Akenside in his *Pleasures of Imagination*, with which Wordsworth was acquainted. In Book III, Akenside recognizes that imagination can be an important aid to moral development but that it can degrade as well as save. In a note appended to the poem, in the edition of 1748, Akenside writes:

> The influence of imagination on the conduct of life, is one of the most important points in moral philosophy. It were easy by an induction of facts to prove that the imagination directs almost all the passions, and mixes with almost every circumstance of action or pleasure. Let any man, even of the coldest head and soberest industry, analyse the idea of what he calls his interest; he will find that it consists chiefly of certain degrees of decency, beauty, and order, variously combined into one system, the idol which he seeks to enjoy by labour, hazard, and self-denial. It is on this account of the last consequence to regulate these images by *the standard of Nature and the general good;* otherwise the imagination, by heightening some objects beyond their real excellence and beauty, or by representing others in a more odious or terrible shape than they deserve, may of course engage us in pursuits utterly inconsistent with the moral order of things.[46]

It is worth noticing that Akenside thinks of imagination as supporting a "standard of Nature." It is then not the ultimate arbiter of right and wrong but an auxiliary function. Moral imagination, as conceived by Boehme and by Akenside, does not seem to possess the intellectual scope which Wordsworth attributes to his ideal. For him, imagination includes a breadth of insight as well as a completeness of concrete detail. Thus, for Wordsworth, moral imagination, so awakened, will not be misled by an attractive show of vivid concrete imagery. It will, if it is truly "reason in its most exalted mood," see

[46] *The Pleasures of Hope, Imagination, and Memory* (Baltimore, 1814), p. 200. Italics mine.

around and beyond the first show of things, even though it sees all, not in abstract terms, but with a sense of actual detail. For Wordsworth, imagination, like Spinoza's intuition, is an infallible guide, once it has been aroused. Boehme, on the other hand, recognizes that imagination may lead us into sin. The truth is that in his moral theory Wordsworth reserves the term *imagination* for the highest power to which it can conceivably be applied.

At any rate, Boehme and his followers, such as William Law, agree with Spinoza and with Wordsworth that virtue is not purely a matter of understanding. As Law writes in *The Way to Divine Knowledge* (VII, 225): "For Reason like the Eye is only an outward Looker on,[47] and can no more form, or model, or alter the Life of the Soul, than it can alter the Life and Vegetation of the Body."

For Boehme, salvation depends upon health of imagination, which must embrace spiritual objects and cling to them. In this way is the soul transformed. The following excerpts, taken from M. Koyré's most excellent study of Boehme, illustrate his theological interpretation of the imagination's function:

Le sens spécial que Boehme attribue au terme *imaginatio* = *Einbildung* lui permet de dire que Lucifer ou Adam ont imaginé *dans* le *centrum naturae*. . . . En effet, non seulement, avec tout le moyen âge et toute son époque, Boehme croit à la puissance magique de l'imagination qui peut produire des effets parfaitement réels, mais il l'envisage comme un acte *sui generis* qui assimile le sujet imaginant à l'objet imaginé. L'imagination est ainsi une force qui peut s'exercer dans différents domaines de l'être; on peut imaginer *dans* quelque chose comme on peut regarder dans quelque chose, avec cette différence toutefois que le simple regard ne produit aucun effet, tandis que l'imagination fait participer le sujet à la qualité de son objet, et, en même temps, modifie cet objet conformément à l'imagination du sujet. Imaginant dans le *centrum naturae*, Lucifer, par l'action (réelle) de son imagination, a modifié l'équilibre des puissances de ce *centrum*; il l'a "embrasé," parce qu'il était lui-même "embrase" par l'orgueil; inversement l'imagination a embrasé en lui son propre *centrum*, l'assimilant et même l'incorporant

---

[47] Compare Coleridge's censure of Newton's theory of mind as a "lazy-looker-on" (*Letters*, 1796, I, 353).

au *centrum naturae.* La conception boehmiste de l'imagination est, selon toute probabilité, favorisée par le sens du mot *bilden,* qui veut dire *former,* d'où l'on peut tirer *einbilden═informer* et *sich einbilden═se former* en et *s'incorporer à.* Ce calembour, à vrai dire, ne se trouve pas chez Boehme—nous l'avons trouvé chez Hegel—mais il est tout à fait boehmiste.

La foi véritable est une puissance et une action. Elle est, dit Boehme, en reprenant une conception de Paracelse, "une forte imagination." C'est là sa vraie nature. Il ne suffit point, en effet, de dire que la foi est un acte de volonté. Certes, elle est cela, et c'est pourquoi elle est—en tant que spirituelle et pénétrée d'amour—un don de soi. Un don confiant, un abandon de l'âme à Dieu qu'elle aime, vers qui elle tend et avec qui elle cherche à s'unir. Mais nous ne le savons que trop: la volonté, en elle-même, est impuissante, tenue et faible "comme un néant." Pour qu'elle agisse, il faut qu'elle se donne, ou qu'elle trouve, une puissance, un mécanisme d'action qui n'est, nous l'avons vu, rien d'autre que l'imagination.

L'âme—l'homme pour être plus exact—"imagine" "en Dieu," "imagine" "dans le Christ," ce qui veut dire chez Boehme qu'il "se reconstruit" lui-même selon l'image (Vorblid) du Christ qu'il forme en lui; puissance plastique et magique, l'*imaginatio* "coule" l'homme dans la "forme" imaginée par lui. Elle le transforme en cette image qu'elle lui fait imiter; l'introduit dans le Christ auquel elle le fait participer, et cette transformation n'est autre chose que l'incarnation du Christ dans l'homme qui devient, en un sens direct et positif, image, incarnation et expression de Dieu. On pourrait dire: imaginant "dans" le Christ, le fidèle l'imite, et, l'imitant, il réalise lui-même, l'image de Dieu. On pourrait dire également qu'en le faisant il ne fait que se réaliser et exprimer son propre fond. N'est-il pas, en effet, image de Dieu? Et la similitude divine *(Bildniss)* n'a-t-elle point été implantée par Dieu dans son âme? Exprimer Dieu, n'est-ce point sa vraie fonction, sa véritable mission? Et n'est-ce point le Christ, l'Homme-Dieu, créature dans laquelle s'était pleinement et parfaitement réalisé l'homme en son essence véritable, l'homme tel qu'il aurait dû être dans sa parfaite intégrité, qui représente Dieu sur le plan humain, et, ce qui est la même chose, le représente dans ce monde?

Ainsi, le but et la mission de l'homme sur terre consiste dans l'imitation du Christ. Le thème est fort ancien, mais comme toujours, ce n'est point le thème, c'est son interprétation qui fait l'originalite du penseur.[48]

[48] Koyré, *op. cit.,* p. 218, n. 4, and pp. 481-482.

Wordsworth was not, while at work upon the first draft of *The Prelude*, by any means prepared to accept so apparently orthodox a scheme of morality. Here the pertinence of Spinozism is manifest. Spinozian ethics involves the same emphasis upon a way of knowing more powerful, in its influence over the soul, than is reason; it recognizes that this way of knowing has a contribution to make to religion; but it does not include the welter of biblical and mythological notions with which Boehme's exposition is sprinkled.

* * *

For Wordsworth imagination is the vehicle whereby the great values are brought into the scope of human life. It is the spiritual and psychological matrix of human freedom. Intelligence and foresight may sketch an admirable plan of action, but they cannot always translate it into terms of actual volition. Intelligence may be willing and the emotions confused, or again the emotions may be right and intelligence narrow and abstract. It is imagination that reconciles the trio, emotion, intelligence, and volition, and frees the soul from conflict. It is also the surest practical guide in the tangled web of human relations. Imagination supplies the foundation for broader human sympathies and, in the more popular sense of the term, for human understanding; for it can bring us, as it does in a number of Wordsworth's poems, to an appreciation of human beings, seen as individuals in the actual setting of their lives. Furthermore, the imaginative man is never narrowly doctrinaire, and, accordingly, when he is faced by something which he fails to understand, he is capable of detachment and not in haste to condemn. This point of view, Wordsworth presents in *The Prelude*, Book XIII. Having described fancy and imagination in general, Wordsworth turns toward things "nearer to ourselves" and speaks of

> . . . human nature and that marvellous world
> As studied first in my own heart, and then
> In life among the passions of mankind
> And qualities commix'd and modified
> By the infinite varieties and shades

Of individual character. Therein
It was for me (this justice bids me say)
No useless preparation to have been
The pupil of a public School, and forced
In hardly independence, to stand up
Amid conflicting passions, and the shock
Of various tempers, to endure and note
What was not understood though known to be;
Among the mysteries of love and hate,
Honour and shame, looking to right and left,
Uncheck'd by innocence too delicate
And moral notions too intolerant,
Sympathies too contracted. Hence, when call'd
To take a station among Men, the step
Was easier, the transition more secure,
More profitable also; for the mind
Learns from such timely exercise to keep
In wholesome separation the two natures,
The one that feels, the other that observes.[49]

Thus imagination is presented as a steadying influence in moral relations. It is not the expansive power, the irresponsible force, of which the late Irving Babbitt had so much to say in his rather too generalized censure of romantic ethics. But imagination is no "inner check." It is not a negative command that speaks authoritatively to a soul which accepts imperatives whose origin it does not understand. Nor is imagination subject to established conventions. It guides only by enlightening desire: the imaginative man does what, in the light of imagination, he feels that he really wants to do.

From the standpoint of the historian of ethical theory, Wordsworth's ethics of imagination may well be described as an individualism. The decision of the individual is recognized as the ultimate arbiter of right and wrong in human conduct, and the individual must depend wholly upon his own insight or forfeit his moral freedom. When we consider the theory in its fullest context and recognize that Wordsworth believes in a suprapersonal origin of imagination, we must ad-

[49] *The Prelude*, Bk. XIII, ll. 308-331.

mit, however, that this ethical individualism merges with a theory of man and his place in the world system which transcends the limits of individualism as that doctrine is most frequently understood.   Since, according to Wordsworth, the imagination leads us to recognize the unity of the world and the ultimate community of spiritual forces in the world, his ethics does not involve a philosophy of competition nor does it commit him to a spiritual individualism of proud self-confidence of the sort that Nietzsche was later to endorse.   It involves neither hero-worship of the strong man nor any insistence that one should become one's own hero, worthy of self-worship.   For Wordsworth at this period, the individual must make his own decisions and his growth must be an inner one, but the enlightened individual will not consider his own prosperity as the sole end or purpose of his own existence.   Such narrow individualism does appear in Wordsworth's writings, as in *The Borderers*. But here the poet clearly enough condemns the narrow and rationalist selfishness of Oswald.

Again, the ethics of imagination, as Wordsworth presents it, differs, in at least one very important respect, from later ethical teaching which centers about esthetic activity.   Wordsworth is no esthete: his teaching is not that of Walter Pater. He saw, while at work on the first draft of *The Prelude,* no reason for supposing that the man who makes imagination the guide of life must ignore practical affairs or substitute the enjoyment of beauty for participation in the world of human business.   The imagination of *The Prelude* is the very heart of actual, moral practice, although it is true that in looking back upon this period Wordsworth accused himself of something very like the false detachment of the "esthete."   Nothing was, however, further from his intention when he first conceived the ethics of *The Prelude.*

CHAPTER VII

"How Poor a Thing Is Man"

As HE GREW older, Wordsworth's attitude changed, and the ethics of imagination ceased to give him entire satisfaction. In the "Ode to Duty" and in "Elegiac Stanzas" we find a new point of view very consciously set forth.

Before the change, Wordsworth had considered the imaginative life the one true goal of human activity. He was willing, if necessary, to dwell in peasanthood, poverty, and seclusion that he might possess it. After the change, such an ethic seemed narrow and selfish. Man must seek, he came to believe, not his own happiness but the performance of the duty that he owes his fellows.

> Farewell, farewell, the heart that lives alone,
> Housed in a dream, at distance from the kind!
> Such happiness, wherever it be known,
> Is to be pitied, for it is surely blind.[1]

His individualism troubled him. He was no longer willing to trust himself as the "judge and witness" of his life. In *The Prelude* he had sung of the emotions of the free man:

> . . . which best foresight need not fear,
> Most worthy then of trust when most intense.[2]

In the "Ode to Duty" he retracted this trust:

> Through no disturbance of my soul,
> Or strong compulsion in me wrought,
> I supplicate for thy control;
> But in the quietness of thought:
> Me this unchartered freedom tires;
> I feel the weight of chance desires:
> My hopes no more must change their name,
> I long for a repose that ever is the same.

[1] "Elegiac Stanzas, Suggested by a Picture of Peele Castle in a Storm."
[2] Bk. XIII, l. 115.

His earlier ethic seemed too subjective, too uncertain. A moral guide, thought Wordsworth, must be something objective, steadfast, and commanding; for human beings are weak. Perhaps in a perfect state, all talk of duty would be unnecessary. Man would need no guide but his own intelligence and his own desire. But this world is no Utopia where feeling and insight go hand in hand. Wordsworth was oppressed with a sense of human finitude.

Coupled with this sense of finitude, came a realization of the weight of circumstance beneath which humanity must labor. His brother's tragic death and the collapse of the French Revolution may have swayed Wordsworth toward this point of view, but this is a problem of biography to which we shall presently turn. At any rate, he was driven to putting such words as these into the mouth of the Wanderer, a character who, he asserted, in many respects resembled himself:[3]

> One adequate support
> For the calamities of mortal life
> Exists—one only; an assured belief
> That the procession of our fate, howe'er
> Sad or disturbed, is ordered by a Being
> Of infinite benevolence and power;
> Whose everlasting purposes embrace
> All accidents converting them to good.[4]

Here again occurs the thought that man must seek supplementary aid. Through his own efforts he cannot assure his happiness. Influenced by this feeling, Wordsworth turned toward belief in a future life as a recompense for the evils of the present one. This was indeed a drastic step for the author of "Tintern Abbey" to take.

Whereas Wordsworth had once rejoiced in the possibility of man's communion with the infinite, he now deplored man's unhappy finitude, and whereas he had once joyously affirmed the possibility and described the nature of the moral life, he now as during his Godwinian period brooded over the difficulty of its attainment.

[3] Introduction to *The Excursion*.   [4] *The Excursion*, Bk. IV, ll. 10 ff.

Contrast the lines from *The Prelude:*

> . . . to my conscious soul I now can say—
> "I recognize thy glory"[5]

with those from *The Excursion,* quoted from Daniel, which close with:

> ". . . unless above himself he can
> Erect himself, how poor a thing is man."[6]

Here we find the essence of the new attitude.

In this mood Wordsworth sought practical aid from philosophy. A few years before, he had desired only a theory of ethics; he now sought maxims of conduct. Thus he was no longer interested in speculation for its own sake. Contemplation now seemed to Wordsworth of value only as it answers man's needs, only as it gives him hope and helps him to do the right. In fact, pure speculation seemed to him almost indecent, an insult to the universe, which he felt surely does not exist

> Only to be examined, pondered, searched,
> Probed, vexed and criticized.[7]

To one thus anxiously seeking an ethical maxim and despairing of man's lot on earth, the philosophy of Kant, who is often called the modern Stoic, would naturally appear attractive. In Kant's little work entitled *Fundamental Principles of the Metaphysic of Morals,* there are certain ideas that must have pleased the "second Wordsworth." Again the immediate source is probably Coleridge, who, as we have seen, had a high opinion of Kant. Wordsworth at least twice denied any direct acquaintance with German metaphysics.[8] But in 1815, in Chap-

---

[5] Bk. VI, ll. 598-599.
[6] Bk. IV, ll. 320 ff.   [7] *The Excursion,* Bk. IV, ll. 968 ff.
[8] Indeed, it is likely that Wordsworth was never clearly aware of the Kantian source of some of the ideas included in *The Excursion.* He once told Captain Hamilton, the brother of the philosopher Sir William Hamilton, that he had no knowledge of Kant, although it appears that Sir William had been struck by the Kantian tone of certain passages in *The Excursion* (John Veitch, *Memoir of Sir William Hamilton,* Edinburgh, 1869, p. 88). Again in 1840 Wordsworth, writing to Robinson, mentions the charge of plagiarism brought against Coleridge, who was accused in *Blackwood's* of borrowing passages from Schelling without acknowledgment. Wordsworth asserts that he himself has "never read a word of German metaphysics, thank Heaven!" although he does not doubt that

ter IX of *Biographia Literaria* Coleridge wrote to the effect that he had been acquainted with Kantian teaching for fifteen years, after which period he asserted that he still read all of Kant's productions "with undiminished delight and increasing admiration."

Kant, like Wordsworth, had ceased to see in the contemplative life man's highest attainment. He tells us that Rousseau brought home to him the narrowness of such a *summum bonum*. The life of moral relations with one's fellows, the life of duty, began to seem more important.

In the first pages of the *Metaphysic of Morals* occurs a brief argument in defense of this point of view. Nature obviously did not intend man for happiness.[9] For had she wished man to be solely happy and no more, she surely would have intrusted his happiness to instinct rather than to reason, which in man holds but a fluctuating supremacy. But since Nature has given man his reason to pilot him, we may assume that she intends him to live rationally rather than happily. A completely rational life then is the goal that we must endeavor to pursue.

In the *Metaphysic* Kant tries to present a formula, the famous categorical imperative, by which we may test the rationality of our actions. The distinctive character of reason being, he thinks, its universal application, he decides that if we can universalize a contemplated action, i.e., if we can conceive of all men acting thus under similar conditions, without having to admit that the universality of the act undermines the possibility of its performance, we may consider it a good act.[10]

But all activity, thinks Kant, must have an end for the sake of which it is performed. This the first formulation of the imperative does not supply. But as the purpose of Nature seems to be the production of rational life the end of human activity should be the preservation of rationality. Thus we should treat human personality, i.e., potential rationality, al-

---

"they are good diet for some tastes." We must then suppose that Wordsworth drew his Kant from Coleridge, but we need not believe that in 1805 or in 1810 Wordsworth would have "thanked Heaven" for his lack of direct acquaintance with Kant and Schelling.

[9] *Metaphysic of Morals*, pp. 13 ff.   [10] *Ibid.*, p. 22, *ca.*

ways as an end and never as a means.[11] This is perhaps Kant's most important ethical conclusion.

We should live, says Kant, *as if* we were members of a Kingdom of Ends in which everyone's personality is respected. The fact that we are not in such a state matters little; for the value of our actions lies not in the actual results but in the will that prompts us to try our utmost for the good. In this Kingdom of Ends there are two types of wills.[12] A will whose activity necessarily coincides with the moral law, i.e., the will of a personality which of its own desire seeks the good, is a sovereign will, and good absolutely. A will not absolutely good experiences obligation. The moral necessity which this obligation imposes upon the personality is called duty, which occurs only when reason strives to guide a wayward personality. Without duty the will moves in confusion, drawn hither and yon at the call of impulse. Recognizing duty, the will approaches autonomy or stable self-control. Without duty it is—to use the Kantian term—heteronomous. The resemblance of this doctrine to the content of the "Ode to Duty" is obvious, and has been occasionally remarked. The third stanza thereof, which we have already quoted, seems its poetic expression. We shall see below that the doctrine appears again in *The Excursion*.

The problem of human freedom troubled Kant persistently, for he believed that the very possibility of our experience of objects and events in space and time demanded absolute determination of effect by cause. To extricate himself from this difficulty, he postulated another experience, "intelligible" rather than "sensible," and, philosophically speaking, more "real" than the experience of space and time. In the realm of such a purely rational experience, he suggested, human freedom might have its origin. Man, as a metaphysical amphibian, belongs, according to Kant's suggestion, to both these worlds. He is autonomous when he acts rationally, for then he is claiming his right as a member of the intelligible world, and his action is a logical one determined by ground and consequent.

[11] *Ibid.*, p. 78, *ca.*   [12] *Ibid.*, pp. 63, 64-67.

When he fails to use his reason, when he merely obeys impulse, man belongs solely to the sensible world and is determined in his action by the laws of cause and effect. Here Kant followed Rousseau, for whom obedience to impulse was slavery; obedience to law, of which the individual approves and to which he lends his support, freedom.

As regards a future life in which the righteous man is recompensed for the evils and oppression which he has suffered, Kant is skeptical. For Kant—and here, as we shall see, Wordsworth followed him—reason is limited to a narrow sphere, the natural sphere, and when it endeavors to climb beyond, it becomes helplessly involved in contradiction. Thus immortality is like the existence of the intelligible world, a matter for faith to grasp but not for reason to determine. For practical purposes, however, we must assume that the universe is ordered by a wise and a good God who rules from his seat in the intelligible world, caring for the survival of his creatures after death.[13] Otherwise the aim of all activity, a life that is at once rationally moral and materially happy is but a dream; for in this life happiness and morality are incompatible.

As our mention of the "Ode to Duty" has suggested, after 1805 Wordsworth's philosophy was of a very Kantian aspect. He still had faith, however, in his mystical communion with Nature, upon which even at this time he built his philosophy. One of the most beautiful of all Wordsworth's descriptions of this experience occurs in *The Excursion*. The Wanderer, striving to answer the question of the skeptic, exclaims, true to the philosophy of *The Prelude:*

> Access for you
> Is yet preserved to principles of truth,
> Which the imaginative Will upholds
> In seats of wisdom, not to be approached
> By the inferior Faculty that moulds,
> With her minute and speculative pains,
> Opinion, ever changing!

---

[13] *Critique of Practical Reason* (New York, 1927), Bk. II, chap. ii, sec. v, pp. 220-229.

There are times, he holds, when the universe itself

> doth impart
> Authentic tidings of invisible things;
> Of ebb and flow, and ever-during power
> And central peace, subsisting at the heart
> Of endless agitation.[14]

This is the experience of "Tintern Abbey" and *The Prelude*. The presentation here differs in only one essential respect from the earlier ones. Wordsworth feels in *The Excursion* that only to the ear of faith does the universe speak of mysterious union. A skeptic will feel exaltation, but he will not know why he is exalted. He is pious "beyond the intention of his thought."

Such a change is quite in harmony with Wordsworth's attitude at this time. He had ceased to talk, as he did in *The Recluse*, of man's salvation in terms of "nothing more than what we are." The Wordsworth of *The Excursion* is looking for aid, and like Kant he finds it in faith.

At any rate, this mystical experience, confirming his faith as it did, withheld Wordsworth from Kantian doubts as regards a future life and the existence of the intelligible world, which the poet probably identified with the World-Soul of his earlier thought and the "active principle" of *The Excursion*.[15] Thus it is not surprising that we find in Wordsworth less skepticism than in Kant. Wordsworth accepted the latter's severe limitation of human reason, which faculty he condemned when he wrote in *The Excursion*:

> Man is of dust: ethereal hopes are his,
> Which, when they should sustain themselves aloft,
> Want due consistence; like a pillar of smoke,
> That with majestic energy from earth
> Rises; but having reached the thinner air,
> Melts and dissolves, and is no longer seen.[16]

But, for the reasons that we have stated, this did not trouble Wordsworth as it did some Kantians. It is the positive side

---

[14] *The Excursion*, Bk. IV, ll. 1126 ff.
[15] Bk. IX, ll. 1-15.   [16] Bk. IV, ll. 140 ff.

of the Kantian ethics which the Wanderer presents in *The Excursion*.

All the goods of life, the Wanderer maintains, are unstable, and the passions by which we desire them are fickle; rational duty alone transcends this blight and stands forever immutable:

> Possessions vanish, and opinions change,
> And passions hold a fluctuating seat;
> But by the storms of circumstance unshaken,
> And subject neither to eclipse nor wane,
> Duty exists;—immutably survive,
> For our support, the measures and the forms
> Which an abstract intelligence supplies;
> Whose kingdom is where space and time are not.[17]

Here we find what seems obvious reference to the relation between the sense of duty in man and the intelligible world, which transcends space and time.   The first lines of the quotation appear to allude to the condition of the heteronomous will, that moves in confusion unguided by reason.   Some lines below, Wordsworth describes submission to the intelligible order as "constituting strength and power."   Mention of the law of reason is made again in later passages.[18]   In Book IX Wordsworth writes that man was actually created to obey this law of life, a doctrine which, as we have seen, is the very bulwark of the Kantian ethic.

Again in Book IV conscience is spoken of as the image of God in man.

> . . . conscience reverenced and obeyed
> As God's most intimate presence in the soul,
> And his most perfect image in the world.[19]

This is consistent with Kant's teaching concerning the possibility of the intelligible world's influencing the sensible.   When God is considered as the subject which contemplates the intelligible world—and Kant tended toward such a theology—Wordsworth's expression appears clearly Kantian.   For in the

---

[17] *The Excursion*, Bk. IV, ll. 69 ff.
[18] *Ibid.*, Bk. IV, ll. 806 ff., and Bk. IX, ll. 126 ff.
[19] *Ibid.*, Bk. IV, ll. 224 ff.

rational moral life man transcends the sensible world and claims membership in the intelligible. Thus conscience considered as the feeling of compulsion which the reason exercises upon us, may well be termed God's most intimate presence in the soul.

Kant's concept of a Kingdom of Ends in which the intrinsic worth of personality, as the seat of reason, is respected seems to have made a profound impression upon Wordsworth:

> Our life is turned
> Out of her course, wherever man is made
> An offering or a sacrifice, a tool
> Or implement, a passive thing employed
> As a brute mean, without acknowledgment
> Of common right or interest in the end;
> Used or abused, as selfishness may prompt.
> Say, what can follow for a rational soul
> Perverted thus, but weakness in all good,
> And strength in evil?[20]

Between the positions of *The Prelude* and *The Excursion* lies an interesting transition which we have not yet examined in any detail. The outstanding monument of this transition is the famous "Ode to Duty," which, despite its title, contains elements of both romantic individualism and of stoicism.

The "Ode" is really much more than a transition in which conflicting ideas are placed side by side. The doctrines of self-realization and of stoical duty are fairly well woven together. The clearest instance of this harmony lies in stanza six quoted below, which Wordsworth deleted after the first edition. The "Ode" *as it finally stands* is, however, closer to stoicism than to the philosophy of self-realization.

Now, we shall find that the doctrine of the "Ode to Duty" is very similar to Schiller's subtle restatement of the Kantian ethical philosophy.[21] It seems to turn upon the famous doctrine

---

[20] *Ibid.*, Bk. IX, ll. 113 ff.

[21] In his thorough and learned work *Kant in England* (Princeton, N. J., 1932, p. 160) Dr. René Wellek has expressed doubt that the "Ode to Duty" belongs to the Kantian tradition. He feels that Wordsworth might easily have drawn the doctrine of this poem from a general acquaintance with Christianity.

of the *schöne Seele*. In his great life of Wordsworth, Professor Harper has, at the suggestion of Professor Lovejoy, indicated this connection.[22] He quotes the following passage from Schiller's *Anmuth und Würde* and compares it with Wordsworth's treatment of the innocents who "without reproach or blot" dispense with conscientious reflection.

In a beautiful soul the moral feeling in all the emotions has at length grown so secure that it can fearlessly leave to impulse the guidance of the will, without fear of contradiction from the latter. Therefore, in a beautiful soul, particular acts are not properly moral, but the whole character is. . . . With ease, as if mere instinct were at work through her, she performs the most painful human duties . . . she herself never perceives the beauty of her own conduct, and it never occurs to her that there could be other acts and other feelings; whereas a well-drilled pupil in the school of moral rules, obedient to her master's command, will be ever ready to give the strictest account of the relationship of his actions to the law.[23]

Unfortunately Professor Harper seems to interpret *Anmuth und Würde* solely with reference to such passages and thus gives the impression that Schiller's doctrine is present only in the first stanzas of the "Ode to Duty." If we consider, however, other utterances of Schiller's, it becomes obvious that his position is much closer to Wordsworth's than has been admitted. The doctrine of the *schöne Seele* with the qualifications which Schiller attaches to it seems to be reflected throughout the entire "Ode." Thus we need not say that in the first two stanzas Wordsworth reluctantly relinquishes Schiller's doctrine, for the entire "Ode" may easily be interpreted as an acceptance of Schiller's restatement of Kant.

Consider as an introduction to our comparative study of

This hypothesis is perhaps not an impossible one, but the close parallel of Schiller's modified Kantianism, which we shall examine at once, indicates a more definite and tangible origin.

[22] George M. Harper, *William Wordsworth* (3d ed., New York, 1929), p. 442.

[23] *Schiller's Sämmtliche Werke* (Stuttgart, 1862), XI, 294. (The translation is Professor Harper's.) We might consider as similar to this passage, Schiller's poem *Natur und Schule* (or the *Genius*), where the poet describes the graceful and unreflective virtue of those who have not "lost their guardian angel."

Schiller and Wordsworth, the former's little poem "Die Führer des Lebens":

Zweierlei Genien sind's, die dich durchs Leben geleiten.
  Wohl dir, wenn sie vereint helfend zur Seite dir stehn!
Mit erheiterndem Spiel verkürzt dir der eine die Reise,
  Leichter an seinem Arm werden dir Schicksal und Pflicht.
Unter Scherz und Gespräch begleitet er bis an die Kluft dich,
  Wo an der Ewigkeit Meer schaudernd der Sterbliche steht.
Hier empfängt dich entschlossen und ernst und schweigend der andre,
  Trägt mit gigantischem Arm über die Tiefe dich hin.
Nimmer widme dich einem allein! Vertraue dem erstern
  Deine Würde nicht an, nimmer den andern dein Glück![24]

Clearly this peculiar dualism is not precisely Wordsworth's; at least we cannot say that it is the attitude of the final draft of the "Ode to Duty." But it is closer to Wordsworth than the reader may at first suppose, for it becomes obvious that Schiller has been preoccupied with the problem which troubles Wordsworth in the first stanzas. Schiller agrees with Wordsworth in this: man has other supports than the genial sense of youth or happy instinct.

What then is the relation of happy inclination to duty? Schiller in his ethical essays and Wordsworth in the "Ode to Duty" of 1807 answer this question in very similar fashion. Consider the stanza which follows, the one that Wordsworth withdrew after 1807:

> Yet not the less would I throughout
> Still act according to the voice
> Of my own wish; and feel past doubt
> That my submissiveness was choice:
> Not seeking in the school of pride
> For "precepts over dignified,"
> Denial and restraint I prize
> No farther than they breed a second Will more wise.

Certain lines from "The Happy Warrior" indicate a similar attitude. The Warrior has clearly attained the "second Will more wise." He is not under the whip of obligation:

[24] *Ibid.*, I, 343. Italics mine. See also XII, 249 *(Über das Erhabene).*

. . . 'Tis he whose law is reason, who depends
Upon that law as on the best of friends.

In his moral essays Schiller seems clearly to have anticipated this position of Wordsworth's. Schiller, a student of
Kant, combines an element of Stoicism with his doctrine of the
schöne Seele. Thus Schiller in his ethical essays strengthens
his doctrine of the *schöne Seele* with a commendation of conscientious reflection, whereas Wordsworth softens the duty
philosophy of his "Ode" by praising the spirit of free and
even eager acceptance of a moral law which cannot be interpreted as satisfying our immediate desires. The two philosophies coincide, although they have, in this case, approached
one another from opposite directions.

We learn that the *schöne Seele* is not to be confused with
a mere temperamental disposition to follow virtue, or to act
in accordance with virtue. *Schöne Seele* must be able to call
upon a sterner philosophy, as Wordsworth would say, "according to their need."

Die schöne Seele muss sich also im Affekt in eine erhabene (*i.e.* morally self-transcending) verwandeln, *und das ist der untrügliche Pro-
bierstein, wodurch man sie von dem guten Herzen oder der Tempera-
mentstugend unterscheiden kann.* Ist bei einem Menschen die Neigung
nur darum auf Seiten der Gerechtigkeit, weil die Gerechtigkeit sich
glücklicher Weise auf Seiten der Neigung befindet, so wird der Natur-
trieb im Affekt eine vollkommene Zwangsgewalt über den Willen
ausüben, *und wo ein Opfer Nöthig ist* so wird es die Sittlichkeit, und
nicht die Sinnlichkeit bringen.[25]

The two following quotations present Schiller's doctrine in
epigrammatic form: "Überhaupt gilt hier das Gesetz, das der
Mensch alles mit Anmuth thun müsse, was er *innerhalb seiner
Menschheit* hinausgehen muss. . . . Man fordert Anmuth von
den der verpflichtet, und Würde von dem, der verpflichtet
wird."[26] *Anmuth* is the grace of temperamental or spontaneous virtue, pursued without possible conflict. *Würde* is the
dignity of heroic self-command in the face of stern alternatives.

[25] *Ibid.*, XI, 301-302 (*Über Anmuth und Würde*). Italics mine.
[26] *Ibid.*, XI, 306 and 307. Italics mine.

The *schöne Seele* of Schiller's mature position must be capable
of both types of moral action. Compare this with the following lines from the character of the "Happy Warrior":

> Whose powers shed round him in the common strife,
> Or mild concerns of ordinary life,
> A constant influence, a peculiar grace;
> But who if he be called upon to face
> Some awful moment to which Heaven has joined
> Great issues, good or bad for human kind,
> Is happy as a Lover; and attired
> With sudden brightness, like a Man inspired;
> And, through the heat of conflict, keeps the law
> In calmness made. . . .[27]

Although Wordsworth and Schiller may differ frequently on
shades of emphasis and matters of qualification, it is obvious
that they face the same problem and are disposed toward similar solutions.

We are interested here primarily in indicating the profound
similarity of Wordsworth's ethical thought of 1805-1807 and
Schiller's doctrine in such essays as "Anmuth und Würde"
which appeared twelve years earlier. We cannot, however,
avoid commenting upon the possibility of Schiller's having influenced Wordsworth in this matter. Professor Herzberg in
his article "Wordsworth and German Literature"[28] has amassed
considerable evidence which proves conclusively that Coleridge
was acquainted at an early period, 1798, with Schiller's dramatic writings. Furthermore, when, in later years, Coleridge
translated Schiller, he turned to the *Piccolomini* and to *Wal-
lenstein*. Now, conflict between heart and reason, so sharp
that it precludes the possibility of reconciliation, is the theme
of these plays. Thus Coleridge's interest in this aspect of
Schiller's work may well have led him to acquaint Wordsworth
with Schiller's prose in which this problem is discussed systematically.

[27] Ll. 45-54.
[28] Max F. Herzberg, "Wordsworth and German Literature," *PMLA*, XL,
302 ff. In a letter to Cottle, 1798, Coleridge compares Schiller's *The Robbers*
with Wordsworth's *The Borderers*, praising "those profound touches of the human heart" which both works contain (*Early Recollections*, I, 250).

Let us analyze the philosophy of the "Ode to Duty" and then compare it point by point with Schiller's ethics. There are three types of character described in the "Ode." (1) There is a spontaneous goodness of heart:

> Glad hearts without reproach or blot;
> Who do thy work and know it not.

Mention of this is offset by (2) an enthusiastic apotheosis of conscience, of self-control which is "victory and law." (3) Finally, conscience is described as being in its full development not a matter of self-denial and control, but a free and happy choice of alternatives.

1. Wordsworth admits that the first character, however lovely to witness, is not alone strong enough to face grave moral problems. The genial sense of youth is not reflective enough to comprehend the need of deliberate self-sacrifice. It is in its proper element only "where no misgiving is." This type of character—the *schöne Seele* quite unaided by conscience which, as we have just seen, falls below Schiller's ideal—is not the one celebrated in *The Prelude*, for there Wordsworth has insisted upon the importance of "clearest insight," upon "reason and its most exalted mood." There are, however, passages in *The Prelude* which seem to describe such a state of mind. These passages are inspired by Dorothy Wordsworth, and thus they in some measure corroborate Professor Harper's suggestion that, in describing the innocent and unreflective goodness of heart of the "Ode to Duty," Wordsworth had his sister in mind:

> . . . far less did critic rules
> Or barren intermeddling subtleties
> Perplex her mind; but, wise as Women are
> When genial circumstances hath favor'd them,
> She welcom'd what was given, and craved no more.
> Whatever scene was present to her eyes,
> That was the best, to that she was attuned
> Through her humility and lowliness,
> And through a perfect happiness of soul
> Whose variegated feelings were in this

Sisters, that they were each some new delight:
For she was Nature's inmate. Her the birds
And every flower she met with, could they but
Have known her, would have lov'd. Methought such charm
Of sweetness did her presence breathe around
That all the trees, and all the silent hills
And every thing she look'd on, should have had
An intimation how she bore herself
Towards them and to all creatures. God delights
In such a being; for her common thoughts
Are piety, her life is blessedness.[29]

Upon this passage at least one comment is in order. It is interesting to notice that Schiller considered grace, as distinct from rigidly conscientious integrity, to be a feminine characteristic in which men are frequently lacking. Although perhaps more capable of heroic self-command, men lack the harmony of sensation and intelligence, or of duty and desire, which becomes a gracious woman. Thus women possess beautiful souls more often than men. Man is less easily at peace, more doctrinaire and rigidly conscientious. He thus has a tendency to destroy what he produces. Schiller attributes this to restless pride in the poem "Würde der Frauen," but here for the moment his sympathies are clearly turned against his own sex. It is noteworthy that Wordsworth in "Tintern Abbey" had already described Dorothy as an unreflective person of quick sensibility. The *schöne Seele* is usually guided by taste rather than by principle, though capable of correcting taste when harsh problems arise.

2. The Wordsworth of *The Prelude* believed firmly that imaginative insight, the sort of creative interpretation which reveals the beauties of Nature and the characters of men, is a sufficient guide of life. As the illuminative source of virtue and of freedom, this faculty makes clear to us what we really

---

[29] *The Prelude*, Bk. XI, ll. 203 ff. In this connection, we must not forget Coleridge's first description of Dorothy included in a letter to Cottle (July, 1797):

"In every motion, her most innocent soul outbeams so brightly that who saw would say

    'Guilt was a thing impossible in her.' "

desire. In the "Ode to Duty," Wordsworth deserts this esthetic morality. Subtle sensibility may render a person gracious and attractive, even happy, but never profoundly moral. For this, the "firm support" of duty is necessary. We have already heard Schiller render the same decision. He has presented it as emphatically in the following:

Das Sittliche darf nie einen andern Grund haben, als sich selbst. Der Geschmack kann die Moralität des Betragens begünstigen . . . aber er selbst kann durch seinen Einfluss nie etwas Moralisches erzeugen.[30]

Wordsworth's "Ode" embodies sincere respect for duty conceived as an objective law, infinitely more important than our own private interests. Self-transcendence with its resulting impartiality of judgment is in itself a richer thing than "uncharted freedom." By submitting to moral law, one is freed from the weight of chance desires, acquiring a stability of character and true peace of mind. This fortitude must transcend the desires and rule them according to conscience. Even the *schöne Seele* cannot always accomplish this without moral effort. Here we find Wordsworth's "Ode" in its most truly stoical moment. In this belief he is at one with Kant, who values such autonomy as the triumph of human nature. The "measures and the forms" of duty are revealed to us by reason whose strict impartial universality will not tolerate an exception in our own favor. Thus the almost impersonal freedom of moral autonomy is supported by the "confidence of reason."

3. But consider once more the finally rejected stanza which contains the lines:

Denial and restraint I prize
No further than they breed a second Will more wise.

This attitude toward "denial and restraint" is precisely that of Schiller. Kant had maintained that actions possess moral value or merit only when performed solely out of respect for duty: if inclination and duty happen to coincide, no moral value attached to the act. Schiller admitted that no mere inclination can be described as moral, but he insisted that a character whose

[30] *Op. cit.*, XII, 235. *(Über den Moralischen Nutzen ästhetischer Sitten.)*

desires and interests have grown to coincide with duty itself
possesses a peculiar value. To overcome temptation is a victory over the enemy, but perhaps it is only an isolated victory.
Victory coupled with real enjoyment permanently vanquishes
the foe; it even reconciles him, as in the formation of a "second
will more wise."

It is only when man's moral attitude results from the united action
of the two principles (of desire and reason) and thus becomes the expression of his entire humanity—when it becomes natural to him—
that it is secure; for as long as the spirit employs violence, so long must
instinct use force to resist it. The enemy who is only overpowered
and cast down can rise again, but the enemy who is reconciled is truly
vanquished.[31]

Such free inclination toward duty may be illustrated by the
attitude of a kindly and courteous man who avoids giving
others pain or embarrassment, not solely because he believes
it wrong to do so but because he is freely inclined toward such
suavity and values this atmosphere in his personal relations.
This evaluation is essentially esthetic—an enjoyment of harmony, harmony of desires, interests, and sympathies within
one's own character. There may, of course, be times when
such a person finds himself faced with a "painful duty," and
then he must act upon a sterner motivation. But just as long
as duty remains painful we may say that he has still to recon-
cile the enemy. This inclination toward duty is clearly not the
ideal of *The Prelude,* where Wordsworth boldly maintains
that the pursuance of enlightened desire is in itself virtue.

In this discussion of the finally rejected stanza, we must
not forget that Wordsworth did at last remove it and that,
aside from its rejection, its content must be interpreted as an
ideal not yet realized by humanity. To construe it otherwise
would involve us in contradiction with the beginning of the
third stanza: "Serene will be our days and bright. . . ." It is
interesting to notice that Wordsworth thinks of this ideal as

        [31] *Op. cit.,* XI, 291. ("Über Anmuth und Würde.") The translation is that
of Professor Wilm, from whose work *The Philosophy of Schiller* (Boston, 1912)
I have drawn many helpful suggestions.

some day to be realized—though he once wrote, "serene *would be* our days."

Wordsworth's final invocation to duty as the beautiful revelation of deity as well as his use of the Hebraic "daughter of the voice" has no precise counterpart in Schiller's writings. The latter, unlike Wordsworth, was too thorough a Kantian to interpret his feelings in so boldly cosmic a fashion, whereas for Wordsworth, with his background of Nature mysticism, this was to be expected. And yet Schiller was not unaware of the beautiful aspect of sheer duty. In fact, recognition of this glorious aspect of moral character was in his eyes one of great motivating force supporting human virtue. Here it is not the purely esthetic ideal of graceful conduct, which motivates less heroic actions, but recognition of the power and the intrinsic dignity of moral autonomy.

Wordsworth's "the most ancient heavens through thee are fresh and strong" recalls, although perhaps it does not echo, Kant's famous passage in which he celebrates the sublimity of austere moral integrity—the starry heavens above and the moral law within.[32] In later life, this seems to have been the aspect of morality which most impressed Wordsworth. This significant change is heralded by Wordsworth's removal of stanza six of his first published draft of the "Ode to Duty." Without these lines the doctrine of the "Ode" inclines sharply towards a rigorous stoicism, unqualified by the doctrine of the *schöne Seele*. Thus the "Ode to Duty" marks even more clearly than has been supposed, a great turning-point in Wordsworth's thought, as he passed from a philosophy of sheer self-realization through the doctrine of the *schöne Seele* to the severe and rigorous stoicism of his later life. The final position is

---

[32] Kant writes in the conclusion of the *Critique of Practical Reason*: "Two things fill the mind with ever new and increasing admiration and awe, the oftener and the more steadily we reflect on them—the starry heavens above and the moral law within." The late Paul Elmer More has pointed out in his *Skeptical Approach to Religion* (Princeton, N. J., 1934), p. 116, that these words are little more than a prose version of the nineteenth Psalm:
> "The heavens declare the glory of God;
> And the firmament sheweth his handiwork.
> The law of the Lord is perfect, restoring the soul;
> The testimony of the Lord is sure, making wise the simple."

well exemplified in *The Excursion* and in such poems as *The White Doe of Rylstone* and "Laodamía" where the austerity of the later ethics is clear. Of the many passages that could be quoted from the last two poems to illustrate our point, let us be content with these: ". . . the Gods approve the depth, and not the tumult, of the soul"; and

> Her soul doth in itself stand fast,
> Sustained by memory of the past
> And strength of Reason; held above
> The infirmities of mortal love;
> Undaunted, lofty, calm, and stable,
> And awfully *impenetrable*.

CHAPTER VIII

Summary and Evaluation: The Tragic Flaw in Wordsworth's Philosophy

> . . . That was the curse prepared
> For me: I would not listen to my voices.
> —E. A. ROBINSON

MUCH OF THE noble enthusiasm which inspires *The Prelude* is of a social and political origin, and no one can say that Wordsworth's earlier writings are not to a large degree strengthened by his political interests. The ideal of liberty is taken up and absorbed into the development of Wordsworth's early philosophy, becoming inseparably united with the bold romantic individualism of *The Prelude*.

The mind of man, the locus of liberty, is the glory of the world, an awe-inspiring subject for contemplation.[1] Man is worthy of himself only when he realizes the dignity and power of which his mind is capable, owing to his essentially human endowment.[2] This power, the proper energy of mind,[3] is manifest in the creations of the imagination and the syntheses of the inquiring intelligence. It is, indeed, what Coleridge called the *esemplastic* power. Unlike the association of ideas or the unconscious forming of habits, this power is not borne in upon the mind by mechanical repetition: it is the fundamental assertion of the mind itself, genuine liberty, the full exercise of which is at once moral freedom and happiness. The philosophy of *The Prelude* centers upon this concept. The theories of education,[4] of art,[5] and of democratic politics[6] are founded upon it.

---

[1] *The Recluse*, ll. 788 ff.; *The Prelude*, Bk. III, ll. 178-194.
[2] *The Recluse*, ll. 811 ff.
[3] *The Prelude*, Bk. XI, ll. 270 ff.; Bk. II, l. 381, and elsewhere.
[4] Bk. V, esp, l. 499.
[5] Bk. II, l. 381; Bk. XI, ll. 269 ff., and elsewhere.
[6] Bk. XII, ll. 185-286, esp. ll. 249-277.

> . . . We added dearest themes,
> Man and his noble nature, as it is
> The gift of God and lies in his own power,
> His blind desires and steady faculties
> Capable of clear truth, the one to break
> Bondage, the other to build Liberty
> On firm foundations, making social life
> Through knowledge spreading and imperishable,
> As just in regulation, and as pure
> As individual in the wise and good.[7]

This inner nobility of man as man is the very first principle of a democratic philosophy which must ignore

> The differences, the outward marks by which
> Society has parted man from man,
> Neglectful of the universal heart.[8]

This principle of mental power is not to be nourished solely upon learning or the amassing of knowledge. It is imagination[9] and it can be aroused only by Art and Nature. But give the human mind the opportunity of an awakening, allow Nature quietly to stimulate the imagination and education humbly to further this development—in short, let the essential power of mind be released—then moral excellence, happiness, and a profound wisdom will follow of themselves. For the "human soul is good and graciously composed" and wants only the enlightenment of its own imagination.

Of course, the dominion of imagination cannot be established by the exercise of an abstract intelligence such as Godwin had advocated. Imagination flowers in the insight of the poet and the artist, orderly and comprehensive yet rich in concrete detail. It is often awakened by natural beauty, but it may also be inspired by human affairs, by the heroic or pathetic fact of human life itself. And this was indeed the case with Wordsworth during his first residence in London. We must understand people, not sheerly by classification and analysis, but by characterizing them as a disinterested novelist might

---

[7] Bk. IX, ll. 360 ff.
[8] Bk. XII, ll. 217 ff.
[9] Bk. XIII, ll. 84-210.

attempt to do, marking and evaluating their manners, interests, and ideals against the full and enduring background of their common life.[10] Once we have taken this attitude, we have solved the greatest of our practical problems. We find that we can follow our impulses and treat our fellow men literally as we want to treat them; and that we need never regret our actions, if only we can preface our desires by clear imaginative vision of our fellows and of their lives.

Surely then the human "frame is good and graciously composed"; human beings are worthy of self-government and, once truly awakened, quite capable of it. Such is the noble humanism of *The Prelude*, a philosophy of self-confidence and of enlightened self-assertion, which distinguishes its doctrine from the somewhat too conventional admonitions of *The Excursion* and later poems. But despite the energy with which the teaching of *The Prelude* was presented, its doctrine could not have had so profound a seat in Wordsworth's mind as we often suppose. As we all know, the ink was hardly dry upon the first draft of *The Prelude* when Wordsworth in no equivocal fashion repudiated its philosophy, for "Elegiac Stanzas" and parts of the "Ode to Duty" amount to a recantation. Furthermore, a careful survey of the last books of *The Prelude* itself indicates at least two or three passages where traces of a latent skepticism and dissatisfaction may be found. In Book XII, good men are recognized as the genuine "wealth of nations," but Wordsworth mentions his anxious meditations upon equalitarianism:

> . . . I could not but inquire,
> Not with less interest than heretofore,
> But greater, though in spirit more subdued,
> Why is this glorious Creature to be found
> One only in ten thousand? . . .[11]

Again we must remember that the virtues of the full imaginative life are in the last book of *The Prelude* attributed only to "higher minds,"[12] although no mention is here made of any

[10] Bk. XII, ll. 15-44.
[11] Bk. XII, ll. 87 ff.   [12] Bk. XIII, l. 90.

possible conflict between this doctrine and the democratic tenets of earlier passages.[13]   In "Elegiac Stanzas," however, there is no difficulty of interpretation. A wholly new attitude appears:

> Farewell, farewell the heart that lives alone,
> Housed in a dream, at distance from the Kind!
> Such happiness, wherever it be known,
> Is to be pitied; for 'tis surely blind.[14]

Here Wordsworth is repudiating the philosophy of *The Prelude,* which has come to appear as selfish and socially unobservant. Again in the "Ode to Duty" occurs a similar repudiation:

> I, loving freedom, and untried;
> No sport of every random gust,
> Yet being to myself a guide,
> Too blindly have reposed my trust:
> And oft, when in my heart was heard
> Thy timely mandate, I deferred
> The task, in smoother walks to stray;
> But thee I now would serve more strictly, if I may.[15]

The doctrine of *The Prelude* is spoken of with tolerance but is nonetheless found to be wanting. It seems to the Wordsworth of 1805-1806 to be pitifully subject to self-deceit and the weakness of rationalization. Man requires a standard of morality so firmly defined and rigorously stated that he can in no way alter its *dicta* or tamper with its integrity by a rationalizing interpretation. We shall presently question the validity of this criticism which Wordsworth directs against his own thought.

But now let us consider Wordsworth's first bit of self-criticism, the notion that in *The Prelude* he had entertained a philosophy "housed in a dream, at distance from the Kind." Certainly a perusal of the magnificent conclusion of *The Prelude* suggests to the reader no strain of selfishness, and, if we understand its doctrine, we can hardly feel that it is based upon a sheltered ignorance of human life. Surely Wordsworth

---

[13] For instance, with *The Recluse,* ll. 811 ff.
[14] "Elegiac Stanzas," ll. 53-56.   [15] Ll. 25-32.

does not deny the existence of evil or of suffering. He insists only that we enrich our understanding of life through concrete insight and so widen our sympathies before judging our fellow men or attempting to influence their lives. Where then lies the flaw in his thinking? I, for one, believe that there is in the conclusion of *The Prelude* no serious or fundamental flaw. The weakness of Wordsworth's philosophy is most clearly manifest not here but in the great ethical poems which follow, in "Elegiac Stanzas," "Ode to Duty," *The Excursion,* and "Laodamía."

There are, most broadly speaking, two attitudes of the intellectual towards democracy: one in which he would raise all men, who, he recognizes, are equal in fundamental capacity, toward a life of responsible self-government; the other in which he recognizes in many if not all of the humble and untutored a strength and wisdom which he may not himself possess, an ability to face the real world, born of stress and its complementary fortitude.

The first of these appears clearly in *The Recluse* and the second occasionally in *The Prelude*[16] and in such poems as "Resolution and Independence" and "Elegiac Stanzas." These two points of view are not necessarily contradictory. They can exist side by side as they do in Wordsworth's earlier thought. After all, men of intellectual and of moral virtue have much to learn of one another. But there is possible a confusion of these elements, and this we may call the *democratic fallacy,* a sadly perverted form of equalitarian doctrine, which, although frequently arising in democratic communities, is by no means essential to democracy or indeed a necessary outcome of it. This fallacy appears when the gifted man hesitates to make full use of his gifts, is even suspicious of them, because they are not universal. This line of thought becomes even more dangerous if the man of genius has at one time overestimated the power of his less endowed fellows. He may finally come to suspect even his own strength. This I believe to have been the case with Wordsworth.

[16] Bk. XII; Bk. IX, ll. 387 ff.

As we have seen, Wordsworth had drawn from Godwin, if only for a brief period, a certainty that man must free himself from convention and sentiment and solve his problems, individual and social, solely by the aid of analytic intelligence. This philosophy he shortly repudiated, having recognized, not without bitter disappointment, that reason by itself, working as it does with abstract terms, offers but meager motivation for man's emotions and engenders but little strength of will.[17] He then supplemented his Godwinism with his own doctrine of the ethical imagination above described. In this doctrine Wordsworth retained something, however little, of Godwinism. The individual remains his own arbiter of right and wrong, and man's mind, albeit his imagination rather than his reason, remains its own court of highest appeal. What I really want to do when I have envisaged my situation and the people involved in the full clarity of concrete imagery—that is the right thing to do. There is no other way, rational or traditional of determining right or wrong. I must face the world, "being to myself a guide." And so must all men who are capable of moral life.

While working upon *The Prelude*, Wordsworth had, as we have seen, pondered the problem: How many men are capable of such responsibility? All, of course, possess the capacity, for all men possess the nucleus of imagination or they would be incapable of the simplest acts of knowing, of the most rudimentary awareness of unity in variety. This fact was at one time enough for Wordsworth. In time, under democratic ideals and wholesome education guided by sound romantic teaching, genuine moral liberty would be the possession of all. Furthermore, men would learn to appreciate the natural religion which must accompany the dominion of imagination. We have already seen that Wordsworth believed all human beings to be at least *capable* of some mystical insight. This hope for the future was enough, and until this happy consummation, the "higher minds," the few romantic intellectuals and the rarely gifted children of Nature, untutored but happily inspired, must preserve this substantial wisdom.

[17] 1850, Bk. XI, ll. 309 ff.

The unenlightened must be brought slowly to the position of the elect, such is the faith of 1800. This belief is tempered somewhat by doubts and qualifications expressed in *The Prelude*. Some men are perhaps almost incapable of enlightenment, and some fortunate souls need very little enlightening. But the faith remains throughout unretracted: Virtue is the the child of imagination and the only path to virtue and wisdom lies through expansion of the individual's imaginative powers. The poet, the true romantic poet, the imaginative man par excellence, is the proper teacher of the human race. Thus Wordsworth writes of himself in the last lines of *The Recluse* fragment:

> . . . may my life
> Express the image of a better time. . . .

Suddenly, at least in appearance, this faith is retracted: the poets must discipline their wayward genius and assume the patient fortitude and sturdy endurance of the humble. They have withdrawn themselves and housed their ideals in a dream, and their ideals are selfish and futile. They must go to school to the very people that they had once considered their rightful pupils. They must assume the "unfeeling armor of old time," so admired in the "Elegiac Stanzas."

Even so, the time may come when a romantic individualism, the ethics of imagination, may become feasible:

> Serene will be our days and bright,
> And happy will our nature be,
> When love is an unerring light,
> And joy its own security.

But this Utopian state can apparently arise only as the result of long years of self-discipline on the part of mankind in general. And in Europe of the Napoleonic era, even "higher minds" are incapable of such free self-assertion. They must subject themselves to the authority of a law of duty. Essentially, this doctrine is repeated in *The Excursion*, Book IV, where the Wanderer rebukes a presumptuous generation for having expected to accomplish too much.[18]

[18] Ll. 260-331.

To account for this *volte-face*, we find available three or four possible explanations which have been offered at one time or another by Wordsworth's biographers. (1) In the first place, we may attribute it to the temporary failure of French democracy, and its passage under Napoleon into imperial dictatorship. The philosophers seemed to have betrayed the people or, at least, advised them so badly that the people became willy-nilly the victims of an archadventurer. Certainly at this time the human virtues might easily appear to advantage in contrast with the ideals of revolutionary individualism which seemed to have been treacherously perverted to such foul ends.

(2) Again it may be true that, brooding over his unhappy relations with Annette Vallon and considering the suffering and unhappiness which impulse had produced, Wordsworth may have come to believe that human nature is fundamentally incapable of "being to itself a guide." This unfortunate affair, however, lay well in the past, dating from a time when even the philosophy of *The Prelude* was unformulated. Hence had remorse for the desertion of Annette exercised any effect upon his philosophy, it would have checked the first development of such thinking rather than have caused its decline. Furthermore, impulsive weakness may easily enough be explained according to the psychology of *The Prelude*. We often act impulsively when our impulses are unenlightened by full comprehension, expressed in concrete imagery, of their present significance and possible consequences.

(3) Perhaps most important of all the reasons advanced is that expressed in "Elegiac Stanzas": "A deep distress hath humanized my soul." Under the emotional strain of a cruel bereavement, the loss of his brother John, Wordsworth came to value more highly the virtues of endurance and resignation. This, to be sure, is a natural and quite comprehensible development of his personality. It is only when such insight leads to repudiation of the efficacy of a philosophy of self-enlightenment that we must put it down as a counsel of despair. After all, Wordsworth's bereavement really widened his imaginative

sympathies, as the "Elegiac Stanzas" eloquently tell, and included within the sphere of his understanding attitudes never before so clearly envisaged.

(4) It is also important to remember in the above connection that at this time, as the "Intimations Ode" suggests, Wordsworth recognized a certain decline in his own gifts of intense esthetic sensibility and of mystical exaltation. The resultant loss of self-confidence might well be reflected in his emphasis upon the humble virtues and the philosophy of duty. Duty may then appear as the one sure foundation of human dignity, without which man is a poor creature, weak and insignificant:

> Possessions vanish, and opinions change,
> And passions hold a fluctuating seat:
> But, by the storms of circumstance unshaken,
> And subject neither to eclipse nor wane,
> Duty exists. . . .[19]

We might call this a philosophy of self-defense as opposed to the philosophy of self-confidence, so clearly expressed in *The Prelude*.[20]

These reasons, offered frequently as explanations of Wordsworth's change of heart, are most assuredly not to be dismissed. Certainly the first, third, and fourth seem to bear out our problem. But it seems clear that no one of these influences could have determined Wordsworth's thinking profoundly had it

---

[19] *The Excursion*, Bk. IV, ll. 69 ff.

[20] If the reader will turn to Professor Gilbert Murray's famous essay on Stoicism, he will find a masterful account of the psychology underlying acceptance of a philosophy of self-defense. Professor Murray's phrase "loss of nerve" is especially significant and, I think, applies to Wordsworth. I cannot refrain, in passing, from offering an adverse criticism of all philosophies of duty which try, so to speak, to make of some rational principle or formula a rock upon which human nature may rest secure. The theory is simply that by surrendering ourselves to the dictates of an absolute principle of duty, we transcend ourselves and escape the weaknesses of an unaided human nature. But these principles, modern categorical imperatives or more ancient formulas, must, of course, be interpreted to meet concrete situations. In this very interpretation there lies the danger of rationalization, certainly as great as that attendant upon determining what we really want to do. If the reader doubts this, he has only to consult the textbook criticisms of Kant's categorical imperative. In a word, practical ethics cannot be reduced to a discipline, however much the weary and the timid may desire to have it so simplified.

not been for his unhappy readiness to entertain what we have called the democratic fallacy. Had these circumstances arisen before a thinker quite free of any merely sentimental interest in praising his fellow men or of any desire to be as like them as possible, the outcome must have been very different. And, be it said in defense of *The Prelude*, the benevolence which it teaches does not necessarily involve such a sentimentalism.

II

Much can be said, despite the above, in defense of the "Ode to Duty," even by a Wordsworth enthusiast whose center of gravity lies deep in *The Prelude*, especially if he reads the "Ode" in the version published in 1807, which, alone of all the editions of the poem, contains as its sixth stanza the following lines:

> Yet none the less would I throughout
> Still act according to the voice
> Of my own wish; and feel past doubt
> That my submissiveness was choice:
> Not seeking in the school of pride
> For "precepts over dignified,"
> Denial and restraint I prize
> No farther than they breed a second Will more wise.

Here duty and enlightened inclination seem capable of reconciliation in the life of the morally successful man. The rigor of a categorical imperative and the "confidence of reason" which such a formula is said to supply are seen as preliminary or probationary supports of the comparatively immature moral agent. At least the above stanza suggests such doctrine. Thus Wordsworth seems to have hesitated between a philosophy of complete stoicism and a reformed version of the humanism of *The Prelude*. As late as 1809, the date of the pamphlet on the Convention of Cintra, there remains some trace of the earlier philosophy. The people are in many cases, we are told, greater than their leaders who, being immersed in political competition, quite fail to understand and often betray them. Wordsworth speaks enthusiastically of the foundations of popular virtue, "the instincts of natural and social man, the deeper emotions, the simpler feelings, *the spacious range of the disinterested imagination,* the pride in country for country's sake, when to serve has not been a formal profession . . ." (italics mine).

But, we may comment, if leaders are not to be trusted, the people in their homely wisdom, ought not to follow them. The moral is clear. Since the people cannot lead themselves, there should be no change in social and political life. And Wordsworth was soon to recognize this conclusion, implicit in the development of his thought. The Cintra pamphlet presents a truncated form of the philosophy of *The Prelude.* Popular virtue is recognized and similarly explained in both writings; but in the later work there is obvious a suspicion concerning the very possibility of great, radical leadership. This is symptomatic of Wordsworth's development, as he passes from *The Prelude* to *The Excursion,* where reactionary politics begin to be clearly manifest. This retreat is inevitable; for unless some individuals are recognized as possessing the right and the strength to consider themselves as prophetic reformers, distinct from the multitude, no philosophy of revolution or even of progress is possible. Nothing could emphasize the development of this later attitude more sharply than Wordsworth's appreciation of Burke inserted in *The Prelude,* according to De Selincourt, not before 1820. Here Wordsworth praises the philosopher who

> Declares the vital power of social ties
> Endeared by Custom; and with high disdain,
> Exploding upstart Theory, insists
> Upon the allegiance to which men are born. . . .[21]

In the last book of *The Excursion,* some few years previously, Wordsworth had insisted that "The primal duties shine aloft—like stars" and that knowledge of right and wrong based upon reason, imagination, and conscience are vouchsafed alike to all. But in praising Burke, a few years later, he was willing to emphasize Custom as the great teacher.

[21] 1850, Bk. VII, ll. 527 ff.

The triumph of the democratic fallacy, with its pernicious leveling of great minds and small, leads to an inevitable and ironic conclusion. It finally destroys faith in democracy. If we are to identify ourselves with "the Kind" and accept the virtues of endurance, we will come to accept the traditional supports of the humble and gather stoically beneath the orthodox and conservative strongholds of church and state. With these great fortresses of security we shall not care to tamper. In fact, there seems something indecent in any attempt to recast the scheme of things. Of such development in Wordsworth's thinking we are all only too well aware. The extreme illiberalism which resulted in his political thought is too well known to require much comment. His opposition to reform, expressed with timid and suspicious querulousness, is almost identical with the attitude of an aristocratic arch-conservative, although the fear of change which is its usual aspect has an ultimate origin quite distinct from any aristocratic sentiment. This fear of change led Wordsworth to oppose universal education and the freedom of the press, and this latter as early as 1814, within ten years of the completion of the first draft of *The Prelude*. But Wordsworth's intellectual progress from "Elegiac Stanzas" was an inevitable one. Once doubt the value of the intellectual and spiritual independence of the individual, and the rest follows.

We have described the vacillations of Wordsworth's thought while he passes from *The Prelude* to *The Excursion* as a wavering between the philosophies of "I *want*" and of "I *must*," between the ideal of self-realization and the ideal of self-transcending duty. In this his thought is clearly less balanced than that of Dante or even of Goethe, if we consider the latter's thought as expressed in such a poem as his "Vermächtniss." It is this vacillation that reveals the tragic flaw in Wordsworth's philosophy. The moral insight so brilliantly presented in *The Prelude* is very shortly marred and finally, in the later poems, wholly obscured by Wordsworth's failure to perceive that these two approaches to morality can be rendered mutually consistent. Wordsworth faces a fatal disjunction: either we are to develop ourselves, our insights and our sympathies and proceed according to a romantic version of Augustine's formula, *Ama et fac quod vis,* or we are to submit ourselves wholly to the discipline of an established principle of duty. There can be no alternative or middle course. This becomes clear when we consider Wordsworth's final deletion of the important sixth stanza of the 1807 "Ode to Duty."

We have only to compare the moral tone of "Laodamía" with that of the "Ode to Duty" to recognize how significant a turning-point the repudiation of this stanza marks. After all, in the "Ode" duty is presented, as also in the letter to *Mathetes,* as an attractive and beautiful ideal in harmony still with Wordsworth's natural religion. The ideal of "Laodamía" is heroic but forbidding, almost dour; the gods frown more readily than the flowers laugh.

In the 1807 "Ode," respect for temporarily unpleasant duty may through our appreciation of its full significance be transmuted into a "second will" free from the earlier tensions. This is in no very important respect inconsistent with the doctrine of *The Prelude,* where Wordsworth admits that in ethical development we must "complete the man . . . made imperfect in himself."[22]

Had Wordsworth proceeded in this way and expanded the important ideas involved, the philosophy of *The Prelude* might well have been richly supplemented. But here Wordsworth failed. Imagination and spontaneous enjoyment are discounted in favor of stoic endurance such as appears in the *White Doe.* And I very much fear that this evaluation is founded largely upon the feeling that in accepting dutiful endurance as the prime virtue, we are identifying ourselves with "the Kind." Thus the democratic fallacy seems to triumph.

Wordsworth's failure to integrate the philosophy of *The Prelude* with a theory of duty constitutes a real loss to our modern culture. It is one of our fundamental weaknesses that we habitually see life as divided between play and real enjoyment on the one hand and important work and duty on the

[22] Bk. XIII, l. 202.

other. What we want to do and what we ought to do stand
apart even in theory. This is perhaps inevitable in an irreligious and commercial civilization. But against this error
Wordsworth's teaching might well have proven to be a great
force had he overcome his own confusion, for he at least faced
our problem and in his happier periods held a key to its
solution.

But let us here in fairness to Wordsworth admit that the
democratic fallacy, as we have described it, confused and perverse as it is, rests upon one sentiment among others, which is
clearly an honorable one. This is an intense dislike of making
an exception of oneself. It is from this underlying motive,
which in the minds of rationalist philosophers may be interpreted as a respect for strict logical consistency in practical life,
that the real power of Kant's categorical imperative derives.
Consider Walt Whitman's famous resolve to accept nothing
that all men might not enjoy on the same terms. This may
be a sound foundation for equalitarian ethical doctrine, but of
course it should be read as requiring equal opportunity rather
than any limitation of achievement to the common level.

Wordsworth's later attitude toward religion is worth attention. We may grant that the need of a spiritual security to be
drawn from sources external to the self initiates a sound approach to religion. But Wordsworth becomes too eager to
accomplish his pilgrimage, too dogmatically certain of what
is to be learned from humility. He will take no chances, so
strong is his philosophy of self-defense, in religion any more
than in politics. The "wise passiveness" of his earlier philosophy, the willingness to follow where his richly expanding
experience might lead him is now quite vanished. His religion lacks plasticity and what Professor A. E. Taylor has called
the element of surprise.

Compare the fourth "Evening Voluntary" (1834) with
any poem which expresses a genuinely active religion, say
Blake's *Sunflower* or Herbert's *The Pulley*:

> But who *is* innocent? By grace divine,
> Not otherwise, O Nature! we are thine,

Through good and evil thine, in just degree
Of rational and manly sympathy.
To all that Earth from pensive hearts is stealing,
And Heaven is now to gladdened eyes revealing,
Add every charm the Universe can show
Through every change its aspects undergo—
Care may be respited, but not repealed;
No perfect cure grows on the bounded field.
Vain is the pleasure, a false calm the peace,
If He, through whom alone our conflicts cease,
Our virtuous hopes without relapse advance,
Come not to speed the Soul's deliverance;
To the distempered Intellect refuse
His gracious help, or give what we abuse.[23]

What mechanical piety this is!   As mechanical as the verse.
But we must look for little else. For the Wordsworth of this
period faith is no longer seeking understanding. It repudiates
the very sources from which understanding once sprang. All
is fixed and unquestionable. Doubt and intellectual independence have no real function, not even that of leading us toward
profounder insight. Nor does the poet listen with "wise passiveness" for the old Eolian visitations.[24] Neither reason nor
inspiration is needed now.

But such considerations only convince us how much the
English-speaking world has lost by the tragic failure of Wordsworth's philosophy.

* * *

When we contemplate the grave difficulties which Wordsworth's ethical philosophy encounters, and when we consider
that at one time he was willing to condemn his earlier philosophy as a mere rationalization of selfish impulse, we are reminded of the new humanist criticisms of romantic ethics,
presented in recent years by the late Irving Babbitt and the

[23] "Evening Voluntary," IV, ll. 16-31.
[24] We have only to recall Wordsworth's growing emphasis on craftsmanship
and the "art" of poetry—his comments on which, as his letters show, could grow
pedantic—to recognize that he quite "outgrew" the philosophy of poetry and of
life expressed in the lyrics of 1798. See especially the letter to Sir William M.
Gorman, April 16, 1834.

late Paul Elmer More. These writers, at once, critics and philosophers, have found much to condemn in the ethical teaching of romanticism. And, after observing the instability of Wordsworth's ethical thinking, we are in no position lightly to pass over their comment. Perhaps we shall have to conclude with the admission that the new humanist evaluation of romantic ethics is very similar to Wordsworth's own repudiation of his earlier theory of morals. At any rate, the point will bear investigation.

But while we are stating the points at issue between the new humanism and romanticism, it will be wisest to consider the ethics of imagination as a trend of thought which is by no means exhaustively presented in the work of any one thinker.

Like all great ways of thought, romantic ethics has passed through a period of dogmatic enthusiasm and then slowly collected itself into a more consistent and systematic form. The Romantic poets, influenced in one way or another by such divergent thinkers as Plato, Boehme, Spinoza, Shaftesbury, Rousseau, Kant and Schiller, first clearly stated the romantic theme in modern ethics. In recent times this theme has been restated in a more consistent manner by such thinkers as Bergson and Croce and by their many followers. These later formulations should by no means be overlooked by those of us who are tempted to dwell solely upon the earlier and less coherent statements of the poets although the latter are, to be sure, artistically much more powerful.

Again, in judging romantic ethics, we must not censure it because it has been misunderstood or because grave abuses, which it is eager to condemn, have at times arisen in its name. It seems that the devil can quote Wordsworth and Blake today as glibly as he once quoted Scripture. In fact, he is, I suspect, soon to become an apt, if perverse, scholar in the school of the new humanism itself. He will find in certain criticisms of humanitarian doctrine several texts as easily distorted as any which his nimble brain has ever twisted into plausible caricature. There has never been a fool-proof philosophy, romantic, classical, or humanist, and I shudder to think of the banalities to which we should be committed were we to attempt to construct one.

All great philosophies involve a theory of man. The romanticist theory of man is most pithily expressed by Croce when he writes in his *Esthetic: "Homo nascitur poeta."* By this he means, if we may translate his terminology into one with which we are familiar, "man is an imaginative animal that he may become a rational or a moral animal." Imagination is not daydreaming, it is not reverie. Reverie makes no effort to attend to one object, but surrenders to association and is borne along upon its stream. Reverie lacks the internal coherence of imagination, which either by conscious effort or uncontrolled interest attends to one object which may or may not be present in the physical environment. Of course if one wishes to speak of sheer reverie as a lower form of imagination, say, the "pathetic" imagination, one is within his rights. But these two things must never be confused.

If we ignore the problem of imagination's mystical origin, we may describe this function as the activity which selects and unites words, images, ideas, or plans of action so that they shall reveal a significance or realize a purpose which in their isolation they cannot achieve. Imagination is the fundamental principle of the human mind. It underlies all the other mental activities, including analytical reason which is so frequently described as its opposite. We must all imagine or we must be silent and inactive, for imagination is indispensable to all interpretation, expression, and communication. Indeed, the most pedantic scheme of classification, the most pedestrian exercise of labeling and pigeonholing, owes its origin to a once fresh imaginative vision now long forgotten.

Art differs from commonplace communication only in degree. The poet is, so to speak, the athlete of imagination. Sedentary or commonplace expression is imagination that falls into habitual routine, imagination which repeats itself and becomes mechanical. It is imagination in bondage to its own past. Pure imagination struggles against this countertendency and seeks to maintain a dominion over habits of speech and of action which, if uncontrolled, tend to repeat the past. Pure imagination employs and transforms routine rather than succumbing to it.

Imagination pursues a free search for meaning. By *free search* I do not mean to include capricious or irresponsible groping. I mean activity free from mechanical repetition, dominated by no authoritarian methods or standards, something that is at once autonomous and spontaneous. Successful imagination renders meaning in a form that is inseparable from the words or images employed. The words and images are not ready-made but moulded and fused together in a unique ensemble. That is why poetry, or the more concentrated embodiments of imagination, cannot be successfully translated.

The power of pure or unrelaxed imagination lies in this. We are aware, when we participate in it, not only of ideas but of ideas which seem to present themselves as concrete realities. And it is this lively presence of the imaginative object which may awaken man to decision and to action. The products of pure imagination, even when they are not highly sensuous in style, offer a compact ensemble of detail which the schematic patterns and formulas of analytical reason nearly always lack. Thus enthusiasm can rarely be awakened and never long sustained by sheer reasoning. No ideal can transform life that fails to receive imaginative embodiment. Hence the wise reluctance on the part of so many to substitute more scholarly and accurate prose for the concentrated imagination of the King James Bible.

Plato, Napoleon Bonaparte, the poet Shelley, and Babbitt agree on one thing. Imagination can rule mankind. Man differs from the animals in that he can pursue or seek to avoid objects and situations which are not present in his immediate environment. And he tends to pursue or avoid those things which he clearly and vividly imagines. This led Plato to the conclusion that freedom of imagination should be suppressed. He found no room in his ideal republic for self-made and unacknowledged legislators who might mould the imaginations of their fellows. Shelley, on the other hand, whose Platonism

springs rather more from the *Phaedrus* and the *Symposium*
than from the *Republic,* finds in robust imagination the one
great instrument of moral development:

Ethical science arranges the elements which poetry has created, and
propounds schemes and proposes examples of civil and domestic life:
nor is it for want of admirable doctrines that men hate, and despise,
and censure, and deceive, and subjugate one another. But poetry acts
in another and diviner manner. It awakens and enlarges the mind
itself by rendering it the receptacle of a thousand unapprehended com-
binations of thought. . . .[25]

Shelley continues:

The great secret of morals is love; or a going out of our nature,
and an identification of ourselves with the beautiful which exists in
thought, action, or person, not our own. A man, to be greatly good,
must imagine intensely and comprehensively; he must put himself in
the place of another and of many others; the pains and pleasures of
his species must become his own. The great instrument of moral
good is the imagination; and poetry administers to the effect by acting
upon the cause. . . . Poetry strengthens the faculty which is the organ
of the moral nature of man, in the same manner as exercise strengthens
a limb. . . .

We have more moral, political, and historical wisdom than we
know how to reduce into practice; we have more scientific and eco-
nomical knowledge than can be accommodated to the just distribution
of the produce which it multiplies. . . . But we let "I *dare not* wait
upon *I would,* like the poor cat in the adage." We want the creative
faculty to imagine that which we conceive; we want the poetry of life:
our calculations have outrun conception; we have eaten more than
we can digest. The cultivation of those sciences which have enlarged
the limits of the empire of men over the external world, has, for want
of the poetic faculty, proportionally circumscribed those of the internal
world; and man, having enslaved the elements, remains himself a
slave.[26]

Without a robust imagination man is the slave of the
civilization which he has produced. But Shelley has not con-

[25] J. Shawcross (ed.), *Shelley's Literary and Philosophical Criticism* (London, 1909), p. 131.
[26] *Ibid.,* p. 151.

sidered the possibility that man may become the slave of imagination. Will imagination always conduct itself as happily as Shelley seems to think? Imagination is the soul of persuasion, it is the very life-blood of communication. Its instrumental value is unlimited. But can imagination judge the ends and ideals which it presents so vividly? For Shelley, poetry or imagination must determine these ultimate values or they must remain undetermined, for ethical science, according to Shelley, can only arrange the elements which poetry has created. Can we safely trust our destiny to the guidance of what Shelley calls "poetry"?

On this point Shelley and the new humanists disagree. But in Shelley we find an early and perhaps overenthusiastic form of romantic ethics. We shall find that the disagreement is not so sharp, if we consider other romanticists. But even here there will be evident an important if not irreconcilable opposition. For the new humanist, imagination is to be recognized as powerful and therefore as dangerous. It is a manifestation of the expansive forces, the *élan vital* of the human spirit. If human nature is conceived as essentially good, its expansive affirmations are thought to be completely trustworthy; and this for the humanist is the origin of an anarchic ethics of self-expression and self-realization which in his eyes is only the apotheosis of caprice, strengthened by an irresponsible imagination. This centrifugal force must be withstood, and indeed in the conduct of anyone who is not wholly corrupted by romantic error it *is* to some extent withstood, but not by imagination. It is by conscience, known to the humanist as the *frein vital* or inner check, that this may be accomplished.

This inner check is introduced with both traditional and psychological credentials. We are referred to the demon of Socrates and to the still small voice of Scripture, on the one hand, and on the other to the immediate data of consciousness which since the time of Descartes have been often thought to constitute a source of philosophical authority. To be sure, the humanists admit that the inner check is not equally obvious to all human beings. But those who lose sight of it have been benighted by false teaching. For the humanist all healthy traditions involve some emphasis upon conscientious restraint. The concept of moral law is universally human, and those who do not feel the presence of a restraining law have distorted their essential human nature. It is also asserted as a corollary that those who lose sight of their own weakness, of their tendency to know the better and do the worse, are deficient in introspection. Babbitt viewed even Socrates with mild suspicion because he tended, despite his demon, to identify virtue and knowledge and argued that to know the good is to follow it. For the humanist, to know the good and to follow the worse course is the essential human weakness against which the force of the inner check must ever be directed.

With all this I can find little fault. Certainly no serious student of morals wishes to ignore the important experience of self-restraint. But there are two questions which we must consider carefully before we accept or reject the humanist criticism of romantic ethics: (1) What is the inner check? and (2) Has romantic ethics any place for the inner check once it is properly interpreted?

These two questions lead to a third: If the inner check exercises restraint upon so powerful a faculty as imagination, what is its relation to imagination? We may be aided in answering this by returning once more to the thought of William Wordsworth, who after 1805 had as much to say about conscience as any modern humanist. Since Wordsworth is also a prophet of the imagination, we should expect to find in his thought something that is relevant to our inquiry. In *The Prelude* Wordsworth glorifies the ethical power of imagination, the full exercise of which will insure the autonomy of the individual soul, the inner sovereignty and peace of will which has so long characterized the philosophical ideal of human life.

> Emotion which best foresight need not fear,
> Most worthy then of trust when most intense.[27]

In this view of conduct there is little mention of conscience, nor is there any consistent recognition that conscientious re-

[27] *The Prelude*, Bk. XIV, ll. 122-123.

straint is necessary once the imagination has been aroused and holds dominion over the affections.

But, as we have seen, hardly had Wordsworth expressed this view of life and of conduct than he repudiated it, seemingly frightened by the very aspect of what he had produced. He concluded that only under Utopian conditions can imagination and desire, enlightened by imagination, be laws unto themselves; and he suggested that his earlier too eager idealism had led him into a life of narrow and selfish concerns, when he had ignored the "timely mandate" of the sense of duty. Quiet endurance of human lot, the dignity of renunciation and submission appeared as far stabler virtues than the expansive freedom of *The Prelude*. A philosophy of inner check seemed almost wholly to supersede the earlier ethics.

But this second position of Wordsworth's is not strictly, humanistic. It is rather stoical. The individual insures himself against despair by substituting resignation, by renouncing personal ambition and refusing to allow himself the privilege of criticizing the great traditions. In such a scheme an impersonal conscience quite overrules the imagination of the individual. We have noted that Wordsworth in swinging suddenly from romantic individualism to stoicism reveals a certain instability of vision. He has become acquainted with the two great forces of moral life, with imagination and with conscience. But he does not know how to make the two live together and so he swings from one extreme to another. And we have seen that Wordsworth never wholly freed himself from this perplexity, for he retreated, as the years went by, further and further into his stoicism. But even this stoicism finds an important ally in imagination, in what Wordsworth called the "imaginative will" which upholds "principles of truth." Thus the ultimate ideals of life are affirmed by an ethical will which has need of imagination to support its dictates in a form palpable to the affections. Imagination seems, as is suggested in *The Excursion* (Bk. IX, l. 223), to assure freedom in that it makes feasible our control of emotion and desire. But it is not the function of imagination to guide: this is reserved for conscience, which is frequently identified with moral or practical reason, somewhat according to the Kantian pattern.

In *The Excursion,* Book IV, conscience is described as a manifestation of something substantially permanent and eternal; whereas desire is thought to be unstable and changing, even within the life of one individual. Hence conscience is granted the paramount position in human life, nor is imagination at this time considered even as a likely candidate for this honor. Conscience, so exalted, is no longer an inner check or timely mandate but the very guide of life to which all human energies should, it is thought, submit.

This position is no more satisfactory to the new humanist than is the earlier position of *The Prelude.* The humanist has no more faith in a dominant conscience than he has in a dominant imagination. For him moral health requires an interplay of the two. Those who emphasize the exclusive importance of a rational conscience produce formulas comparable to Kant's categorical imperative, the application of which to actual situations is notoriously a matter of gravest difficulty. Babbitt was never weary of censuring philosophies of this type in which a rigid rationalism dominates, just as Paul Elmer More spoke sharply of the "fiat money" of metaphysical speculation. So our problem still stands. A study of Wordsworth may help us state our difficulties, but we shall not find in this early stage of the development of romantic philosophy any wholly satisfactory solution. How are we to describe the interplay of conscience and ethical imagination without surrendering one wholly to the domination of the other? In other words, what is the inner check, and how is it related to imagination?

We shall not find that the new humanists themselves offer an adequate answer to this question. They try to silence our doubts by speaking of the inner check as an immediate datum of consciousness, thereby seeking to suggest that it requires no further explanation and that its status in the phenomenology of the spirit is evident. But if we decline to analyze the *frein vital* we shall never know what it is, even though we feel its presence as vividly as we experience love or hatred. And if we do not analyze, we shall often confuse genuine conscience with its most specious counterfeit, timidity engendered by the pressure of convention and the fear of disapproval. Philosophy should never renounce its rights to examine and to ponder, although the philosopher must recognize that there is a time for contemplation and a time for action and belief.

In the sequel I shall suggest, following Croce's lead without adopting his terminology, a line of thought which distinguishes imagination from conscience and shows how genuine conscience arises from the working of imagination, in one sense depending upon imagination although exercising an influence upon it. Conscience is the consciousness of the limitations of our imagination. It is simply the admission that we may be ignoring an important point of view, that there may be many other ways of interpreting our situation, ways which we have not explored. Conscience becomes a sense of guilt when we recognize that greater caution or greater persistence—in short, more light and less heat—would have made another mode of action appear as the satisfactory one. In other words, conscience, as the name implies, is self-knowledge. This self-knowledge is necessary if we are to correct imagination's tendency to ignore everything but the vision of the moment. To quote R. G. Collingwood:

In thinking something out, as Kepler thought out the paths of the planets, we imagine the alternatives and then accept one and reject the rest; but in imagination the first stage does not exist. In making up a tune, we do not try the various notes to see which to put next; we imagine the whole tune, and then, if we are dissatisfied with it, re-imagine it afresh with some change which in altering a single note alters the quality of the whole. Hence the will to imagine is a will which does not contemplate alternatives; it is an "immediate" will, a will merely to do what one is doing. And in this way art is the most primitive practical activity, just as it is the most primitive theoretical activity.

In imagining, we do not contemplate the alternative possible imaginations. It follows that the coherence or unity which is the goal of imagination is a coherence of this individual imagination with itself, and not with any other. So far as it is a successful piece of imagining considered in itself, it is beautiful; and this beauty is quite unaffected by the question whether anybody else or I myself at another time have imagined anything compatible or incompatible with it. In this, imagining is sharply opposed to thinking.[28]

Thus thought must strengthen ethical imagination by reminding us of imagination's limitations. But thought alone cannot successfully move the human will nor can it adequately reduce morality to a formula. All it can do is to remind us that no one moment of imagination offers a complete vision of life in all its aspects and dimensions. Intelligent conscience must urge imagination to complete its work. It can do this best by reminding us of the many times in the past when we have allowed decision to follow hastily upon the first look. Thus conscience does not really check imagination. On the contrary, it urges us to employ imagination more amply. The fault of much romanticism is simply that conscience has not urged the romanticist to be imaginative enough. If we are to realize Shelley's ideal and imagine intensely and comprehensively, putting ourselves in the place of another and of many others, we must employ more than mere imagination. Our imagination must be stimulated by a thoughtful conscience.

To sum up: romanticists and new humanists agree in recognizing the enormous power of imagination which rules mankind. The earlier exponents of romanticism erred in that they overlooked the importance of conscience. The new humanists err in that they tend to consider conscience as something so fundamental that it cannot be analyzed and thus they fail to describe its true status. After analysis we learn that if we are to call conscience an inner check we must remember that it is not a check upon imagination but upon volition which it at times retards in order to allow the ethical imagination to survey its world more amply. Thus the new humanist criticism of romantic ethics, although not without justification of a sort, is incomplete. It is also beside the point, insofar as final evaluation is concerned, because thinkers working within the romantic position may find it possible to correct the immature but

[28] *Outlines of a Philosophy of Art* (London, 1925), pp. 22-23.

almost inevitable extravagance of romanticism as it first reacted against earlier ways of thought.

In *The Prelude* Wordsworth seems to have included within the scope of ethical imagination some such conscientious check upon narrow or hasty decision. Let us examine with this in mind the following passage from Book XII (ll. 24-44):

> And it was proved indeed that not in vain
> I had been taught to reverence a Power
> That is the very quality and shape
> And image of right reason, that matures
> Her processes by steadfast laws, gives birth
> To no impatient or fallacious hopes,
> No heat of passion or excessive zeal,
> No vain conceits, provokes to no quick turns
> Of self-applauding intellect, but lifts
> The Being into magnanimity;
> Holds up before the mind, intoxicate
> With present objects and the busy dance
> Of things that pass away, a temperate shew
> Of objects that endure, and by this course
> Disposes her, when over-fondly set
> On leaving her incumbrances behind
> To seek in Man, and in the frame of life,
> Social and individual, what there is
> Desirable, affecting, good or fair
> Of kindred permanence, the gifts divine
> And universal, the pervading grace
> That hath been, is, and shall be.

Consider also the lines (Bk. XIII, ll. 325 ff.) from the conclusion of *The Prelude*, where Wordsworth clearly recognizes the value of restraint which enables us, in moments of doubt

> . . . to keep
> In wholesome separation the two natures
> The one that feels, the other that observes

thus avoiding the dangers of selfish rationalization. It is to be regretted that considerations such as these did not withhold Wordsworth from renouncing the scheme of ethical thought developed in *The Prelude*.

In closing, let me mention another topic which would be interesting to develop, namely, a romantic criticism of the new humanism. I cannot expand this theme here, and I shall condense my remarks to the following: Humanist philosophy, if untempered by other ways of thought, will emphasize our respect for moral integrity at the expense of our spontaneous sympathies which are aroused by the joys and sorrows of the just and of the unjust alike. These sympathies may even be atrophied in the souls of those whose enthusiasm has been held within the narrow channels of humanist doctrine. I can imagine a new humanist admiring the noble sentiment of Mark Antony's eulogy of the slain Brutus, for this is, so to speak, a rationalist sentiment. But this is one thing and the *lacrimae rerum* is another. We know that "human hopes defeated and overthrown are mourned by man," and the universal sympathy of Robert Burns is a human thing, whatever one may say about humanitarianism. I cannot imagine a strict new humanist deeply appreciating Wordsworth's "Simon Lee" and its unforgettable exclamation "Alas! the *gratitude* of men. . . ." The new humanist is in danger of forgetting that, although imaginative love affords not always an unerring light, it is nonetheless the motive power without which there is nothing generous or noble in the world. When a moralist forgets this, he has come very close to forgetting everything of importance.

Appendices

The notion of "objective metaphor" and of Nature's plastic power over both esthetic objects and the human mind may have been, in part, *suggested* to Wordsworth by Archibald Alison's *Essays on the Nature and Principles of Taste,* which was first published in 1790. Wordsworth, however, goes far beyond Alison when he includes in his theory the mystical doctrine of Coleridge's Eolian Harp. In the conclusion of his book[1] Alison presents a doctrine, drawn from Reid's "invaluable work *On the Intellectual Powers of Man,*" to the effect that "matter is not beautiful in itself but derives its beauty from the expression of *mind.*" Alison does not mean that we actually and validly recognize the presence of mind in Nature, but that Nature in some of its forms subtly suggests through various means a *power* or *affection* of mind, i.e., a type of purposive action or of emotional response. Alison is not a mystic, but a fairly cautious eighteenth-century psychologist of the associationist school. He believes, to be sure, that we feel ourselves to be immediately aware of God's wisdom and power of invention when we contemplate the works of Nature and their intricacy of design. And he believes:

. . . there is no man of genuine taste, who has not often felt, in the lone majesty of Nature, some unseen spirit to dwell, which in his happier hours, touched, as if with magic hand, all the springs of his moral sensibility, and rekindled in his heart those original conceptions of the moral or intellectual excellence of his nature, which it is the melancholy tendency of the vulgar pursuits of life to diminish, if not altogether to destroy.[2]

This is remarkably Wordsworthian in sentiment, but Alison's explanation is not mystical. He insists that such sentiment is

[1] Essay II, chap. vi, sec. 6.   [2] *Ibid.*

owing to the fact that the forms of Nature express (i.e., power-fully suggest) animation, which appears for instance in the sun as the "cheerfulness of his morning," the "splendor of his noon-day" and the "tenderness of his evening light." Now, Wordsworth does not stop at the suggestion or expression of animation but boldly insists that "the forms of Nature have a passion in themselves." On the other hand, Alison insists that it is in the human form and countenance that we most perfectly sympathize with the object of our contemplation.

Despite these important differences of interpretation, there can be no doubt that Alison is describing experience remark-ably similar to Wordsworth's and that Wordsworth may have drawn many important suggestions from him, suggestions which may well have illuminated the poet's experience and sharpened his insight. Consider, with reference to what we have called objective metaphor, the following passage. The expression of mental qualities in Nature may be drawn

from analogy or resemblance; from that resemblance which has every-where been felt between the qualities of matter and of mind, and by which the former becomes so powerfully expressive to us of the latter. It is thus, that the colours, the sounds, the forms, and above all, perhaps, the motions of inanimate objects, are so universally felt as resembling peculiar qualities or affections of mind, and when thus felt, are so productive of the analogous emotion; that the personification of matter is so strongly marked in every period of the history of human thought; and that the poet, while he gives life and animation to every thing about him, is not displaying his own invention, but only obeying one of the most powerful laws which regulate the imagination of man.[3]

The last sentence indicates the important difference of inter-pretation that distinguishes the poet from the psychologist. Dean Sperry, in his recent volume *Wordsworth's Anti-Climax*, has wisely emphasized the importance of Alison's work for interpreting Wordsworth, but he fails to notice in this connec-tion that for all the many points of interesting resemblance, Wordsworth is a romantic mystic and Alison an eighteenth-century associationist, that for Wordsworth the imaginative *act*

[3] *Ibid.*

really constitutes the momentary identity of man and the
World-Soul, while for Alison imagination consists in the "indulgence of a train of thought," subject to the laws of
association.

There are several other points of possible contact between
Wordsworth and Alison which must not be overlooked. Alison
argues, much as does Wordsworth, that the enjoyment of an
object as beautiful requires an earlier nonesthetic interest in the
object. Imagination is not aroused until an object presents
itself which awakens in us a definite emotion and in this way
holds our interest. We have seen that Wordsworth recognizes
such a pre-esthetic interest as a stimulus and as an auxiliary of
genuine esthetic enjoyment. He seems inclined, however, to
find this supporting interest as especially important in childhood development. This Alison does not mention.

Nor does Alison describe esthetic enjoyment itself in a
manner likely long to hold Wordsworth's interest. In fact, he
considers imagination to be little more than a play of images
aroused by association. These images tend in successful artistic
achievement to maintain a uniform emotional tone.

Another doctrine of Alison's that must be mentioned appears in his insistence that enjoyment of beauty is incompatible
with practical concern or with scientific or philosophical interest. One cannot consider an object as useful for some definite
purpose and at the same moment enjoy its beauty, nor can one
search for the causes of an event and at the same time appreciate its beauty. These important doctrines are considered although quite without reference to Alison in the thinking of
both Wordsworth and Coleridge, as we shall presently see in
detail. But this is of no great significance since the ideas in
question appear elsewhere especially in Kant.

* * *

I have found in conversation and correspondence that some
students of Wordsworth have been puzzled by Mr. Whitehead's quotation of *The Prelude* (1850), which begins:

> Ye Presences of Nature in the sky
> And on the earth. . . .[4]

[4] Bk. I, ll. 464 ff.

These students have been inclined to interpret this passage, not without some reason, as an example of the associationist philosophy. It is therefore difficult for them to read it as an instance of Mr. Whitehead's more novel theory, although some of them have tried to simplify matters by arguing that Mr. Whitehead is himself an associationist in modern dress!

Certainly Mr. Whitehead does not find in the passage quoted any complete and unconditional acceptance of a strictly associationist philosophy. In his comment upon this passage, he speaks of the "entwined prehensive unities each suffused with *modal* presences of others." [5] The term *modal* is derived from Spinoza, and Whitehead has chosen it with this fact explicitly in mind.[6] Apparently Whitehead interprets Spinoza pretty much as Coleridge interpreted him when he paraphrased Spinozism as follows: "Each thing has a life of its own, and we are all one life." Whitehead has stated the same thing in his highly technical vocabulary:[7] "Each event is an individual matter of fact issuing from an individualization of the substrate activity. But individualization does not mean substantial independence."[8]

Mr. Whiteheads's philosophy is really very Wordsworthian in spirit. Even if we ignore the very explicit mention of Wordsworth in *Science and the Modern World*, we still are able to find important analogies between the two ways of thought. And this is not surprising: both thinkers turn resolutely away from mechanism and determinism, and neither is afraid of panpsychism. Mr. Whitehead has insisted that the "key-notion" with which a philosophy of Nature should start is "that the energetic activity considered in physics is the emotional intensity entertained in life."[9] And with this notion we can well imagine the Wordsworth of *The Prelude* heartily

[5] Italics mine. [6] *Op. cit.*, p. 102.
[7] See especially the end of his essay "Nature and Life."
[8] *Ibid.*, p. 103. It is curious to note, in the light of Whitehead's employment of a Spinozian concept, that Professor Beatty commends very highly Chapter V of *Science and the Modern World* ("William Wordsworth: His Doctrine and Art in Their Historical Relations," p. 192). It seems that to ignore Spinozian elements in Wordsworth is one thing, while to keep them from slipping in unnoticed is quite another.
[9] *Modes of Thought* (New York, 1938), p. 252.

concurring. But we may go even further. Consider the following passage of Mr. Whitehead's:

There is a unity in the universe, enjoying value and (by its immanence) sharing value. For example, take the subtle beauty of a flower in some isolated glade of a primeval forest. No animal has ever had the subtlety of experience to enjoy its full beauty. And yet this beauty is a grand fact in the universe. When we survey nature and think however fitting and superficial has been the animal enjoyment of its wonders, and when we realize how incapable the separate cells and pulsations of each flower are of enjoying the total effect—then our sense of the value of the details for the totality dawns upon our consciousness. This is the intuition of holiness, the intuition of the sacred, which is at the foundation of all religion. In every advancing civilization this sense of sacredness has found vigorous expression. It tends to retire into a recessive factor in experience, as each phase of civilization enters upon its decay.[10]

The passage which Mr. Whitehead quotes from Book I of *The Prelude* contains concepts quite foreign to the philosophy of a strict associationist, as Mr. Whitehead has noticed when he employs a Spinozian concept in connection with Wordsworth's thought in this passage. It is only by ignoring these concepts that we can reduce the passage to an expression of an associationist theory of knowledge. Of course, after we have once witnessed characters of hope, fear, triumph, or the like embodied or expressed in natural objects, we may tend to feel such emotions in the presence of other natural objects linked to the first by association. Thus our emotional consciousness in the face of Nature may become very complicated. And furthermore, an almost constant sense of sympathy with Nature may be established. Also, many glimpses of natural objects are not at once fully appreciated but are enjoyed only at a later time when association recalls them to attention. There is no denying the importance of association in the growth of a poet's mind, or of any mind. But, if you say that the *whole process* by which Wordsworth comes to feel the "entwined prehensive unities" and "modal presences" is a matter of association in his own mind, and if you believe him to be aware of this, then I

[10] *Ibid.*, p. 164. Italics mine.

do not see how you are going to explain Wordsworth's tendency to personify the power that impresses characters upon objects. We know from the Preface of 1800 that Wordsworth disliked rhetorical personification. On the other hand, all this is clearer if we find here a reference to what I have called "objective metaphor," for in that case the personification is not merely rhetorical.

Had Wordsworth believed that his experience was wholly to be explained in associationist terms, his view of life would have been quite other than the one with which we are familiar. Thus I am convinced that, had his attitude toward natural objects been strictly limited to that which he describes in *The Prelude* (Bk. II, ll. 181-202), where he tells us that the moon was dear to him because of feelings analogous to patriotic and domestic love, we should hear nothing of the "soul of all the worlds." It is interesting to notice that, in the passage just below that mentioned, Wordsworth's affections are described as attached to "rural objects," while Nature herself is "intervenient"[11] and "secondary."

> Those incidental charms which first attach'd
> My heart to rural objects, day by day
> Grew weaker, and I hasten on to tell
> How Nature, intervenient all this time,
> And secondary, now at length was sought
> For her own sake. . . .[12]

Here we come upon a very important comment made by the poet himself. Association by itself attaches the affections to particular objects like the sun and moon. Nature herself, as distinct from "rural objects," is then *secondary*, but not, be it noted, wholly absent from experience. The fact that she is not wholly absent suggests some source of insight other than association. And this other source is, I believe, just what Whitehead has been trying to describe. Wordsworth himself recognizes the delicate complexity of the origin of his insight and

[11] The terms *collateral* and *intervenient*, used by Wordsworth in describing secondary interests, appear in the same significance, although in a different context, in Bacon's *Advancement of Learning*, II, VIII, 2, *ad finem*.

[12] *Loc. cit.*, Bk. II, ll. 204 ff.

warns us in the lines immediately following (208-237) against partitioning the mind, describing its development in clear-cut stages, and deriving each particular thought from a *single source*. It is not surprising then that even in the account of his earliest experience, Wordsworth suggests a feeling for the organic unity of Nature present along with and related to the enjoyment of expressive imagery.

Thus I certainly do not believe that, when Wordsworth speaks directly of the Presences of Nature as working upon external objects, he is merely straining a figure of speech. Indeed, we are told in language true to Boehme that the mind of a child

> Even as an *agent of the one great mind*,
> Creates, creator and receiver both,
> Working but *in alliance with the works*
> Which it beholds.[13]

Despite all this, we need not argue that Wordsworth's theory of objective metaphor indicates that he has not profited by studying Hartley and the associationists. Far from it. We have just indicated that Wordsworth may well have gained some confidence in this belief from a reading of Alison, and in this matter Hartley's influence would tend to be somewhat similar. Let me add some further material on this point. If the reader will study Part I, Proposition LXXXII of *Observations on Man*, where Hartley ·develops his interesting theory of natural analogies, which are apprehended directly by the human mind, and which only later, as I understand it, give rise to associations, he will find a passage that may very well have helped Wordsworth to arrive at the theory of objective metaphor. We quote only a few sentences of a very interesting discussion:

Analogy is that resemblance, and in some cases sameness, of the parts, properties, functions, uses, etc. any or all, of A to B, whereby our knowledge concerning A, and the language expressing this knowledge, may be applied in the whole, or in part, to B, without any sensible, or, at least, any important practical error. Now analogies, in this sense

---

[13] *Ibid.*, Bk. II, ll. 272 ff. Italics mine.

of the word, some more exact and extensive, some less so, present themselves to us every where in natural and artificial things; and thus whole groups of figurative phrases, which seem at first only to answer the purposes of convenience in affording names for new objects, and of pleasing the fancy in the way to be hereafter mentioned, pass into analogical reasoning, and become a guide in the search after truth, and an evidence for it in some degree. I will here set down some instances of various degrees and kinds.[14]

Of course, Hartley does not suggest Nature as the *author* of these analogies. He also warns that the human mind may overstep itself and distort the analogies which it apprehends. In this latter process association seems to be involved.[15] I suspect that Wordsworth had this passage in mind in A, Book II, lines 396-430. The "affinities" (1. 403) are, I suggest, the natural analogies. In lines 407-411 he voices the fear that he may have been subject in his seventeenth year to the gross distortion of these analogies, of which Hartley says that "the properties, beauties, perfections, desires, or defects and aversions, which adhere by association to the simile, parable, or emblem of any kind, are insensibly as it were, transferred upon the thing represented."[16] But even in the above-mentioned passage Wordsworth seems to incline to the belief that he converses with "things that really are," and he adds:

> From Nature *and her overflowing soul*
> I had received so much that all my thoughts
> Were steep'd in feeling.[17]

The apprehension, at least the early apprehension, of objective metaphor is a by-product of Wordsworth's boyish sports. He notices the impression of various characters in natural objects and enjoys them while he is engaged in quite unesthetic pursuits. The characters observed are often appropriate to the emotional tone of the accompanying activity. Furthermore, these characters become associated in the boy's mind with the activities themselves. But he at times also enjoys a less obvious

[14] *Observations on Man* (London, 1801), I, 293.
[15] See the last paragraph under Proposition LXXII, pp. 296-297.
[16] *Observations on Man*, I, 297.   [17] Italics mine.

beauty, when pure form which exercises a minimum of expressive power catches his attention. Thus he takes a "pure, organic pleasure in the lines of curling mist." Such charm is intellectual, since the objects, let us say, like many mathematical figures, do not suggest or participate in familiar and much loved things. This would seem to be a more difficult form of enjoyment, which marks a maturer stage of the individual's development, where the interfusion and "mutual domination of things" is harder to grasp.

It would, I think, be unwise to deny that such writers as Hartley and Alison exercise an influence on Wordsworth that penetrates to the very heart of *The Prelude*. But this influence is almost everywhere "transcendentalized." In Chapter IV we return to some of the material here presented and search for the historical origin of the transcendental element which it contains.

APPENDIX TO CHAPTER IV

IMAGINATION IN *BIOGRAPHIA LITERARIA*

The student of *The Prelude* will find himself on familiar ground when he turns to Coleridge's theory of imagination as presented in *Biographia Literaria* (1815). This will be especially true, if he considers carefully not only the summary statements so often quoted but also the rather more obscure exposition of transcendental idealism which introduces these summaries and affords them a philosophical background and orientation.

Two quotations from the *Biographia* will help to center our discussion upon the more important topics involved.

These (the human faculties) I would arrange under the different senses and powers: as the eye, the ear, the touch, &c.; *the imitative power, voluntary and automatic; the imagination, or shaping and modifying power; the fancy, or the aggregative and associative power;* etc., etc.[1]

[1] *Biographia Literaria* (Oxford, 1907), I, 193. Italics mine. mine.

Also the more famous passage in which Coleridge distinguishes the two phases or levels of imagination and makes clear that this "faculty" is, so to speak, the fundamental motive power of conscious awareness.

The Imagination then I consider either as primary, or secondary. The primary Imagination I hold to be the living power and prime agent of all human perception, and as a repetition in the finite mind of the eternal act of creation in the infinite I AM. The secondary Imagination I consider as an echo of the former, co-existing with the conscious will, yet still as identical with the primary in the *kind* of its agency, and differing only in *degree*, and in the *mode* of its operation. It dissolves, diffuses, dissipates, in order to recreate: or where this process is rendered impossible, yet still at all events it struggles to idealize and to unify. It is essentially vital, even as all objects (*as* objects) are essentially fixed and dead.

FANCY, on the contrary, has no other counters to play with, but fixities and definities. The fancy is indeed no other than a mode of memory emancipated from the order of time and space; while it is blended with, and modified by that empirical phenomenon of the will, which we express by the word Choice. But equally with the ordinary memory the Fancy must receive all its materials ready made from the law of association.[2]

This statement follows upon and is thoroughly to be explained only with reference to Coleridge's brief but firmly drawn exposition of transcendental idealism which precedes it. Here the influence of Schelling and of the Behmenist tradition is certainly clear enough. And against this background, Coleridge's theory of imagination is far more illuminating than it at first appears to be, even though his account of imagination has been a source of much profit to many students of esthetics and to many critics who have not accepted his system of idealism. But many students would understand Coleridge more readily were they willing to consider with more patience the philosophy which completes his theory of criticism.

This transcendental philosophy, as presented in Chapters XII and XIII of *Biographia Literaria,* finds its central object in the fact of self-consciousness, the "*act*" of self-consciousness

[2] *Ibid.*, p. 202.

Coleridge might prefer to say. This act is summarized in the utterance *I am*. It is, indeed, at once the assertion of the *I am* and also a prominent feature of the object to which that assertion refers, for consciousness invokes a recognition of itself. Thus philosophy depends upon a sort of intuitive self-knowledge from which it draws the material for its speculative system-building.

Consciousness, centering in the assertion of its own identity, cannot enjoy an isolated existence: there must be an object standing within the scope of mental activity. This object may, of course, include the fact of consciousness itself, the recognized identity of the knower. But the transcendental idealist locates the *complete* union of subject and object only in the infinite *I am*, the creative mind of God, whose being in no way depends upon a conditioning environment. This theology has little directly to do with esthetics. It is, of course, toward the finite, human mind that our attention must be directed. We find the finite subject of consciousness maintained by a dual activity, whose opposed tendencies Coleridge describes as "centrifugal" and "centripetal" powers. This is in keeping with the "polar logic" which, Coleridge tells us, he found in Bruno and Boehme. As we have seen above, for Boehme all created being, including most especially the life of the human soul, involves the interplay of two opposed forces, one passive, the other active.

Following in the path of this philosophy which builds its theory upon the coincidence of opposites, Coleridge describes the interplay of two forces. These two forces together maintain the conscious *I am* and constitute the primary imagination which is the central agency of all awareness, as also the secondary or voluntary and creative imagination. The *I am* is accordingly the product of two tendencies. The first of these, the centrifugal, or passive, would, in isolation, wholly "objectize" the mind. But this tendency is offset by another which brings the mind to "recognize" itself in the manifold of objectivity so introduced:

Bearing then this in mind, that intelligence is a self-development, not a quality supervening to a substance, we may abstract from all *degree,* and for the purpose of philosophic construction reduce it to *kind,* under the idea of an indestructible power with two opposite and counteracting forces, which by a metaphor borrowed from astronomy, we may call the centrifugal and centripetal forces. The intelligence in the one tends to *objectize* itself, and in the other to *know* itself in the object.[3]

In the production of finite consciousness, which is an "echo" of the infinite *I am,* a suprapersonal power is at work. From this power the two opposed tendencies, which together constitute or produce the finite mind, are first separated out and then united with one another. For Coleridge, as for Wordsworth, our awareness depends· upon an activity, vastly greater in scope than our own, which is involved in the life of the subject and in the very existence of the object. It is this wider power which initiates interplay between the two. This dependence of the finite self upon a transcendent power finds its place in Coleridge's little system of "dynamic philosophy" as the *scholium* to Thesis VI:

> If a man be asked how he *knows* that he is? he can only answer, *sum quia sum.* But if (the absoluteness of this certainty having been admitted) he be again asked, how he, the individual person, came to be, then in relation to the ground of his *existence,* not to the ground of his *knowledge* of that existence, he might reply, *sum quia Deus est,* or still more philosophically, *sum, quia in Deo sum.*[4]

With this we should compare Wordsworth's very similar doctrine expressed in *The Prelude:*

> Hitherto,
> In progress through this Verse, my mind hath look'd
> Upon the speaking face of earth and heaven
> As her prime Teacher, intercourse with man
> Established by the sovereign Intellect,
> Who through that bodily Image hath diffus'd
> A soul divine which we participate,
> A deathless spirit.[5]

Thus consciousness seems to identify itself with many objects, and the nature of a moment of consciousness is best

[3] *Ibid.,* p. 188.
[4] *Ibid.,* p. 183.   [5] Bk. V, ll. 10-17.

described by listing its objects. And yet the conscious being can say *I am*, for it does not lose itself in these objects but discovers itself as an identity or continuity present with and mirrored in them.

For God, or the Absolute Mind, diversity and unity may exist in perfect balance and the whole may constitute a magnificently integrated organic system. But the finite mind is in no such splendid equilibrium. As the finite subject comes to consciousness, it must yield itself to a field of objectivity through which it then asserts itself as a unity, maintaining or recognizing itself as an ego, in contrast yet in contact with these objects.

Without some array of objectivity, no finite consciousness is possible; and unless this objectivity is so organized that it supports the ego's recognition of its own identity and continuity, there is again no consciousness. Here, of course, the Kantian theory of synthetic unity is most relevant. The objects of which the ego is aware are themselves involved in the dual activity which supports consciousness. Thus Coleridge is able to insist that his theory of knowledge is not a subjectivism: the table of which we are aware need not be called a "representation"; it is the real table. The process of knowing is no more limited to the knower than to the known. The two participate in one activity, and it is wrong to suppose that the self is the only source of energy. The world makes a claim upon the subject, and the subject in turn seeks to possess its world. This process repeats itself in a new setting as the secondary or creative imagination arises. Here the stages or moments of activity are more easily recognized. In the origin of the primary imagination, no consciousness is possible except as both moments complete themselves. But the secondary imagination has an origin within consciousness, or at any rate with some effort it is possible for us to recognize distinct levels of consciousness in the growth of the secondary imagination. The artist must be fascinated by objects and he must submit his attention to them. But he must do more than this. A person of alert sensibility is not necessarily an artist. The artist must assert his own spiritual mastery over objects. The creative mind's power of self-organization draws objects into its own life and assimilates them. But the creative mind has already been awakened and enriched by the objects which have held its attention. Thus the act of creation is an outcome emerging from the world as well as from the self. We are reminded of the passage, quoted above, with which Wordsworth closes Book XII of *The Prelude:*

> I seem'd about this period to have sight
> Of a new world, a world, too, that was fit
> To be transmitted and made visible
> To other eyes, as having for its base —
> That whence our dignity originates,
> That which both gives it being and maintains
> A balance, an ennobling interchange
> Of action from within and from without,
> The excellence, pure spirit, and best power
> Both of the object seen, and eye that sees.[6]

In *The Prelude,* Wordsworth presents this theory in figurative and informal fashion. Coleridge tries in the *Biographia* to develop it in a series of philosophical propositions, for which he humorously apologizes by means of the "letter from a friend" in Chapter XIII. Wordsworth shows the influence of Boehme; Coleridge has absorbed that influence and, so to speak, tempered its quality by blending it with Schelling's more systematic idealism.

The first moment of esthetic awareness may be called that of sensibility. But this does not refer to any unusual acuteness of the sense organs. It is a mental attitude, a naïve, or, if deliberate, a "wise," passiveness. Nonetheless, without sensation no mind could exist as passive. Hence for the Coleridge of *Biographia Literaria* the philosophies of Hartley and of Hobbes are by no means wholly irrelevant. But this sensibility can be best described by reference to the analogy of the "Eolian Harp" and to Wordsworth's "Eolian visitations." The influence which objects exercise over the mind suggests

[6] Bk. XII, ll. 370 ff.

that they too are dependent upon a power which manifests itself through finite mind and finite object. In later years Coleridge seems to have felt that he could perhaps somewhat clarify the analogy of the "Eolian Harp":

The mind does not resemble an Aeolian harp, nor even a barrel-organ turned by a stream of water, conceive as many tunes mechanized in it as you like, but rather as far as objects are concerned a violin or other instrument of few strings yet vast compass, played on by a musician of Genius. The Breeze that blows across the Aeolian harp, the streams that turned the handle of the barrel-organ might be called *ein mannigfaltiges*, a mere *sylva incondita*, but who would call the muscles and purpose of Linley a confused manifold?[7]

Despite all this neither Wordsworth nor Coleridge, but their successor in the romantic tradition, John Keats, has given us the most memorable statement of the operation of esthetic sensibility:

As to the poetical Character itself (I mean that sort, of which, if I am anything, I am a member; that sort distinguished from the Wordsworthian, or egotistical Sublime; which is a thing per se, and stands alone), it is not itself—it has no self—it is everything and nothing—it has no character—it enjoys light and shade; it lives in gusto, be it fair or foul, high or low, rich or poor, mean or elevated—it has as much delight in conceiving an Iago as an Imogen. What shocks the virtuous philosopher delights the chameleon poet. It does no harm from its relish of the dark side of things, any more than from its taste for the bright one, because they both end in speculation. A poet is the most unpoetical of anything in existence, because he has no Identity— He is continually in for and filling some other body. The Sun,—the Moon,—the Sea and men and women who are creatures of impulse, are poetical, and have about them an unchangeable attribute; the poet has none, no identity—He is certainly the most unpoetical of all God's creatures—If then he has no self, and if I am a poet, where is the wonder that I should say I would write no more? Might I not at very instant have been cogitating on the Characters of Saturn and Ops? It is a wretched thing to confess; but it is a very fact, that not one word I ever utter can be taken for granted as an opinion growing out of my identical Nature—how can it when I have no Nature? When

[7] Miss A. D. Snyder, in *Revue de Littérature Comparée*, VII (1927), 529.

I am in a room with people, if I ever am free from speculating on creations of my own brain, then, not myself goes home to myself, but the identity of everyone in the room begins to press upon me, so that I am in a very little time annihilated.[8]

This is what Coleridge meant when he said that the mind is "objectized."

It is important to notice that in this passage Keats does not describe the activity of composition, but a preliminary state of mind. However, sometimes a work of art, even when completed, will reveal the artist's sensibility more fully than his creative ability. Such is the case, for instance, in many of Walt Whitman's poems, and, we may add, in the journals of Dorothy Wordsworth:

> . . . wise as Women are
> When genial circumstance hath favor'd them,
> She welcom'd what was given, and craved no more.
> Whatever scene was present to her eyes,
> That was the best, to that she was attuned
> Through her humility and lowliness,
> And through a perfect happiness of soul
> Whose variegated feelings were in this
> Sisters, that they were each some new delight:
> For she was Nature's inmate.[9]

But it is the active phase of esthetic activity that most interests Coleridge. When he speaks of imagination it is usually this moment that he has primarily, almost exclusively, in mind. The poet, as distinct from the esthetically sensitive person, "brings the whole soul of man into activity, with the subordination of its faculties to each other according to their relative worth and dignity. He diffuses a tone and spirit of unity, that blends, and (as it were) *fuses,* each into each, by that synthetic and magical power, to which I would exclusively appropriate the name of Imagination."

This "tone and spirit of unity" is the poet's contribution. It is, in a sense his signature, by means of which the poet

---

[8] *Letters of John Keats,* ed. Sidney Colvin (London, 1891), pp. 184-185, May 3, 1818, to J. H. Reynolds.   [9] *The Prelude,* Bk. XI, ll. 205-214.

asserts his identity and exercises a creative, but by no means an arbitrary, freedom. This contribution, of course, varies in quality from poet to poet. Coleridge indicates something of this wide range of possible variation in his contrast of Shakespeare and Milton:

What then shall we say? even this; that Shakespeare, no mere child of nature, no *automaton* of genius, no passive vehicle of inspiration, possessed by the spirit, not possessing it; first studied patiently, meditated deeply, understood minutely, till knowledge, become habitual and intuitive, wedded itself to his habitual feelings, and at length gave birth to that stupendous power, by which he stands alone, with no equal or second in his own class; to that power which seated him on one of the two glory-smitten summits of the poetic mountain, with Milton as his compeer, not rival. While the former darts himself forth, and passes into all the forms of human character and passion, the one Proteus of the fire and the flood; the other attracts all forms and things to himself, into the unity of his own ideal. All things and modes of action shape themselves anew in the being of Milton; while Shakespeare becomes all things, yet for ever remaining himself.[10]

But all this has to do with the subtleties of a supreme self-expression. The secondary imagination usually has humbler tasks to perform. It must sustain a minimum of esthetic and logical continuity without which the self is lost in the things which capture its attention. Thus the function of the secondary or esthetic imagination corresponds, so to speak, on a higher plane, with the more fundamental activity of the primary imagination. This latter, the agency of perception, must preserve the continuity of consciousness throughout the flow of time, so that the *I am* and the objectivity which it holds before it may be recognized as continuous with the past, both of the self and of the object. As Coleridge has pointed out in a passage which echoes Kant and anticipates Bergson, "The act of consciousness is indeed identical with *time* considered in its essence. I mean time *per se*, as contra-distinguished from our *notion* of time; for this is always blended with the idea of space, which, as the opposite of time, is therefore its *measure*."[11]

[10] *Biographia Literaria*, ed. Shawcross, II, 19-20.
[11] *Ibid.*, I, 87.

The secondary imagination must sustain another less obvious continuity, that of esthetic relevance. It is thus that it performs its best-known function, that of establishing unity in variety. When this unity is organic, so that the elements united are transformed by their union, the process is properly called *imagination*. When the union is less fundamental, when it does not transform or mould the elements but leaves them as they were, the process is called *fancy*. Imagination produces a system of internally related objects, which are altered by the relations that they bear to one another. Relations established by fancy are external to the objects related and do not transform them.

According to Coleridge the two functions, imagination and fancy, may be employed together, but as two distinct tools. Wordsworth, on the other hand, is inclined to insist that the "associative" power, granted by Coleridge exclusively to fancy may also be exercised by imagination. The difference may, after all, be little more than one of terminology, although it is interesting to notice, as Mr. Clarence Thorpe has pointed out,[12] that Wordsworth is willing to include within the scope of imagination a faculty which Coleridge describes in terms so nearly those of an associationist philosophy. But since Wordsworth by no means limits imagination to the associative power, we must hesitate to draw too sharp a conclusion.

APPENDIX TO CHAPTER V

It is interesting to note that Coleridge seems to have attempted, years after writing "Dejection," to explain Wordsworth's "Ode" upon epistemological grounds. At least, he quotes the poem as if he believed that it expressed the principles of a theory of knowledge. It may seem surprising that his suggestion is really helpful toward understanding a difficult passage. Wordsworth's magnificent phrases "the fountain-light of all our day" and "a master light of all our seeing" may be rescued from obscurity by consideration of Coleridge's use of a

[12] Clarence D. Thorpe, "The Imagination: Coleridge *versus* Wordsworth," *Philological Quarterly*, XVIII (Jan., 1939), 1-18.

selection from the "Intimations Ode" in Essay XI of the second section of *The Friend*. Here Coleridge writes of the "one principle of permanence and identity, the rock of strength and refuge, to which the soul may cling amid the fleeting, surge-like objects of the senses." Thus Coleridge tries to cast an epistemological interpretation upon the "Ode," for even in later life, years after he wrote "Dejection," Coleridge continued to find the mysticism of the poem unsatisfactory, doubting (in *Biographia Literaria*, Chapter XXII) that children are ever "seers blest." He admits, however, in the same chapter that to those who are acquainted with the "twilight realms of consciousness" the meaning of the poem is sufficiently plain and, he seems also to suggest, its validity apparent. If this interpretation is correct, the "recollections" of the "Ode" are similar to Plato's reminiscence in that they lie at the very foundations of knowledge, at the groundwork of rational certainty, which would be impossible without them, as logic is impossible without the principles of contradiction and identity, recognition of which comprises the permanence of thought as opposed to the flowing inconstancy of the senses. Insofar as the phrases "the fountain-light of all our day" and "a master-light of all our seeing" are concerned, it is clear that Wordsworth attached some such meaning to his poem. Certainly the lines are otherwise wholly obscure. But, of course, Wordsworth could not have *limited* the meaning of the "Ode" to any such notion. The "imperial palace" and the "clouds of glory" are more than a speculative justification of the laws of logic!

As a matter of fact, the experience behind these passages in the "Ode" should not puzzle one who has made a thorough study of *The Prelude*. Such experience is nothing more nor less than the sentiment of Being, the sense of the concrete universe in its spatial extension and temporal endurance, which constitutes a permanence and identity as important as anything that Coleridge may have had in mind. As we have seen, the sentiment of Being involves panpsychism; and in the "Ode," as also in *The Prelude*, Book V, Wordsworth sees the World-

Soul as the matrix or living environment from which the soul issues forth. This matrix is never sharply isolated from the finite mind. It stands as the background of every soul. It is the soul's "immensity," its "immortality," its divine "home."

In the "Ode," the experience elsewhere described as the sentiment of Being is recorded against a set of concepts which yield, upon superficial examination, a more conventional and orthodox aspect than most of Wordsworth's earlier utterances. This is owing almost entirely to the mention of immortality, although even here the notion of pre-existence is likely to trouble many. But there is really far less orthodoxy in the "Ode" even than appears. Thus it is doubtful that Wordsworth thought, at the time when he wrote the "Ode," primarily of a personal pre-existence or even of a personal post-existence. He was thinking rather more of the finite soul as issuing forth from its eternal home, the "immortal sea."

The sentiment of Being becomes clearly apparent not only in the "Ode" itself but also in the subsequent essay on "Epitaphs" (1810) where Wordsworth once again considers the notion of immortality and the intuitive origins of human belief in the eternal nature of the human soul. Here he emphasizes more persistently the idea of personal immortality. But he insists that the basis for such belief lies in what we may call the sense of eternity or, as Wordsworth preferred to put it, of "immortality." This sense, even when present in childhood consciousness, is not the result of "unthinking gaiety or liveliness of animal spirits." It is not the outcome of the child's ignorance of physical death. It is rather a positive intuition which may be expressed in any number of images. "Never did a child stand by the side of a running stream, pondering within himself what power was the feeder of the perpetual current, from what never-wearied sources the body of water was supplied, but he must have been inevitably propelled to follow this question by another: 'Toward what abyss is it in progress? what receptacle can contain the mighty influx?' And the spirit of the answer must have been, though the word might be *sea* or *ocean*, accompanied perhaps with an image gathered from a map or from the real object in nature . . . a receptacle without bounds or dimensions—nothing less than infinity. We may then, be justified in asserting that the sense of immortality, if not a co-existent and having birth with Reason, is among the earliest of her off-spring."[1] If this sense of immortality is to be considered as a "master-light of all our seeing," as indeed it is in the "Ode" itself, then we must believe that it is indeed "co-existent and having birth with reason."

From this immortal sea, its eternal home, the soul must issue forth and possess a finite individuality of its own. Such a notion is in harmony with the neoplatonic doctrine of emanation and with the Behministic emphasis upon divine "out-breathing." Consider, for example, Plotinus' statement of mysticism in the *Sixth Ennead:*

God is external to nothing that exists, he resides in all things; but they know him not. They fly his presence, or rather they run away from themselves. They cannot, of course, seize the being from whom they fly; nor can they find another like him since they have lost themselves. Will a son, having in madness forgotten his own identity, recognize his father? But the man who at last discovers who he is, will know also whence he comes.[2]

This reminds us of Wordsworth's "consciousness of Whom we are."

We must also remember that William Law held a view of immortality very similar to that of the "Ode"[3] and that, as is well known, the gnostic Hermes Trismegistus[4] in ancient times, and in modern Vaughan and Traherne[5] employ very similar ways of describing mysticism, emphasizing the glory of childhood and its high privilege of contact with divine power. Mr. John D. Rea has added the name of the later neoplatonist, Proclus, to the list of possible sources and urges that we compare the following passage:

[1] *Prose Works,* II, 29.
[2] VI, 9, 7.
[3] See above, pp. 104-105.
[4] Scott (ed.), *Hermetica* (Oxford, 1924), I, 197, and II, 261, n.
[5] T. Traherne, *Centuries of Meditation* (London, 1927), III, secs. 1-5 and espec. sec. 12.

Descensus animae in corpus seiunxit quidem illam a divinis animis, a quibus intelligentie, et potestate, puritateque implebatur. Coniuxit vero generationi, et naturae, materialibusque rebus a quibus oblivione, et errore, et ignorantia est imbuta.

with Wordsworth's

> Our birth is but a sleep
> and a forgetting.

Mr. Rea quotes in Ficino's Latin translation of Proclus, which is included in a little volume purchased by Coleridge in 1796: *Iamblichus de Mysteriis Aegyptorum, Chaldaeorum, Assyriorum, Proclus in Platonicum Albiciadem de Anima, atque Daemone . . .* Lugduni . . . , 1777.[6]

Even Boehme himself suggests the great wisdom of children in *The Aurora:*

For the corrupted nature in this world *labours* in its utmost power and diligence, that it might bring forth heavenly forms, and many times little children might be their parents' school-masters and *teachers,* if parents could but understand, or would but take *notice* of them: But nowadays the corruption is unfortunately with both young and old, and the proverb is verified.

> Wie die Alten singen,
> So lerneten die Yungen.

> As the old ones sing,
> So th' young learn to ring.[7]

---

[6] See John D. Rea, "Coleridge's Intimations of Immortality from Proclus," *Modern Philology*, XXVI (1928-1929), 208. That Wordsworth might easily come upon many congenial thoughts in Plotinus, and hence have listened patiently to all neoplatonism, is evident from a passage like the following, which distantly reminds us of Wordsworth's faith that "Nature never did betray the heart that loved her."

"There are in man two distinct things, . . . Nature and the body which through it becomes a living being; Nature precedes the body which is its creation, made and shaped by it; it cannot originate the desires; they must belong to the living body meeting the experiences of this life and seeking in its distress to alter its state, to substitute pleasure for pain, sufficiency for want. This Nature must be like a mother reading the wishes of a suffering child, and seeking to set it right and to bring it back to herself. In her search for the remedy she attaches herself by that very concern to the sufferer's desire and makes the child's experience her own" (*Enneads*, IV, 20). The language of this passage is perhaps closer to Wordsworth than is the thought, but it clearly shows that Plotinus must have been a welcome guest in the philosophical conversations of Wordsworth and Coleridge.

[7] *The Aurora*, chap. xii.

But search as we may for echoes, the fact remains that the tone of the "Intimations Ode" is neoplatonic, if we take that term in its broader sense to represent a tradition that has never died out. To be sure, Wordsworth's experience does not move strictly according to the neoplatonic program as it appears in Plotinus, where, under ideal conditions, the philosopher gradually regains his power of intuitive vision, as his soul recovers its birth-right, first relinquished after early childhood. For Wordsworth, however, ecstasy is gradually replaced by a philosophic resignation and understanding. There is, of course, no question of identifying the intimations of immortality directly with Platonic reminiscence, as it appears in Plato's own work, for, according to this version of the doctrine, no special privilege is granted to the experiences of childhood.

It is interesting to notice that in the "Tintern Abbey" lines, Wordsworth does not grant early childhood any extraordinary power of insight. Mystical vision is here described as a product of maturity. But we must remember that in "Tintern Abbey" little attention is paid to childhood. The poem centers upon the contrast of a serene and mystically enlightened maturity with a sort of emotional *sturm und drang* which precedes it and which disturbs the mind so greatly that the development of a broad, synoptic philosophy is retarded. In Wordsworth's own life this almost desperate attitude was produced by the moral and spiritual confusion which followed his experiment with Godwinian rationalism. It was accompanied by a restless and fanciful exercise of the poet's esthetic powers.

Thus I do not find Mr. Beatty's theory that Wordsworth tended to divide human life into three periods, childhood, youth, and maturity, or the ages of sensation, emotion, and reason respectively, as very helpful. Wordsworth's view of his own life is more complex than this, the presence of periods of mystical illumination in its several forms excluding any such threefold division as far too simple. To be sure, we have seen that mystical enlightenment is in its origin connected with the sensuous alertness that supports esthetic enjoyment. And thus mysticism is not out of place in a period of personal development that is primarily characterized by sensation. But the "wisdom" of Wordsworth's maturity is not a matter of reason as distinct from intuitive or mystical vision, and in Wordsworth's career the independent exercise of the rational faculty belongs to the *middle* period when rationalism actually precipitates a crisis. Mr. Melvin M. Rader's tabulation of the "stages" in the development of the poet's mind is more complete than Mr. Beatty's and preferable in that he recognizes a mystical element in the early years.[8]

In conclusion, let me suggest that *The Prelude*, which is explicitly and systematically biographical, affords a far more adequate account of the stages and periods of Wordsworth's spiritual growth and of the interpretation which he put upon the growth than anything that is to be found in more topical and less complete statements such as "Tintern Abbey" and the "Intimations Ode."

APPENDIX TO CHAPTER VII

Several students of Wordsworth, notably Legouis, Harper, Babbitt, and more recently J. W. Beach, have suggested that Wordsworth wrote to some extent under the influence of Rousseau's philosophy as presented in *Emile;* his suspicion of abstract ideas, which are for him the main source of human error, his insistence that all philosophy, indeed all logical argument, must be based ultimately upon feeling, if it is to escape a chaos of utter relativism and disagreement, his theory of conscience as an inner revelation of feeling, his obvious enjoyment of reverie and his opposition to formal education—all seem pertinent enough to any consideration of Wordsworth's way of thought. Indeed, it would be most foolhardy to deny that Wordsworth falls under the wide influence of Rousseau, whose philosophy exercises, as Babbitt used to insist, a very pervasive power throughout all subsequent thinking. And certainly Wordsworth had ample opportunity to become acquainted with his thought. But some important considerations remain which prevent our listing Wordsworth confidently as one of the

[8] See Rader, *op. cit.*, p. 131.

"sons of Rousseau." In the first place, Rousseau is no pan-psychist, but a very convinced dualist who owes much to Descartes, distinguishing sharply as he does between extended or physical matter and thinking substance:

. . . pour moi, je n'ai besoin, quoi qu'en dise Locke, de connoître la matière que comme étendue et divisible, pour être assuré qu'elle ne peut penser; et quand un philosophe viendra me dire que les arbres sentent et que les rochers pensent, il aura beau m'embarrasser dans ses arguments subtils, je ne puis voir en lui qu'un sophiste de mauvaise foi.[1]

Thus I cannot believe that the spirit of the lyrics of 1798 is Roussellian as one critic has suggested. In view of the Behmenist echoes that we have pointed out, there seems to be no reason for considering Rousseau as a possible source of the ideas contained in these poems.

To be sure, when we study Rousseau's *Reveries*, in particular the seventh "Promenade," we may feel at first that his attitude toward Nature is close to that of Wordsworth. But, when Rousseau begins to explain himself, his motives frequently appear very unlike those of the English poet. Rousseau tells us that he prefers botany to mineralogy or zoology, as a way of studying Nature, because it is easier to pursue, being the work of a leisurely solitude free from social contacts. Again botany does not force us to consider disgusting objects as does zoölogy, and unlike mineralogy it does not depend upon human labor miserably performed in the mines. None of these reasons is essentially Wordsworthian. Wordsworth is not looking for an agreeable pastime. Nor does he love Nature primarily because it helps him to forget himself. Wordsworth is searching eagerly for "things that really are." Rousseau is not always interested in such things. As M. Maritain has pointed out, he is something of a pragmatist insofar as religion is concerned. Speaking of Christianity, Rousseau once said, "It is perhaps an illusion; but if I had a more consoling illusion I should adopt that."[2] The Wordsworth of *The Pre-*

---

[1] J. J. Rousseau, *Emile* (Paris, 1827), Book IV, "Profession De Foi Du Vicaire Savoyard," p. 251.

[2] Pierre-Maurice Masson, *La Religion de J. J. Rousseau* (Paris, 1916), I, 185.

lude would have found such a statement simply irresponsible. To be sure, Wordsworth often talks of transcending analytical reason; but this is only because he feels that he has found a higher cognitive function, not because he wishes to repudiate knowledge. Again, Rousseau's oft-repeated formula, "Only what is not, is beautiful," is wholly at odds with the spirit of *The Prelude* and of *The Recluse* fragment where Beauty is "a living presence of the earth."

Of course, there is no denying that Rousseau's contribution to democratic theory, the concept of the *general will,* is reflected in Wordsworth's thought, as in that of so many revolutionary thinkers. This is particularly true of the revolutionary philosophy which Wordsworth brought with him from France. This philosophy immediately preceded his acceptance of Godwinian ideas. We know from Book IX of *The Prelude* that Wordsworth had been deeply impressed by the ideal of popular sovereignty and by the growth of national spirit and genuine community of popular interest. In all this Wordsworth had been greatly influenced by the inspiring unselfishness and humanitarian idealism of his friend, Michael Beaupuy; and furthermore, as he tells us, he had been disposed toward equalitarianism from boyhood.

But there seems to be little evidence that Wordsworth borrowed these notions directly from Rousseau or that he followed in detail, or was even well acquainted with, the fringe of problems surrounding Rousseau's discussion of the *general* will and its relation to the *will of all;* i.e., between the expression of a widespread spirit of popular agreement and recognition of common interest, on the one hand; and a mere compromise between special sectarian demands on the other. This problem, which Wordsworth hardly notices, constitutes the heart of Rousseau's political teaching.

APPENDIX TO CHAPTERS IV AND VII

WORDSWORTH AND ROMAN STOICISM [1]

We have argued that from the time of the composition of the *Ode to Duty*, Wordsworth's philosophical orientation became for some years increasingly Stoic in character. Indeed, we have described this period of Wordsworth's thought as a modern or romantic Stoicism. We have found it likely that in the *Ode to Duty* and *The Excursion* Wordsworth reflects an acquaintance with the moral philosophy of Immanuel Kant which may be justly described as Stoic, centering as it does about a doctrine of duty or rational obligation that is said to surpass all the other values of human life. In recent years, however, it has been argued that Wordsworth's debt to Stoicism is a more direct one and that we should look primarily to ancient thinkers, especially to Roman philosophers such as Seneca and Cicero. The evidence in support of this theory has been ably marshalled by Professor Jane Worthington Smyser in her monograph *Wordsworth's Reading of Roman Prose*.[2] She reminds us that the motto which Wordsworth affixed to the *Ode to Duty* in the edition of 1836-37 is adapted from a sentence in Seneca's Epistle CXX, "On Virtue." Again the important lines in Book Four of *The Excursion*, quoted by Wordsworth from Daniel—

> And that unless above himself he can
> Erect himself, how poor a thing is man!

contain, as Wordsworth noted, an echo of Seneca's "O quam contempta res est homo, nisi supra humana surrexit!" which appears in the Preface of *Naturales Quaestiones*. This information has always been available. None the less, most scholars have been inclined to treat these references to Seneca as no more than quotations from the classics added by the poet as

---

[1] This appendix has been added in the second edition.
[2] Jane Worthington, *Wordsworth's Reading of Roman Prose*, Yale Studies in English, Volume 102, Yale University Press, New Haven, 1946.

a sort of superficial adornment. Professor Smyser has made it clear that this attitude, shared as it was by the present author, is an uncritical one. She argues cogently that the *Ode to Duty*, the *Happy Warrior*, and other poems of this period contain certain turns of thought and expression that may well reflect a genuine and sympathetic familiarity with the Roman Stoics. Consider the following as a particularly striking example, involving once again Seneca's Epistle CXX. Referring to the *Ode to Duty*, Professor Smyser has written:[3]

To the poet who longs "for a repose that ever is the same" no philosophy could offer more than Stoicism. The Stoical way of life relieves a man of "chance-desires" and strengthens him to the point where his "hopes no more must change their name." "Nemo non cotidie et consilium mutat et votum . . . Magnam rem puta unum hominem agere. Praeter sapientem autem nemo unum agit, ceteri multiformes sumus." (Seneca, Moral Epistles, CXX, 21-22.) Also "sola sublimis et excelsa virtus est, nec quicquam magnum est nisi quod simul placidum." (Seneca, *"De Ira,"* Dialogues, III, I, xxi, 4.)

Either of the above sentiments would, it might seem, have constituted a more appropriate motto for the *Ode* than the quotation actually chosen, which, with its emphasis upon custom,[4] offers perhaps a less characteristic expression of the Stoic ideal. This ideal is essentially a matter of rational consistency, reflecting the "confidence of reason" rather more than the security of custom or habit, although the latter are important auxiliaries. Perhaps had Wordsworth chosen the motto thirty-odd years earlier, while writing the *Ode*, he would have made a somewhat different selection. But in any case, there is much in Seneca to satisfy the moral interests that Wordsworth entertained at this period. This is manifest not only in the *Ode to Duty* but equally in *The Happy Warrior*,[5] who in his fortitude meets danger

attired
With sudden brightness, like a Man inspired.

[3] *Op. cit.*, p. 62.
[4] This motto is adapted from Seneca's "iam non consilio bonus, sed more eo perductus, ut non tantum recte facere posset." *Ep.*, CXX, 10.
[5] *Op. cit.*, p. 66.

This recalls a splendid passage from Seneca's *Moral Epistles:*

. . . ad omne pulchrum vir bonus sine ulla cunctatione procurret; stet
illic licet carnifex, stet tortor atque ignis, perseverabit nec quid passurus,
sed quid facturus sit, aspiciet. (*Ep.*, LXVI, 21.)

We may summarize by saying that Wordsworth's almost
religious emphasis upon the tranquillity and glad confidence
that spring from an enduring rational self-control and his suggestion that this way of life is in harmony with the law-abiding
system of nature are especially characteristic of Seneca, whom
Wordsworth recognized as an author worthy of his attention
and respect.

I do not believe, however, that the texture of Wordsworth's
Stoicism is wholly of Roman origin. His philosophy of duty
is by no means merely a revival of ancient ways of thought.
Wordsworth's Stoicism is modern, even romantic in aspect,
just as his Platonism in the *Intimations Ode* is romantic in
treatment. This seems true even if we ignore the growing
emphasis on Christian attitudes and modes of expression already
apparent in *The Excursion*. To be sure, such modern Stoicism,
whether we find it in Wordsworth, in Kant, or elsewhere, will
resemble in broad outline its ancient counterpart. But it will
often develop characteristics of its own. Let us consider a
few examples of such development apparent in Wordsworth.

In the first place, there is the doctrine of the *schöne seele*,
characteristically romantic and without anticipation in ancient
Stoicism. Recall

> Glad Hearts! without reproach or blot
> Who do thy work, and know it not.

Here Wordsworth considers with respect a morality founded
upon a "genial sense of youth," upon spontaneous sympathies
that coincide with the dictates of a rational obligation. This
is not ancient doctrine. It is an important modern or romantic
variation upon the Stoic theme as stated by Kant. The burden
of proof will fall, I think, very heavily upon anyone who would
dismiss the apparent references to Schiller's moral philosophy

in the second stanza of the *Ode to Duty*. Even so, it hardly matters whether we recognize an influence of Schiller or accept simply the presence of a parallel. In either case, we have before us a typically modern or romantic idea.

As another example, let us consider once more a passage from *The Excursion* where a Stoic ethics is presented in a modern setting.

> Possessions vanish, and opinions change,
> And passions hold a fluctuating seat:
> But, by the storms of circumstance unshaken,
> And subject neither to eclipse nor wane,
> Duty exists;—immutably survive,
> For our support, the measures and the forms,
> Which an abstract intelligence supplies;
> Whose kingdom is, where time and space are not.
> (Book IV, 69 ff.)

Here, in the Wanderer's discourse that corrects and supplements the philosophy of the Solitary, we are presented not only with a Stoic theory of obligation but also with an idealist metaphysic that serves as a background. We come upon a doctrine of an intelligible world that lies beyond the phenomenal limitations of space and time. This notion plays an essential role, as we have seen, in the Kantian philosophy of moral freedom. This is a modern development of the Stoic theory of moral value, supported by a metaphysics that reaches far beyond ancient Stoicism with its naive concept of the *logos* or governing principle that pervades the material world as an indwelling fire. This fiery *logos*, or principle of order, may be thought to extend throughout the space and time of the physical world but certainly not to transcend them. Ancient Stoicism does not present us with an ultimate reality standing beyond or above the physical order. On the other hand, Wordsworth's Stoicism, like that of Kant, is set within a background of idealism rather closer to Plato's than to the orthodox doctrine of the ancient Stoics themselves.

Finally, let us consider a passage that Professor Smyser

has chosen to illustrate a Stoic influence. She argues [6] that the opening lines of *The Excursion*, Book IX (see above, p. 131), indicate a direct acquaintance with the Roman Stoics, for whom the concept of an "active principle," *principatus* or *hēgemonikon* is a central one. We are directed primarily to Cicero's *De Natura Deorum*. Let me suggest that the reader consider the following passage from this work in contrast with the quotations from Shaftesbury which we have already called to the reader's attention in this connection (see above, pp. 134 ff.). Cicero thinks in terms of the four elements, earth, air, water, and fire.

The fourth elemental substance of the universe remains to be discussed: its whole nature is fiery, and it shares this salutary and vital warmth with all things. We may, therefore, conclude that, inasmuch as all the parts of the universe are sustained by heat, the same identical element has maintained and preserved the universe itself through the unnumbered centuries; and our conclusion becomes the more logical when we reflect upon the incontrovertible fact that this glowing and fiery substance is infused into the totality of Nature in such a manner as to exercise at once the powers of procreation and of conception; all living beings, therefore, and all plants whose roots go down into the earth necessarily derive from it their life and their growth.

This substance, then, is the cohesive and conserving force in the universe, and it possesses both sensibility and reason; for everything which is not simple and pure but which is composed of commingled and united elements must have within it some governing principle. In man, it is mind; in beasts, it is something similar to mind, in which is to be found the origin of appetite; in plants and trees, the governing principle is thought to dwell in the roots. By "governing principle" I mean that which the Greeks call *hēgemonikon*, and nothing on any plane of life can be or ought to be more exalted than this. Hence, that substance wherein resides the governing principle of all Nature must be the most exalted of all things and also in the highest degree worthy of universal power and dominion. We perceive, then, that in the component parts of the cosmos (and there is nothing anywhere in the cosmos which is not a part of the whole) sensibility and reason abide. In that part, therefore, in which the governing principle of the cosmos has its seat, these qualities must of necessity be present—and in more intense and sublime guise. And so, we are forced to ascribe intelligence

[6] *Op. cit.*, pp. 52-53.

to the cosmos, and to admit that this substance which encompasses and embraces all things likewise surpasses all things in the perfection of its reason, and therefore that the cosmos is God and that all its powers are sustained by the divine nature.

Besides, this cosmic heat is purer, more radiant, more agile, and thus far more potent in its impact upon the senses, than the earthly warmth by which objects that are familiar to us are animated and supported.[7]

The reader will, I think, be quite ready to admit that the lines from Book IX of *The Excursion* are closer both in content and in tone to Shaftesbury than to Cicero. For one thing, neither Shaftesbury nor Wordsworth identifies the "active principle" with the element, albeit the "divine" element, of fire. This concept will remind us that, moral philosophy aside, there is much in ancient Stoicism that must appear crude and naive to one who, like Wordsworth, admires Newtonian science and has conversed with Coleridge on ancient and modern idealism.

To be sure, we may suspect that Wordsworth was aware of the Stoic origin of his "active principle." But this is a far cry from our insisting that no other influence is discernible in Wordsworth's treatment of the concept. Wordsworth's philosophy during his Stoic period seems to have been drawn from a number of sources. The more recent of these, namely Kant and Shaftesbury, are themselves in the Stoic tradition and contribute toward the formulation of a modern Stoicism, a way of thought to which Wordsworth has given so memorable an expression.

[7] *De Natura Deorum*, Bk. II, 10-11, Poteat's translation, University of Chicago Press, 1950.

Index

(Concepts, Proper Names, and Titles)

Index

Index

tude to pantheism, 16, 25, 42, 69, 73, 107-108, 124, 128, 144, 174, 195; attitude to the philosophy of Coleridge's "Dejection," 170-171; attracted by mystical pantheism of Spinoza, 176-177, 182, 195; belief in the unity of Nature, 6, 9-10, 11, 21, 73, 83, 85, 90, 100, 254, 256; borrowings from Schiller's theory of the *schöne Seele*, 25, 212-216; concept of "intellectual love," 24, 180-183, 190-193; concept of objective metaphor, 86, 86 n., 165 n., 250, 255, 256, 257; concept of "wise passiveness," 3, 4, 9, 12, 54, 87, 236, 237, 263; critical interpretation of doctrine of "Dejection" in the "Intimations Ode," 160-171; debt to the Associationists, 34, 37, 39, 256-258; denial of Spinozian nature of *The Excursion*, 174-175; dissatisfaction with his former ethics of imagination, 204 ff.; doctrine of World-Soul, 20, 21, 88, 252; early enthusiasm for Hartleian psychology, 34-35, 37, 39, 40; echoes of Behmenistic thought in *The Prelude*, 110-112, 114 ff.; in *Lines Written in Early Spring*, 107-108; in "To My Sister," 109; in "Wisdom and Spirit of the Universe," 113-114; in the "Ode to Duty," 128-130; in *The Excursion*, 132-134; in the "Intimations Ode," 270-271; experience as a Godwinian, 22, 24, 96, 97, 183-186, 188, 189, 196-197, 205, 228; explanations of his *volte-face* from a philosophy of self-confidence to a philosophy of self-defense, 230-232; his central precepts, 3-4; his cosmic idealism and scientific naturalism, 19-21; his democratic fallacy, 227 ff., 234, 236; his idea of "the sentiment of Being," 30, 33, 76, 77-79, 80, 83, 89, 90, 91-92, 93-94; expressed most nobly in "The Solitary Reaper," 97, 172, 182, 268-270; his insistence upon panpsychism, 78, 83, 89, 90, 92-93, 95; his modernity, 11; his mysticism, 12-13, 14-15, 21, 24; decline of, 25-26; heightened by natural beauty, 99-100; allied with esthetic insight, 15 ff., 55,

61, 62 ff., 66, 67, 117, 141, 251; his sense of unity of world, 47, 56 n., 57-61, 73, 83, 85, 96, 100; Huxley's hostile misinterpretation of, 5-9; images and figures of speech explained by reference to passages from Boehme, 120-128; influence of British empiricists of 18th century, 23-24; influence of Rousseau's philosophy, 12, 184, 273-275; intellectual debt to Coleridge, 71-72, 141, 142-143, 144, 189, 206-207, 207 n., 216; Kantian aspects of his philosophy, 206-213, 245; latent skepticism in last books of *The Prelude*, 225-226; later shift from too obvious pantheism, 124, 128; Newtonian echoes in Wordsworth's thought, 135-137, 140; parallels with Boehme's thought, 44-71; philosophy of "Ode to Duty" compared with Schiller's ethics, 217-222; philosophy of *The Prelude* and interpretation of the *Ancient Mariner*, 150-159; positive side of Kantian ethics in *The Excursion*, 210-212; praise of Shaftesbury, 11-12, 23; prophet of romantic individualism, 26, 88, 223; rejection of Godwin for Boehme and Spinoza, 31, 66; for pantheism, 42; repudiation of Cartesian dualism, 21; retractions from his early individualism, 25-26; search for maxims of conduct, 206; search for philosophical medium, 27; Shaftesbury's influence on *The Excursion*, 134-140; similarity of his philosophy to that of Whitehead, 81-83, 91, 116-117, 253-256; similarity of his repudiation of his early theory of morals to new humanist critique of romantic ethics, 238-248; similarity to Herder's thought, 178-180; Spinozian aspect of his thought, 20, 23-24, 84, 172-173, 174, 175-176, 177, 180-183, 189-197, 201 ff., 253 n.; Stoicism in his thinking, 25, 206, 212, 215, 219-222, 235, 244; theory of the imagination, 23-24, 33, 34, 37-38, 39-40, 43, 73, 87-88, 119, 126, 148, 156, 162, 169, 170, 182, 183, 188, 194, 196, 198-199, 201-203, 204-206, 223, 224, 228, 229,